PURSUING GOD'S OWN HEART

JERRY VINES

PURSUING GOD'S OWN HEART

*Lessons from the
Life of David*

BROADMAN
&HOLMAN
PUBLISHERS

NASHVILLE, TENNESSEE

© 2003 by Jerry Vines
All rights reserved
Printed in the United States of America

0-8054-2619-1

Published by Broadman & Holman Publishers
Nashville, Tennessee

Dewey: 248.84
Subject Heading: DAVID, KING OF ISRAEL \ CHRISTIAN
LIFE \ GOD—WILL

Unless otherwise stated all, Scripture citation is from the Holy Bible, New International Version, © 1973, 1978, 1984 by International Bible Society. Italic in Scripture text has been added by the author for emphasis.

1 2 3 4 5 6 7 8 9 10 07 06 05 04 03

Contents

Introduction

There are some commercials on television these days for Dodge automobiles. They're memorable ads. I think I remember them because they end with the phrase, "We're changing everything." That's quite a thought-provoking statement.

Dodge may be changing everything about the cars they make, but there's quite a bit of change going on in our world today from all quarters. In fact, I think much of the change going on comes from a growing tendency for people to question everything.

Have you ever questioned something? Perhaps you've questioned a policy at your job. Or maybe you've questioned a grade given to you by a teacher. Perhaps you've even questioned your faith in God.

Generally speaking, people reach a kind of questioning peak in their lives where they examine the world around them. They might ask why they exist or what their lives mean or what their contributions to the world are going to be. This peak is an important time in a person's life and a time when important decisions are made.

Based on forty years of experience in the pulpit, I believe that people usually reach this peak around age 18, 19, or 20. Young people may leave for college or start a job at this age. They usually begin to question their background, their upbringing, and even their faith.

This time of questioning may well be crucial for young people. Without it, a person might never develop or become conscious of his or her own worldview. And, if a person never defines his perspective on the world, he may never become well grounded in a belief system.

Want proof? Just visit a college campus coffeehouse. You'll hear talk of old and new rhetorics, of shifting paradigms, and of feminist revisionism, among other things. You also may get the sense that young people are searching for meaning and direction. We all need something to believe in and a guide for our lives. Some may choose alcohol, others may choose Eastern philosophies, and still others may choose intellectualism.

Many modern scholars and intellectuals are questioning the Bible. Is it really the Word of God? Is it totally free of mistakes or errors? Is it dominated by a certain point of view? Does it represent truth?

None of these questions is new, of course, but they do tell us that we are living in an extremely relativistic culture. Since everything is subject to question, some might say, then everything is open to new interpretation and everything is relative to everything else.

An article entitled "King David: Not the Man He Used to Be?" was published in the March 19, 2001, edition of *U.S. News and World Report*. According to its author, Jeffrey Shuler, there are many archaeological and biblical scholars questioning King David of Israel.

In the article, Shuler reported that many scholars are asserting the opinion that David was not a great king at all. Some say he was just a tribal chieftain, and others say he was simply a folk hero. Shuler goes on to report that while archaeological proof does exist to indicate that David actually lived, no persuasive evidence has been found to show that he led a powerful military regime or enjoyed a peaceful reign as a king.

Now, let me state where I'm coming from. I believe the Bible's account about David is completely accurate because I believe the Bible is divinely inspired.

In this book, we will be examining the life and times of David based on the biblical account of his life. He is the most mentioned person in the Old Testament. He is mentioned six hundred times in the Old Testament and sixty times in the New Testament. There are several great men in the Old Testament. Think of Abraham, father of the nation of Israel. Think about Moses, great lawgiver of the children of Israel. Then, there's David. He was the second king in the land of Israel and their greatest king ever. In many ways, you could say that David was the greatest man of the Old Testament. He's in the New Testament as well. His relationship to the Lord Jesus Christ is mentioned there over and over again. In fact, the link between David and the Lord Jesus is unmistakable in the Bible.

It is my aim in this book to try to answer some of your questions about David, his life, and his heart. David was certainly not a perfect man, but he was a man with a heart that was sensitive to God. His heart was tender toward God. God wants us to have that kind of heart as well. By studying David's life, we can learn how to be used of God more and more in our own lives. It is my conviction that God has a plan for the life of every Christian. If you are a Christian and you seek to make your heart sensitive to Him, then He will use you in a great way, just as He used David so many centuries ago.

Author's Note to Readers

It may be helpful to read the books of 1 and 2 Samuel, 1 and 2 Kings, and 1and 2 Chronicles either before you read this book or while you are reading it. I will make specific references to Scripture throughout the book, but if you want to know the full context of David's life, you should read these passages for yourself.

CHAPTER 1

Career Matters,
or Braveheart

"The LORD does not look at the things man looks at.
Man looks at the outward appearance, but the LORD
looks at the heart."
—1 SAMUEL 16:7

1 SAMUEL 16   A few years ago a movie entitled *Braveheart* hit movie screens around the world. Mel Gibson played a historical Scotsman named William Wallace. Although I did not see this popular movie myself, I heard many people speak of it, and I know Wallace's story from history. All of their talk interested me, and I found out more.

According to one plot summary of the movie, a young Scottish rebel named William Wallace leads an uprising of Scots against a cruel English ruler. William's quest is one of revenge because his own father and brother, along with many other people, lost their lives trying to keep Scotland free. So William dedicates his life to free his country at whatever cost and by doing so proves he has a brave heart. Because of his conviction and dedication, he becomes known across the land as Braveheart.

Israel's King David also had a brave heart. Remember him? The kid who knocked Goliath's block off? Well, he also fought several bloody wars and kept peace in Israel for years. History and recent archaeological findings show us he was an accomplished king. Yet, more than any victory or land acquisition or reign of peace, King David was and is known as a man after God's own heart. David sought to please God even though he was human and he made mistakes.

In fact, David's relationship to God is one that can be used as a model for relationships today. David did make mistakes. He was a sinner. Nevertheless, he was always a man after God's own heart. His heart was tender and sensitive toward God. His heart was brave because of his desire to be close to God and to do His will.

You may wonder what it means to be a person after God's own heart. You may question how and why David was chosen by God to be a great king of Israel. Was it because he was bold or extremely intellectual? Was it because he was handsome or came from a good family? How did he land that job?

This chapter considers David's election process, his selection process, and finally his connection process.

David's Election

Do you remember our 2000 presidential election? That was a roller-coaster ride for supporters of both political parties. Elections can be that way.

Did you know the ancient Greeks scorned elections because they felt that elections could be swayed or rigged too easily? The right idea, maybe? Elections can be grueling, dishonest experiences. Yet for David, the boy who would be king, the election process was different.

Let's talk a little bit about the setting. According to 1 Samuel 16, it all begins out in a field. Picture some sheep, some grass, and a few hills. Throw in a sunny day and a kid in the field working as a shepherd—some summer job, huh? When he gets bored, he plays his harp and writes songs. Got it? Good. We know from reading the Bible that God is about to show David what his career is going to be.

First Samuel 16 shows us how David's election process happened. It might help if you think of this chapter of the Bible as our newspaper or our twenty-four-hour cable news channel for the time.

Do you remember Samuel? He was a great prophet of God. Being a prophet of God was no cushy job. It was tough. If you were a prophet, you *had* to do what God told you to do—like it or not. Being a prophet was probably like being a spy—agent 007 for God accepting seemingly impossible missions all the time. Prophets had no time to say, "Excuse me, God, but I can't do what You're asking me to do because it violates my civil rights," or "Um, God, I can't do that because You're asking me to do something that is not in my job description." No way!

So Samuel had to go to Saul, the king at the time, and inform him that God was booting him out as king because he had been disobedient. Samuel didn't really want to do this, but he did it.

What happens next? God basically tells Samuel to deal with it. God says to Samuel, "I have provided for me a king and I'm sending you to Bethlehem, and we are going to find out who he is."

Do you think Samuel is thrilled with this information? Nope! Samuel asks, "How can I go?" (v. 2). Samuel has it all figured out. He knows this assignment is dangerous. Why? Because King Saul was one of those really suspicious people. He was one of the people Elvis Presley was describing in his song, "Suspicious Minds." Not really! But Saul really did have a suspicious mind.

Saul knew his number was up and that he was being downsized. He was being laid off as king. In other words, in an unstable political climate (much like our 2000 election), anything unusual would be suspicious to Saul. So Samuel is not too thrilled about his mission.

Samuel asks God how he's supposed to get started on his mission, and God says, "Take a heifer." Say what? Yes, a heifer, a young cow. Maybe the cow thing doesn't make much sense to you now, but hang on, it will.

Picture Samuel on his mission to the little village of Bethlehem. What happens when he arrives? "The elders of the town trembled" (v. 4). Yep! They were scared when Samuel came to town. See, Samuel wasn't just Mr. 007, prophet of God; he was also the civil magistrate. He was the judge! The town was probably wondering what was up. A murder? A robbery? What was going down?

Well, you and I know that God is working out His plan here. All of God's plans dealing with human beings have two parts: God's part and the human part. God's part of the plan in a human life is a heavenly call. There are also the earthly circumstances. All of these earthly events converge or come together because God is working behind the scenes.

So here comes Samuel. The folks in town are scared. They ask him, "Do you come in peace?" Then, they see the cow! A cow had probably never looked so good to them before. In their culture, when a prophet came to town with a cow, it meant time for church. It was time for a church service. I wonder if I should come to church in downtown Jacksonville next Sunday with a cow. No, we don't worship that way today. But in Old Testament days, a heifer or cow or other type of animal was a part of the worship. The animal was a part of the sacrifice.

Samuel then tells some of the townspeople to get a man named Jesse and his sons because they are going to be a part of this worship service. Samuel is doing his part of God's plan. He's arranging the earthly circumstances so God can appoint His new leader. The Bible teaches us that God takes leadership very seriously. When leadership becomes unacceptable or undesirable to God, then God examines the situation and provides new leadership.

So Jesse and his sons come to see Samuel. They come in with the oldest son lined up first. The oldest boy's name was Eliab. Picture Eliab as your typical tall, dark, and handsome guy. He could have been the running back on the Bethlehem High School football team. Samuel looks at this ruggedly handsome boy and thinks, "That kid reminds me of Saul. He's got to be the one. He must be God's choice as the next king" (v. 6).

Not exactly. In effect, God says, "Next!"

Exit Eliab. Then, the second son appeared before Samuel. His name was Abinadab (v. 8). That sounds like a good name for a rap music star, huh? Watch out, Sisquo! No threat here. This dude is a complete geek. He's got the thick black glasses, an IQ above 140, and a college education. Surely Samuel must think Abinadab is the man. A guy that smart must be the next king. Well, not too fast. Samuel says, "The LORD has not chosen this one either." Next! (v. 8).

I heard about this family where the parents had seven kids. The mom was so busy that she sometimes called the kids by the wrong names. Finally, the kids just started referring to themselves as their birth order numbers!

So here's number 3 (see v. 9). His name is Shammah. Girls, this guy was Mr. GQ. He's wearing his Tommy clothes and his alligator cowboy boots. He's way cool. Samuel thinks to himself, "Well, a king needs to get along with people and have people think of him as being classy or stylish." But in verse 9, Samuel says, "Nor has the LORD chosen this one."

Ready for number 4? Sorry, the Bible doesn't mention Jesse's other sons. What's up with that? Samuel was one puzzled prophet.

Here's a chance to talk about another vital spiritual principle. "The LORD said to Samuel, 'Do not consider his appearance or his height, for I have rejected him. The LORD does not look at the things man looks at. Man looks at the outward appearance, but the LORD looks at the heart'" (v. 7). That is what it's all about with God—the heart.

Sometimes the Bible uses the word *heart* to refer to the spiritual center of your life. Proverbs 4:23 declares, "Above all else, guard your heart, for it is the wellspring of life." The wellspring of life. There it is. Those issues are what make our lives happen. A good topic for the Oprah show—the wellspring of life. Oprah doesn't need to explain what our spiritual hearts are all about because the Bible does.

As human beings, all we can see of each other is what's on the outside. God sees the inside. You know what I mean. Picture a single working mother, for example, who sees a stay-at-home mom. This mom who doesn't have to work appears to have everything—country club membership, new car, housekeeper to take the kids to school, and a husband with a good job. The tendency in our culture is to be impressed by and to strive to impress others with what's on the outside. If a woman is very beautiful or if a man is extremely handsome, we often think they are more valuable as people. We may even think that it's only the young and beautiful people who can be used of God.

In response to that, God says, "Not!" The Bible makes it clear that God is not impressed by our outward decorations. God looks at our hearts. He examines our motivations. He sees what's on the inside.

In my opinion, God seems to have a fascinating tendency to do unusual things with those people whom the world looks down on. First Corinthians 1:27–28 says, "But God chose the foolish things of the world to shame the wise; God chose the weak things of the world to shame the strong. He chose the lowly things of this world and the despised things—and the things that are not—to nullify the things that are."

In other words, God doesn't judge us as adequate based on how we look or on what we earn or even on whether our teeth are straight. God chooses His workers based on what He sees in their hearts.

OK, let's get back to Samuel. He is probably scratching his long beard in puzzlement right about now. He just can't figure this out. Samuel asks Jesse, "Are these all the sons you have?" Jesse responds by saying, "There is still the youngest, but he is tending the sheep" (v. 11). Can you guess his name? We're talking about David. At this point in time, he would be about sixteen years old.

David is doing ordinary things with his time. He's a teenager who is working, just like many I know. He wouldn't have been dreaming of a car, but maybe he was dreaming of buying a donkey. To his father, Jesse, David may have seemed too young or too lacking in any potential to even be considered to come before Samuel. Yet, when Samuel hears about this sheep-keeping boy, he says to Jesse, "Send for him; we will not sit down until he arrives" (v. 11).

I have a theory about families because I've seen patterns emerge after forty years of preaching. Sometimes a young couple will have a few kids and then think they're finished having children. The wife might go back to work after her kids are in school, and life settles in to a routine. Then, surprise! The wife is pregnant again. Yikes! What a change! But I've seen very special children born as youngest children in families. These children seem to be extremely gifted and talented—perhaps in music or in intelligence or in athleticism.

So here's David, the youngest boy. He probably wasn't taken seriously by his father or his brothers. They probably never asked for his opinion about anything because he was the youngest. They probably never listened to him. Yet, Samuel becomes aware that David is the man. He is appointed by the plan of God. Samuel senses that God is working in the life of this young man.

In our fast-paced, technological world, we may get the idea that we are forgotten by God or that God isn't going to use us. But before you were born, before this world existed, God planned a purpose for your life. Even now, He is working in the circumstances of your life. One day you'll fall right into the groove of God's career and plan for your life. So be faithful. Somebody is watching you. God may be getting you ready for some big job. He may be checking you out to see if your heart is tender and sensitive toward Him.

David's Selection

Here's the big moment. David enters the scene. His day probably started like any other. He got up, washed his face in the nearby brook, fed the sheep, watched for any lions or bears threatening the sheep, and worked on a song or two on his harp. See what I mean about youngest children and talent?

Then, BOOM! Here comes a messenger all sweaty and out of breath. He says, "David! Samuel the prophet has come to town and he has sent for you!"

"Me?" David probably questioned.

"Yes, you!" the messenger probably replied.

And then verse 12 gives a description of David. It says, "He was ruddy." That meant he had red hair and probably a red hot temper! (Shhh. That's another common trait among youngest children, but we won't mention it). The Bible also says that David had "a fine appearance and handsome features." In other words, girls, he was a hunk. But God has said that outward appearance doesn't matter, right? How you look neither qualifies nor disqualifies you for service to Christ. It's just not an issue. It's about your heart.

So David leaves his field and arrives in town to meet Samuel. The Lord says to Samuel, "Rise and anoint him; he is the one" (v. 12).

Can you see the jaws dropping? Jesse and David's brothers must have been beyond shocked! Here is this kid. His muscles are strong from lifting sheep. His eyes are clear from seeing nature. His heart is clean and pure because of his relationship with God. Here he is. Number 8. He's the one.

Back in 1987, I was attending the Southern Baptist Convention in St. Louis, Missouri. On one of the conference days, I preached the convention sermon on the inspiration of the Bible. When it was over, Dr. Charles Stanley came up and embraced me on the platform. He said to me, "God has told me that you will be the next president of the Southern Baptist

Convention." I nearly had a heart attack! Me? No way! Not a chance. Evidently, the Lord did reveal that information to him because I served as president for two terms.

It kind of worked that way with David. The Lord whispered to Samuel, "He's the one." God often puts His hand on the most unlikely people. Think about Jesus. Brought up in Nazareth, which was pretty much the hick town of Israel, He was born into the poor family of Mary and Joseph. And yet, the Savior of the world came from that background. Don't be too concerned about your own background. God has His eyes on you. He has a plan for you, too.

"Samuel took the horn of oil and anointed him in the presence of his brothers" (v. 13). What horn, what oil? Well, there was an animal horn—a flask, really—filled with a specially prepared olive oil. This oil was used to anoint prophets, priests, and kings. In the Bible, oil is a symbol for the Holy Spirit. To be anointed with oil meant one was being prepared to do a job for God.

So Samuel took the oil and anointed, or poured, the oil on David right there in front of everybody. "And the Spirit of the LORD came upon David from that day on in power" (v. 13). Think about that. Those whom God appoints, He also anoints. If God gives you a job to do, He will enable you to do that job.

Want an example? The apostle Paul said he was grateful to the Lord because He had enabled him and called him into the ministry. When God puts you in a place of service, He will also enable you to fulfill that service.

David's Connection

Picture David now. He's been anointed and told that he is the next king of Israel. What do you think he's doing? Calling *Inside Edition* with the scoop? Running to the store to buy the latest in robe attire? Setting up a web page to take questions for David: Future King of Israel? Not exactly.

Look at verse 19. Where is David? He's hanging out with his sheep, doing his job. He simply went right back to the job God had given him to do at that time. God wants David to learn something as he wrestles the lions and bears away from his sheep. God is getting him ready to fight a giant. Get it? You better think about wrestling your lions and bears now, where you are, because God may have bigger giants waiting for you in the future. And if He does, He will give you the ability to overcome them.

What about Saul? That's an interesting part of this story. In verse 13, the Spirit of the Lord comes on David, but look at what happens: "Now the Spirit of the LORD had departed from Saul, and an evil spirit from the LORD tormented him" (v. 14).

How could the Lord send an evil spirit? Since you and I are New Testament Christians, this could never be said of us. Once the Holy Spirit enters the life of a believer, the Holy Spirit is never withdrawn. But in the Old Testament, the Holy Spirit could leave believers.

Saul is fading out of the picture. He had every opportunity as the first king of Israel. But because of Saul's disobedience, the Spirit of the Lord departed from him and an evil spirit from the Lord troubled him.

Saul wasn't just troubled; he was miserable. He was disobedient to God. So one of his servants did some thinking and recommended that a musician be found to play Saul some soothing music. Music has been shown to be therapeutic, and it can certainly soothe us. But it cannot heal us. Only God can heal us.

The instruction was to "search for someone who can play the harp" (v. 16). So they looked for someone who could play the harp. Who do you think it was? You got it! David!

Here's David, a man who is appointed to be a king—and his first assignment is to be associated with a miserable, disobedient king. Why? I think God may have wanted David to make a connection with Saul. Is David faithful to his task? You bet!

He is never unfaithful to Saul. He never becomes hotheaded trying to help God deal with this ungodly king. He just faithfully does what he's been assigned to do. He plays on his harp. He makes a connection.

"Whenever the spirit from God came upon Saul, David would take his harp and play. Then relief would come to Saul; he would feel better, and the evil spirit would leave him" (v. 23). How quickly it will all change. This is the man who will soon hate David and try to kill him.

There is a very unusual verse in the Bible about David, and I think it is the key to the meaning of his life. This statement in 1 Samuel 13:14 is not made about any other person in the Bible. The Lord has said that Saul would be rejected as the king and that another person would be selected: "But now your kingdom will not endure; the LORD has sought out a man after his own heart." This idea is repeated in the New Testament in Acts 13:22. David is known as a man after God's own heart.

What does that mean? Does it mean David was a superman? No. David was in many ways a very weak man. Does it mean David was a perfect man? Not at all. We'll find that David sins in many very human ways. It simply means that David was a man after God's own heart. He was the kind of person who could get God's attention. That's how God wants us to be. God desires that we have a heart seeking His heart—a heart that is sensitive to Him. God wants to be able to make contact with us.

Finally, I will mention one other interesting statement about David from Acts 13:36: "For when David had served God's purpose in his own generation, he fell asleep." That means that David's life was intended to be one of service to other people. David was able to make connections with God and with people.

There are two basic relationships all of us ought to have. The first is a relationship between God and us. The second is a relationship between us and other people. There's the up and down relationship—a heart seeking God. Then there's the outward relationship—one where we serve our own generation in the will of God.

David's life is so rich and full of lessons we can learn and use today. I hope you will continue reading this book to learn more about David's life and times and more about how you can be a man or woman after God's own heart. David's heart was bent toward God just like a flower turns toward the sun. Our hearts should be bent toward the Son. Studying the life of this "Braveheart" can help us have a closer and more rewarding relationship with God and with other people.

CHAPTER 2

Giant Matters,
or Lethal Weapon

*"Challenges are what make life interesting; overcoming them is
what makes life meaningful."*
—JOSHUA J. MARINE

1 SAMUEL 17   We all remember stories of giants from
our childhood days, such as *Jack and the
Beanstalk* and *Gulliver's Travels.* But giants don't exist just in
children's storybooks.

All of us face giants in life. We encounter giants of different
sizes and strengths. What giant are you facing? Sometimes, you
may face emotional giants—a giant of fear or a giant of depression. Other times, you may face a giant of jealousy or of preju-
dice. Maybe your giant is simply another person or problems
you may have with another person. Maybe it's a problem on the
job or something going on at home. Yet, it is a giant and it
threatens you and your life.

As 1 Samuel 17 opens, there is war raging in a wide valley
on the western front about fifteen miles west of Bethlehem, the
childhood home of David. The Israelites and the Philistines are
fighting. The atmosphere is filled with hostility and hatred. The
two armies have gathered in the valley of Elah (v. 2).

As Christians, we know that giants will come into our lives
We also know we will fight battles over these giants. But because

17

we believe in the living God, as David did, we have a lethal weapon that can slay the most wicked and cruel of giants.

Our man David, the one after God's own heart, fought both figurative and literal giants. His first one, interestingly enough, was a literal giant—a man named Goliath who stood more than nine feet tall. Wouldn't the NBA like to nab him!

The biblical account of the battle between David and Goliath is very important. Why? For one thing, we know it is important because of the space given to it. The account consists of fifty-eight verses in chapter 17 of 1 Samuel. It's one of the longest chapters in the Bible. A total of 912 Hebrew words is used to give this account. We also know it is important because it includes detailed descriptions. For example, descriptions are given about the historical location and the military weapons used in the battle.

Do you remember learning about the idea of plot in literature classes as a kid? I do. My teachers would instruct me to search a story for the conflict or problem, the rising action, and then the resolution. To me, this chapter is an example of a perfect plot of a perfect story. My teachers would be happy. The problem is that a giant more than nine feet tall is threatening the Israelites. I think any literature teacher would find a great example of conflict and rising action in this story. And the resolution—well, we will get there.

Picture this. They are in battle on the front lines. Jesse's youngest son, David, is back home with the sheep: "But David went back and forth from Saul to tend his father's sheep at Bethlehem" (v. 15). David's job as musician for King Saul was a part-time gig. David was the one who was called to help Saul deal with the demons of misery that were attacking his mind and heart. David's music soothed Saul's conscience.

Jesse tells David to go to the battlefield to check on his older brothers (v. 17). If you're a younger sibling in your family, you're used to this sort of thing. Jesse tells David to take along some "home cooking" of roasted grain and ten loaves of bread.

So David's job is really to supply moral support for the troops. Jesse also sends ten cheeses to the captain. Hey, it can't hurt. Jesse gives David his main goal in verse 18: "See how your brothers are and bring back some assurance from them." In other words, Jesse wants David to bring back some good news about his older brothers.

David's Story

Picture David. He's just a boy. He's not even shaving the peach fuzz on his chin yet. The morning after his dad has given him his assignment, he's up early. He's ready to go to the battlefield to see the action. There's just something in boys that attracts them to fighting. It's just their nature. Sorry, Mom. That's just how boys are. Visit a middle school some time and watch the boys. You'll see what I mean.

David goes and sees the armies of the Philistines on one side. On the other side he sees the armies of Israel. Fear and anxiety are evident in Israel's camp. Why are they afraid? Verse 4 tells us that the Philistines have a great champion. His name is Goliath, and he is a giant of a man. Nine feet and nine inches tall, to be exact.

Goliath is all decked out in brass armor. He wears a helmet of brass and a coat of mail made of brass (see v. 5). Some have said that his brass armor weighed between 120 and 215 pounds. His spear has a head of iron weighing about 25 pounds. He even has a servant standing in front of him holding up his shield. He is huge. Why do you think he wore all this brass that day? Picture the sun shining on that brass causing the Israelites to be blinded. It's psychological warfare. He wore it to play on their minds and to intimidate them before any fighting started. The history of wars and generals shows that this is true. Image is everything some say, even on the battlefield, and it is all a part of the intimidation techniques one army would use on another.

The Israelites were scared out of their minds. Picture Goliath as he raises those prodigious hands like hams to heaven and says, "This day I defy the ranks of Israel!" (v. 10). The Israelites must have been cowering.

Goliath continues to boast and bully with his words. He asks, "Why do you come out and line up for battle?" (v. 8). In other words, he's asking why they even bothered to fight. Battle is useless, according to Goliath. He suggests that each side should select a man and let those two men duke it out, with the winner taking all. Goliath knew he would be the Philistine pick. My guess is he was hoping that King Saul would be the pick of the Israelites. Saul was also a very tall man (see 1 Sam. 9:2).

Do you have any phobias in your life? Do you have a fear of heights or of flying or of roller coasters? I heard about a woman who had a fear of roaches. Unfortunately, she lived in Florida, and she had to face her fear frequently. Israel had what I call "giantaphobia." They were afraid of this giant. Yet, God has already told us in 1 Samuel 16:7 that we are never to look at the outward appearance. God says that the true strength of a person is not what he or she is on the outside, but what he or she is on the inside. This big, brassy giant intimidates Israel. Where's their faith?

Israel isn't down yet. Even though they were afraid, they've got David, and David sees clearly. David sees reality. The Israelite armies are giant-dominated and David is God-dominated. Quite a difference. But sometimes the only people talking in a tough situation are the whiners. The Israelite army sees Goliath, and they whine that he's bigger than any of them. David looks at Goliath and says he's smaller than God. What kind of person are you? Giant-dominated or God dominated?

Think about this. Past victories prepare you for present victories. Giants can be very scary, just like big roaches, but God is the giant killer. God has a big can of insecticide that will exterminate those pests. Trust in God. Remember that if God is for us, who can be against us? We are more than conquerors through Him who loved us. One day the Lord Jesus went to a hill called Calvary to do battle with two huge giants—sin and death.

Then David has a flashback. He sees what has been going on in the years he has been tending sheep in the wilderness: "But David said to Saul, 'Your servant has been keeping his father's sheep. When a lion or a bear came and carried off a sheep from the flock, I went after it, struck it and rescued the sheep from its mouth. When it turned on me, I seized it by its hair, struck it and killed it. Your servant has killed both the lion and the bear; this uncircumcised Philistine will be like one of them, because he has defied the armies of the living God'" (vv. 34–35). David killed a lion and a bear that threatened the sheep in his care.

There are some beautiful spiritual principles here. Little battles in life get us ready for the big battles. God had David fighting a lion and a bear to get him ready to fight a giant named Goliath. The same thing is true in our lives as Christians. God gives you little battles along the way to get you ready for the big battles. Ever wonder why you lose the big battles? Think about the little battles. Are you losing those too?

When you examine your motives at the ground level and you can truthfully say, "Lord, I want you to win this battle so you'll get the glory," everyone around you will see how God is able to win through you.

Another spiritual principle you can find from the David vs. Goliath struggle is that private victories prepare you for public victories. Jesus won the private battle of temptation in the wilderness at the beginning of His ministry. Then He won the public battle on Calvary at the end of His ministry. Public battles come after you've won some private battles.

It's good to learn to draw the parallels between past victories and present victories. Remind yourself what God did for you in the past. If God could give you a victory by faith over circumstances in the past, the same God can give you victory over your current giants and problems. Humans have short memories. We tend to write our troubles in stone and our vic-tories in water. We get discouraged. We forget so easily. But David draws the parallel between what God did in his life in the past and what God will do in his present life. He keeps the faith.

God's Glory

It's really all about power. As humans, we sometimes try to do the impossible in our own power. David's experience with Golaith teaches us that we need to rely on God's power.

"Then Saul dressed David in his own tunic. He put a coat of armor on him and a bronze helmet on his head. David fas-tened on his sword over the tunic and tried walking around, because he was not used to them" (vv. 38–39). Saul is actually trying to be helpful here. Saul tells him that this is the right armor to get the job done. He then suits him up, thinking he's helping out. This is exactly what a carnal or worldly person would do. Saul thinks the way to win against a worldly giant is by worldly methods. Lots of people think this way, don't they? Sometimes, churches think this way.

For example, technology is a wonderful enhancement in many fields (including religion). But its best use, in my opinion, is as an enhancement, not as an end in itself. The victory doesn't come from carnal equipment or carnal "armor"; it comes from the power of the Lord. The armor is simply sym-bolic. David already has the power to win over Goliath because the Spirit of the Lord is in his life.

So David makes a decision. He puts Saul's armor aside, and he goes down to the brook in the valley. "Then he took his staff in his hand, chose five smooth stones from the stream, put them in the pouch of his shepherd's bag and, with his sling in his hand, approached the Philistine" (v. 40). Why five stones for only one giant? David was a thinker. He was good at drawing conclusions. He knew Goliath had four sons, and he might have to fight them as well.

Five smooth stones. Five stones made by God. Five stones probably about the size of tennis balls. David also has his sling. Just the basics. God has provided him with the weapons he needs. No armor, just a sling, five stones, and a belief that God is a living God. David has the knowledge that God has delivered him in the past and will deliver him in the future.

Let's cut to the confrontation. It's David's time. He has a little sermon for the giant. "David said to the Philistine, 'You come against me with sword and spear and javelin, but I come against you in the name of the LORD Almighty, the God of the armies of Israel, whom you have defied. This day the LORD will hand you over to me'" (vv. 45–46). Basically, David is saying, "You can come with all these weapons, but I come in the name of the Lord." As my young friends might say, "That's cool!"

Now the plot thickens; the pace picks up. If this were an action movie with a big-name star, the audience would be riveted right about now. Here comes Goliath taking huge steps in his brass armor. David doesn't walk, but he runs toward Goliath! I can see a smile curling on the corners of David's mouth. In verse 49 David is holding the sling shot and the smooth stone. Can you see it? He starts swinging the slingshot over his head. About the fourth time around, David lets go— and the stone flies straight as an arrow to Goliath's forehead. Boom! Goliath is out! He falls face down. He's a dead giant. What does David do? He runs over and cuts off Goliath's head. Kind of gory, huh. Then David takes the skull to Jerusalem (see v. 54). Why? There's actually a legend that David buried the skull at a place called Calvary, which means "the place of the skull." But that's just a legend.

Think about it. What was David's weapon? He had the five stones, but his real weapon was the name of the Lord. You and I have the same weapon. When you are afraid, speak His name—Jesus. When you get ready to witness, speak His name— Jesus. When you go to sleep at night and you don't know if you'll wake up the next morning, speak His name—Jesus.

What giants do you have in your life? Why do you want to beat them? Why do you want God to give you victory over them? What is your goal? Is it all about you? Are you just seeking relief from your misery? Just so you'll feel better? Just so your life will be easier? Or do you want to beat the giants in your life so God will be glorified?

Maybe you've been through a job loss, and you didn't know what to do. You didn't see any way out. God delivered by providing another job for you. Some of you have lost loved ones, and you didn't think you could make it. But God came through for you. Past victories encourage us to know that God will give us present victories in the circumstances we face. It's difficult, I know, but God is faithful.

Many Christians are loaded down with the world's armor. They're trying to fight their spiritual battles with worldly, carnal armor. That's where David shows such wisdom. He fights his battle against Goliath with the weapons God provides. He uses the right equipment. We should learn to do that as well.

The giants in your live are obstacles that get in the way of the best life you can live. That giant is the blockage in your life that keeps you from God's best for your life. It is that problem that keeps you from going all out for God. It taunts you. It defeats you. It intimidates you and fills you with despair. But it doesn't have to be this way. With the living God on your side, you have a lethal weapon for the battle.

By the way, how's your church attendance? Is that a battle for you? Is that where the rubber meets the road for you? When it comes down to making a decision about whether to be faithful to God's house or to play golf on Sunday, how do you come out? That's a little skirmish, maybe not even a battle. Actually, that one should be a no-brainer for the committed Christian. If you lose a little battle like church attendance, how will you come out in a big battle like sexual temptation? Think about it.

"For the battle is the LORD's, and he will give all of you into our hands" (v. 47). When temptations and difficulties and all the other giants come in your life, remember that the battle isn't yours. It's the Lord's and you will win the victory because the living God is your lethal weapon. He's the one who does the fighting. He's the one who wins the victory.

In the Old Testament, the name of the Lord represented character and ability. It meant everything that God is and every-thing God can do. As you grow in your Christian life, you will learn more and more about who God is and what God can do. Proverbs 18:10 says, "The name of the LORD is a strong tower; the righteous run to it and are safe." There is strength, power, and victory in the name of the Lord.

When God gives us victories, He is cutting off the heads of the giants that torment us. He is our lethal weapon against any giant that may bully us. Use this weapon. When a giant attacks you, cut its head off through the name of the Lord. You can always look back on the skulls of past giants and know that God will give you the victory again.

There are great names in literature such as Shakespeare, Longfellow, and Tennyson. There are great names in history such as Napoleon, Caesar, and Alexander the Great. But in the realm of salvation and the redemption of human souls, there is only one name. You can call any other name in the world and get no answer. But the Bible says, "And everyone who calls on the name of the Lord will be saved" (Acts 2:21; see also Rom. 10:13).

Remember that you can count on God. If you need a reminder, you may want to memorize 2 Corinthians 1:9–10: "Indeed, in our hearts we felt the sentence of death. But this happened that we might not rely on ourselves but on God, who raises the dead. He has delivered us from such a deadly peril, and he will deliver us. On him we have set our hope that he will continue to deliver us." You can have confidence that there was deliverance in the past, there is deliverance in the present, and there will be deliverance in the future. You can count on God, your lethal weapon, and He will help you kill any giants you might face in your life.

CHAPTER 3

Friendship Matters, or Friends

"A real friend is one who will tell you your faults and failures in prosperity and will assist you with his hand and heart in adversity."
—SAMUEL JOHNSON

1 SAMUEL 18–20   I was flying through a busy airport last year. It was a Thursday night. I've always liked Thursdays because they seem calm to me. Maybe it's because Thursday is the day before Friday.

My flight was delayed, so I decided to walk around the airport. I like to observe people and see what they do. Airports are perfect. I think airports are a great place for novelists to get ideas for their novels or for preachers to get ideas for sermons—so many people, so many actions and reactions, so many bits of conversation, etc.

I ventured restlessly from my concourse and to another, using my observation skills. I guess I was looking for a story. I found one. Crowds of people were gathered around three separate television sets.

The people were standing very close to one another, laughing and smiling as if they knew one another. A few people were sitting on their luggage. Others were standing. I saw one man sitting on the floor looking up at a television.

I thought there must be some important news update. I joined the crowd closest to me. Someone in back of me hushed the crowd as a television show came back from a commercial break. I noticed that several people who were talking on cell phones put them away and walked near the crowd. Others closed the newspapers they had been reading. More and more people came over to join the crowds in front of the television sets.

The commercials ended, and a calm settled down upon the crowd. It was almost as if they were expecting to feel soothed by whatever was coming on. When it began, I didn't recognize the show. But I did hang with the crowd for a while to see what it was all about.

I watched with the crowd as the screen showed five or six young adults sitting on a couch drinking coffee. The conversation focused on a date one of the women had gone on the night before. The topic of discussion was whether she had gone to bed with her date.

"I've been there," said one of the women sitting on a suitcase behind me.

"Yeah, really!" said a thirty-something man to my right. "We all have," he added as he sipped coffee from his paper cup.

I looked around. Absolutely everybody around me was tuned in to this show.

"What show is this?" I whispered to a short, red-haired man to my left as I nudged him with my elbow. He didn't even look at me. I asked again.

"Are you for real?" he said as he turned his eyes quickly toward me and then back toward the screen.

"What show is this?" I repeated, not knowing if he was going to laugh at my question.

"It's *Friends.* You know, Monica and Chandler," he looked at me. "And Ross!"

I was beginning to see the big picture. I'm in a busy airport. It's 8:00 at night on Thursday. And most of the adults I see there are making time, even at an airport, to watch a show about six people from Manhattan who are apparently the best of friends.

As I watched the TV with them, I had an idea that hit me harder than a wrecking ball crumbling the side of a building. I was seeing a modern definition of friendship—self-absorption, self-pity, and intense introspection. What a contrast from the biblical accounts of the friendship between David and Jonathan.

If a person does not watch *Friends* on Thursday night, I soon learned, he or she will not be able to converse with coworkers around the water cooler on Friday. There it is, in a nutshell. America goes to work and talks about what? The war against terrorism? No. The environment? Perhaps. Television sitcoms? You got it.

For a long time now, I've realized people in our society have become increasingly isolated. Bank on-line—no need to talk to a teller. Pay for your gas at the pump—no need to say hello to a gas station attendant. Check out your own groceries. I called my granddaughter's school the other day and got one of those automated voice answering machines. I had to wait for the voice to go through eleven options before I knew which button to push.

The point of all this is to say that people today are living extremely isolated lives. Many people actually could be considered fortresses, living day to day behind walls of isolation. It's not that they're not caring or sympathetic toward people, it's just that because we live the way we do today, we don't have the same contact with our fellow human beings that we once did.

I know *Friends* is just a show. People might tell me to lighten up because it's modern entertainment. But in my opinion, the show is not entertainment that helps me walk closer to the Lord. And even though it's called *Friends,* it certainly doesn't teach me how to be a better friend.

Just what is a friend?

Samuel Johnson said, "A real friend is one who will tell you your faults and failures in prosperity and will assist you with his hand and heart in adversity." I wonder what Rachel on *Friends* would think about that statement.

Someone else said, "I love you not only for what you are, but what I am when I am with you. I love you not only for what you are making yourself, but what you are making me." True friends are gifts, and they make us better people.

In 1 Samuel 18–20, example of a friendship between David and Jonathan is portrayed. I've heard people say that "timing is everything." Well, David really needs a friend at this point. Yes, he's a man after God's own heart. Yes, with God's help he killed the giant Goliath, but troubles are brewing.

David is receiving praise and adulation from the women of the kingdom. First Samuel 18:6 says, "When the men were returning home after David had killed the Philistine, the women came out from all the towns of Israel to meet King Saul with singing and dancing, with joyful songs and with tambourines and lutes." In chapter 19, we see how David handles his success and how his friend Jonathan helps him.

Jonathan, Saul's son and the heir apparent to the kingship, befriends young David, the shepherd boy destined to be king and to actually take Jonathan's rightful place as the king's son. In fact, their friendship is perhaps the loveliest picture in all the Bible of the importance of friends.

Friends are important. They help us cope with the troubles of life. You are a blessed person if the Lord has given you godly friends. If you have one or two true friends, then you are a rich person. Proverbs 27:17 says, "As iron sharpens iron, so one man sharpens another." A friend lifts you up and makes you a better person.

David and Jonathan made a covenant together (see 1 Sam. 18:3). The word *made* really implies that they cut a covenant. What does that mean? In those days, it was normal to cut an animal into two pieces as a symbol of a covenant. The two pieces were laid on one side against the other. The two parties entering the covenant would then walk together through the two pieces of the animal as if to say, "We are making our commitment to one another and if we do not keep these words, may we go to pieces like this animal." A covenant is a very special tie. It's a commitment. Friendship is a commitment you enter into with someone else, too.

Friendship isn't just spiritual. It's a covenant. It's sacrificial. In 1 Samuel 18:4, Jonathan takes off his royal princely garments—his robe, his sword, his bow, and his girdle. No, not one of those girdles your grandma wore, but his waistband—almost like a cummerbund. He gives all his garments to David. Friendships are costly. It costs you something to have a friend. And it costs you something to be a friend.

What makes a friendship work? Think about your own friends. Was it something you two had in common that drew you together? Was it working in the same building? Was it a love of Frappucinos? For David and Jonathan, the friendship happened because God gave them to each other as friends, of course, but also because of proximity. Don't you find that your friends are usually those with whom you are in the closest contact? Jonathan was apparently standing nearby one day as he listened to his father Saul and David talk. They were drawn together after that.

Has that ever happened to you? You and a friend were just drawn together, and it seemed as if you two had known each other for a long time? Jonathan seems to be the one who initiated the friendship.

How do friendships come about? How can you gain more friends like Jonathan? Proverbs 18:24 answers that question for us: "A man that hath friends must show himself friendly" (KJV). In other words, to have a friend, you must be a friend.

I had a very good friend when I was about eight years old. His name was Ray. We met playing backyard football. The first thing he ever said to me was a compliment on my running ability. I thought he was one of the best ball players I had ever seen play in the BFL (backyard football league!). We became fast friends.

According to the account in 1 Samuel 18, Jonathan is the one who reached out to David. The Bible says that their souls were knit together. It means they were one in spirit. True friendship is really a spiritual matter. David was a man after God's own heart. He had a relationship with the Lord. Jonathan also had a good relationship with the Lord. So these two friends had the Lord in common. Think about that. It's wise to choose friends from among believers. Let your friends be those who know and love the Lord. A friendship is not a genuine friendship unless it is based on spiritual matters—matters of the soul.

David's Fame—"David Has Entered the Palace"

The development of their friendship happens right after David kills the Philistine giant Goliath. David had become an instant celebrity. His entire country knows his name. David is "the bomb." He's a young man after God's own heart. He is committed to the Lord, and that gives him wisdom to make decisions. He's not proud. He's not arrogant. And he gives the Lord all the glory for helping him through sticky situations.

David now has success and fame and popularity. It's not always easy for a person to have this kind of popularity so early in life. For some people, it's too much too soon. It happens to athletes. It happens to entertainers. Remember Elvis Presley? Remember how they would say, "Elvis is in the building" or "Elvis has left the building"? Elvis was a talented young man, but unfortunately he came to a tragic end like so many others. Did he have too much fame and success too soon? Perhaps.

Christians can take away many profound spiritual truths from David's experience. For example, David continually passes whatever praise he receives to the Lord. Think of praise as a test. When people praise you, it shows what you're made of. Praise is like gold in a furnace. Proverbs 27:21 says, "The

crucible for silver and the furnace for gold, but man
the praise he receives." The praise is the purifying
shows what is truly in your heart.

Here's a little advice. When people praise you, sile.   pass
that praise on to the Lord. You may not want to do that in an
audible voice, because you may unintentionally sound really
pious. God is our *enabler,* in the most positive sense of the word.
Anything we do as humans that has any value proves that the
Lord enabled us to do it. He's the one who gave us the strength,
the power, and the wisdom to carry out whatever action it was.
Just pass on the praise others give you. Pass it back to the Lord.
Here's something cool. When you pass the praise on to the
Lord, you can also pass criticism on to the Lord as well. Put it
all in the hands of the Lord.

So David is famous now. David is receiving exaltation and
glorification from his nation. "As they danced, they sang: 'Saul
has slain his thousands, and David his tens of thousands.'"
(v. 7). They are praising David. To me, this is misdirected praise.
If you study the chapter before this one very carefully, you may
recall that it was not actually David who won the battle with
Goliath. Even David said, "The battle is the LORD's." It was the
Lord who conquered Goliath. It was the Lord who gave the victory, not David.

"The Philistine commanders continued to go out to battle,
and as often as they did, David met with more success than the
rest of Saul's officers, and his name became well known"
(v. 30). His name got bigger and bigger. He could have packed
the Gator Bowl stadium if it had existed in Israel at that time.
All this fame at such a young age. David needed a friend.

This was a test for David. Was David proud about all the
praise he was receiving? No. He was a young man totally committed to the Lord. Verse 5 says that David goes wherever Saul
sends him. David is now working full-time in Saul's cabinet.
He's probably his bodyguard. "And he behaved himself wisely"
(KJV). That's important. Very important. Do we always behave

ourselves wisely? On the job? At home? Verse 14 also says, "David behaved himself wisely in all his ways." It also says, "Because the LORD was with him." He behaved himself wisely and the Lord was with him.

"Saul realized that the LORD was with David" (v. 28). No wonder Saul is feeling a little uncomfortable. What does David do? "David behaved himself more wisely" (v. 30 KJV). Remember, David is a man after God's own heart.

Another profound Christian truth illustrated here deals with jealousy. You may wonder who was exalting David. His test comes from the exaltation of the women of his country. They praise him and what he's done to Goliath: "Saul has slain his thousands, and David his tens of thousands." Hearing these words makes Saul, the king, extremely jealous of David. Verse 8 informs us that Saul didn't like this new song of praise the women were singing about David. "Saul was very angry; this refrain galled him. They have credited David with tens of thousands but me with only thousands. What more can he get but the kingdom?" (v. 8).

Saul carefully watches the situation with David. He may have perceived a shift in the balance of power. In the book *The Caine Mutiny* by Herman Wouk, a young sailor who has served under a mentally unsettled captain becomes captain himself. He then realizes the subtle shifts in his crew, and he realizes that being in the top leadership position is not a peaceful place to be. In other words, serving as a leader is tough.

"Saul was afraid of David" (v. 12). There's that perceived shift in the balance of power. Saul had no need to be afraid of this young man. But Saul is "because the LORD was with David but had left Saul." It's really quite simple. When a person is out of the will of God, he or she may become afraid of someone who is living in the Spirit. Likewise, when a person is doing what God wants him to do, it upsets the comfort zone of those who aren't living God's way.

So what do we learn about Saul here? We learn about jealousy because we see Saul becoming increasingly jealous of David. He doesn't like him, and he especially loathes the praise, adulation, and fame David is receiving. Jealousy has been called the green-eyed monster. That monster is visiting Saul.

"The next day an evil spirit from God came forcefully upon Saul. He was prophesying in his house, while David was playing the harp, as he usually did. Saul had a spear in his hand" (v. 10). Saul reaches over to get that javelin and SWOOSH! David ducks. It doesn't take David too long to realize he's in danger and that Saul is trying to kill him.

"The next day an evil spirit from God came forcefully upon Saul" (v. 10). That same old evil spirit. It came from God in the sense that God is ultimately sovereign over all things. Remember David's first job for Saul was to play beautiful, soothing music on his harp. David was a musician. He wrote songs and then played them on his harp. When David came into the palace, the evil spirit of depression and misery came upon Saul. It calmed Saul's spirit to hear David play his music. All that changes, though. Now David's music angers Saul. As David plays, "Saul had a spear in his hand" (v. 10). Saul is holding the spear—and then he hurls it toward David.

"And he hurled it, saying to himself, 'I'll pin David to the wall.' But David eluded him twice" (v. 11). David barely got out of the way. Can you see that spear quivering as it sticks in the wall? Maybe David gave Saul the benefit of the doubt. Maybe David thought Saul was just having a bad day. Have you ever had to work for a spear-throwing king? Have you ever been around someone who takes their authority and position as an opportunity to throw spears into the lives of others? Sometimes people use their authority as an excuse for their bad behavior. That's what life was like for David in Saul's palace.

What's causing all this? Saul's jealousy. Proverbs 6:34 says, "Jealousy arouses a husband's fury." Song of Solomon 8:6 says, "Love is as strong as death, its jealousy unyielding as the grave."

That is such an appropriate image. Jealousy is a terrible thing. It causes people to imagine and to obsess. It makes people suspicious and causes wrong conclusions to be drawn. And wrong conclusions often lead to bad decisions. This is the scene in Saul's palace because he's jealous of David.

Keep in mind that Saul already knew God had rejected him. He knew he was on the way out. Samuel the prophet had made it very clear to him that because of his disobedience of the Lord, Saul was destined to fall and someone would replace him. As soon as Saul learned this, he began eyeing people suspiciously. He tortures himself wondering who will take his throne. He loses sleep. Then he begins to hear all the praise for the young David. Verse 9 says it best: "And from that time on Saul kept a jealous eye on David." In other words, Saul began to look at David with a jealous and envious eye. It all boils down to the jealousy Saul feels for David.

Jealousy just coiled itself around Saul's heart like a serpent squeezing all the love out. Had David done anything wrong? No. He was faithful to his king. He doesn't undermine him or undercut him in any way. It's all in Saul's heart. King Saul is on his way out, and he sees the power shifting. Saul's sun is setting. David's sun is rising. And Saul knows it.

It is hard for most of us to rejoice in the blessings of others. When God does something for someone else, many of us wonder why it couldn't have happened to us. But God wants and expects us to rejoice in the blessings of others. Why? Because it is a terrible thing to let jealousy roost in your heart. Think about Saul. Was there really any reason for him to be jealous of this kid David? No. David's victory was Saul's victory. David's victory actually strengthened Saul's position. But Saul has departed from the Lord. He is not where he needs to be with the Lord. Therefore, he has an evil spirit come upon him that gives him an evil eye, and this evil eye is full of jealousy toward David.

Saul then demotes David: "So he sent David away from him and gave him command over a thousand men" (v. 13). David has been Saul's personal bodyguard, but now he's being sent away. It's hard to be demoted and embarrassed in front of your peers. Does David become bitter? No way. He gives no indication of any bitterness in his heart. In everything David did "he had great success, because the LORD was with him" (v. 14).

"Saul became still more afraid of him, and he remained his enemy the rest of his days" (v. 29). His enemy? Good grief! This is David we're talking about. So Saul is now thinking of David as his enemy. It's all in Saul's mind—and in his heart.

Saul also sends servants to David to hurt him, but they're prevented from doing any harm to David because the Spirit of God comes upon them. Saul sends three different groups who can't touch him. Saul decides he'll go himself. The Spirit of God comes upon him! Saul chooses to face the raw, irresistible power of the Spirit of God. Saul strips himself of his royal robes. He's already lost the power of a king; now he loses the symbols of a king. He lies in wait for David. Saul is making some poor choices here.

You might wonder how this story relates to us today. On one level, it's a story about protection. God protects David through His Spirit. It's simple, in a profound kind of way! Live your life for the Lord, serve Him, and turn your problems over to Him—and the Spirit of God will camp around your life. The Spirit of God will take care of you just like it took care of David.

Saul thinks he's got it all figured out by sending David into battle. Saul says, "I will not raise a hand against him. Let the Philistines do that!" He's really saying that he would put David in the battle, and the enemy soldiers would slaughter him. In other words, Saul plans to just stand back and let the enemy do the dirty work. Then he wouldn't have to worry about his enemy any more.

Sending David into battle isn't the only trick up Saul's sleeve. He also uses his own family in verses 17–30. Saul wants to get rid of David, this young upstart, this contender for his throne. So he decides he will use his own daughters to

manipulate David into a dangerous situation. Saul offers to
David his oldest daughter Merab: "Here is my older daughter
Merab. I will give her to you in marriage; only serve me bravely
and fight the battles of the LORD" (v. 17). What's up with that?

But this doesn't work. Saul is foiled again. David refuses.
He says, "Who am I, and what is my family or my father's clan
in Israel, that I should become the king's son-in-law?" He's
humble. He's self-effacing. He's calm. He's also being protected
by God. Verse 19 tells us that this eldest daughter was given to
somebody else. But in verse 20 the plot thickens: "Now Saul's
daughter Michal was in love with David, and when they told
Saul about it, he was pleased." So Saul offers Michal to David:
"I will give her to him so that she may be a snare to him and so
that the hand of the Philistines may be against him"
(v. 21). Here's a father who knows his daughter. He knows why
she will be a snare to David. Maybe he had seen troubling ten-
dencies emerge early in her life—hatefulness, contempt for spiritual things. We'll talk about Michal later.

The dowry request is quite crude. David is pleased to carry
it out, however. He actually doubles what Saul requires of him.
Rather than losing his life, David just wins more and more victories and receives more and more praise. "Saul realized that
the LORD was with David and that his daughter Michal loved
David" (v. 28).

Basically, nothing Saul has attempted has worked. Now
David's status changes.

David's Flight—"David Has Left the Palace"

The first years of David's life were formative years. They're
important. He was out tending to the sheep. God was shaping
him, getting him ready to carry out His purposes and plans.
David is now about to go into his fugitive years. He will be
forced to go on the run. So, in effect, he's left the building, or
the palace of Saul.

Jonathan comes back into the story. Verse 1 of chapter 19 says, "Saul told his son Jonathan and all the attendants to kill David." Well, at least it's now out in the open. No secrets. Saul's jealousy has put murder in his heart. Don't let jealousy make a home in your heart. Don't allow jealousy to eat away the love that's in your heart. It will get control and cause you to do things you don't want to do. Misery, heartaches, and sin will stay in your soul if jealousy comes to live there.

So David flees. He escapes. He goes home. He's not even safe there. He goes home with his wife Michal, and Saul sends the death squad out to get him. They surround his house. His wife Michal advises him to escape through a window. David takes off. He's on the run. He's a fugitive. He has left the building! (see vv. 11–12).

What does Michal do? She takes an image, an idol, and she covers it. She grabs a pillow of goat hair and puts it on the idol as a cover. She pretends that the idol is David. She tells the servants that David is sick. Then the servants leave and report to Saul, "David's sick." Saul doesn't buy it. He says, "Bring him up to me in his bed so that I may kill him" (v. 15). So Saul's servants go back to David's house. They pull the covers back and realize David is gone.

David is now feeling fear. Real fear. Fear for his life. In 1 Samuel 20:3, David says, "Your father knows very well that I have found favor in your eyes, and he has said to himself, 'Jonathan must not know this or he will be grieved.'" He's not letting Jonathan in on it. "There is only a step between me and death." There's a sense in which this is true for all of us. We're all one step away from death. Picture yourself out there in highway traffic. In just a split second, a car can come right in front of you and it's all over. One second here, the next second in eternity. This is why it's wise to be saved if you never have been.

First Samuel 19:1–2 says, "But Jonathan was very fond of David and warned him, 'My father Saul is looking for a chance to kill you. Be on your guard tomorrow morning; go into hiding and stay there.'" David is a fugitive on the run. Do you remember that TV show *The Fugitive?* At the end of every episode, the main character had to leave the town or city where he had begun a new job or had begun to make friends. The authorities were always after him. He was always aware he was being watched, so he had to live always as a fugitive. David's life for the next ten years will be similar to this character's existence. David will be literally running for his life.

"When David had fled and made his escape, he went to Samuel" (1 Sam. 19:18). Remember Samuel? The man of God. David's mentor and spiritual advisor. His godly counselor. David tells Samuel what has happened to him. It's a positive thing to be able to talk to someone about what's going on in your life spiritually. It helps to have someone who will pray with you when the tough times come.

Several people have asked me recently why I think it's important for them to be active in a Sunday school class. Here's the answer. In a Sunday school class, you can find a spiritual leader. It may be the Sunday school teacher. It may be the care group leader. In other words, don't let yourself become isolated as a Christian. Don't let yourself become a fortress unto yourself.

"Then David fled from Naioth at Ramah and went to Jonathan" (1 Sam. 20:1). How's that? A friend just appears. Isn't it wonderful to have a friend? It's nice to have a friend you can be yourself with. It's nice to have a friend you don't have to walk on eggshells for. You can be your true self and lay bare your heart to a true friend. David and Jonathan can level with each other. David says to his friend, Jonathan, "What have I done? What is my crime? How have I wronged your father, that he is trying to take my life?" David is under pressure and his words reflect his stress. He's running for his life. He's a fugitive.

Jonathan doesn't necessarily agree with David. He may think David is overreacting. Jonathan says, "Never! You are not going to die! Look, my father doesn't do anything, great or

small, without confiding in me" (v. 2). Jonathan a
that if his father were planning anything, he would

Luckily for David, he had a true friend in Jonath.
Jonathan goes before his father and speaks a word for ᴵ ᴵend
David. "Jonathan spoke well of David to Saul his father and said
to him" (1 Sam. 19:4). Let's stop right there. Here's another
mark of a true friend. I don't mean Ross, Rachel, or Chandler.
I mean a person who thinks of edifying and lifting up his friend
instead of obsessing on his own problems.

A true friend is someone who speaks well of you when you
aren't around. A true friend loves you for what you are on the
inside. Some people only see what is on the outside. They don't
ever see your soul. It's just human nature for people to focus on
what they can get out of you and what you can give them. But
Jonathan is a true friend to David, and he speaks up for his
friend. Proverbs 17:17 says, "A friend loves at all times, and a
brother is born for adversity."

Jonathan delivers a beautiful speech to his father Saul.
Think about it. Jonathan had a delicate balancing act. On the
one hand, there is the love he has for his friend David. On the
other hand, there is the loyalty he should show to his father.
Jonathan maintains that delicate balance. He was never disloyal
to his father. In fact, Jonathan kept a proper relationship with
his father throughout their lives. Yet, he loved his father enough
to be truthful to him and to speak to him about his friend.

Jonathan says, "Let not the king do wrong to his servant
David; he has not wronged you, and what he has done has ben-
efited you greatly." Jonathan is giving his dad good information
about David (1 Sam. 19:4).

Jonathan says, "He took his life in his hands when he killed
the Philistine. The LORD won a great victory for all Israel, and
you saw it and were glad. Why then would you do wrong to an
innocent man like David by killing him for no reason?" (v. 5).
Jonathan may actually be getting to Saul here. Saul "listened to
Jonathan and took this oath: 'As surely as the LORD lives, David

will not be put to death.' So Jonathan called David and told him the whole conversation. He brought him to Saul, and David was with Saul as before" (vv. 6–7). So Jonathan tells his friend to come on back to town because he thinks he has worked everything out.

The two friends cook up a plan. David tells Jonathan he won't be there for the upcoming new moon festival. David asks Jonathan to tell his dad that David's not there. He asks Jonathan to watch how his dad reacts. Jonathan agrees, and he adds to the plan. He and David plan to go out in a nearby field. Then they plan to have Jonathan shoot three arrows as an indication of how Saul has reacted to David's absence.

Jonathan advises David to hide out while he checks out the situation with his dad. Jonathan still doesn't believe David when he tells him he thinks King Saul is after him. But he does agree to help David figure it out. Jonathan tells David that if what he suspects is true, then he will shoot the arrows beyond the boy and tell the boy that the arrows are beyond David.

You know the story. Jonathan goes to the festival the first day, and David's place is empty. On the second day, Saul basically asks, "Where's David?" Jonathan tells Saul what he and David agreed would be said to him.

Saul gets steamed. He is hopping mad. Jonathan then realizes that David has been right and that the threats to David's life are real. King Saul even throws a javelin at his own son. So Jonathan goes out with the little boy with the arrows. He shoots one arrow far into the distance. He says, "Isn't the arrow beyond you?" That arrow represented David. God is getting ready to send him away. It's going to be David's time of flight.

Sometimes God's plans remove us from where we are and place us somewhere new. That's about to happen to David. God's getting him ready to be a king.

Verse 41 of 1 Samuel 20 tells us, "After the boy had gone, David got up from the south side of the stone and bowed down before Jonathan three times, with his face to the ground. Then they kissed each other and wept together—but David wept the most." Isn't it wonderful to have a friend who will weep with you? When you hurt, he hurts.

Jonathan says to David, "Go in peace" (v. 42). But this is not really a peaceful situation. Peace in the biblical sense is not the absence of trouble; it is the presence of God. Jesus said in this world we will have tribulation, but in Him we can have peace. Jesus said in John 14:27, "My peace I give unto you." You can have the peace of God even in difficult, troublesome times.

David was not killed by Saul. In fact, he was going to live fifty more years. He will be reigning as king for thirty of those years. God had a plan for David's life just as He has a plan for your life. You are in the hands and in the care of the almighty God. No weapon formed against you will prosper if you are living in the plan and purpose of God.

David and Jonathan experienced a beautiful friendship. It was so different from some of the friendships we see today. That Thursday night I spent in the airport really made this clear to me. We all have a friend who sticks closer than a brother—and His name is Jesus.

CHAPTER 4

Cave Matters,
or Heart in Darkness

*"The heart is deceitful above all things and
beyond cure. Who can understand it?"*
JEREMIAH 17:9

1 SAMUEL 21–24   *Heart of Darkness* is a novel by Joseph
Conrad that you may have read. It's a
book about the continent of Africa, two men, and their experiences in that part of the world. One of the men, named Marlow,
is on a journey in search of a mysterious character named
Kurtz. Marlow's journey takes him into the heart of Africa,
where he discovers Kurtz's position of power and influence over
the local people. Marlow then begins to question the values of
his culture and of himself.

The plot revolves around physical and psychological jour-
neys. The theme explores the darkness of the human heart.
Remember Jeremiah 17:9 with its statement about the human
heart: "The heart is deceitful above all things and beyond cure.
Who can understand it?" In my opinion, *Heart of Darkness* confirms that Bible verse.

Conrad's book is full of symbolism about Africa, also
known as the "Dark Continent," and about the European impe-
rialism of the last two centuries. The "heart of darkness" literally refers to the geographical heart of the African continent
(where Marlow finally confronts Kurtz), but it also figuratively
refers to the heart of the character, Kurtz. His heart is dark

because it is human, and he sees Africa and her people as an opportunity for his own wealth and profiteering.

We left our Braveheart, David, on the run at the end of the last chapter. He's a fugitive running from a jealous King Saul. Now his story continues. His life is described in 1 Samuel 21–24 as he takes refuge in caves. He still has a heart after God's heart. But his heart, just like his physical body, will be in darkness for some time. David doesn't have a heart *of* darkness like the character Kurtz in Conrad's novel, but he temporarily has a heart *in* darkness because he in hiding, and he's taking refuge in caves.

When I was pastor at my second church, I discovered there were many caves in my community. That was the church where Janet and I met. Some of the guys in the church would get together to explore the caves. Caves are certainly not my dream world because they are cold, dark, damp, and stale. Very little light enters a cave. Stalactites and stalagmites create scary images of large, fiendish mouths with sharp teeth. Only fungi and other organisms that do not require light to live in the dark inner areas of caves.

Bats, spiders, cockroaches, salamanders, and all sorts of fungi and mosses live and grow in the darkness of caves. As Tony Waltham states in his book on caves, "Inside a cave, beyond its entrance zone, it is not just dark, it is totally black. There is no light at all, and this affects nearly all forms of life."[1] Waltham goes on to describe various forms of life that live and thrive in caves, some having no eyes at all because of the constant darkness.

At the time I'm writing this in December 2001, our nation is at war in Afghanistan. Our forces are fighting Osama Bin Laden, who has admitted responsibility for the September 11, 2001 attacks on the World Trade Center and on the Pentagon. Many experts believe Osama Bin Laden is hiding in caves, making it very difficult for him to be discovered. Satan's man, Osama Bin Laden, is on the run. He knows his life is in danger, and he has reportedly taken refuge in caves. God's man, David, also feared for his life and took refuge in caves.

David was a man after God's own heart. The heart is important. The Bible tells us we are to keep our hearts with diligent care because out of the heart come the issues of life. Issues seem to be taking over our lives. We hear about issues on TV all the time—Oprah, Fox News, CNN. All of them pump information about current issues into our brains. Yet, the issues of our heart are different from the issues of peace in the Middle East or the economy or Social Security. The issues of our heart affect the quality of our lives as we make our own choices whether to live as Christians or as nonbelievers. David's life and the issues he faces, especially during his time in the caves, teach us many lessons today.

David's cave experiences are those times in his life when he is living more in the darkness than in the light. He is a fugitive, a runaway living in fear for his life. David's life could well be summarized by 1 Samuel 21:10: "That day David fled from Saul." David is wanted dead or alive. Saul is after him. The insane jealousy King Saul feels for this younger man is fueling his desire to chase and kill David.

Geographically, David will be in and out of various caves during this time. He will also hide in the woods and in the mountains. His life during these years reminds me of the young man, Eric Robert Rudolph, who escaped from authorities after being accused of various bombing incidents.

Allegedly, Rudolph lived or is still living in the mountains of North Carolina. According to the official web site for the FBI (www.fbi.gov), Rudolph is one of America's ten most wanted criminals at this time. He's on the run, and many experts think he may be seeking refuge in mountain caves. Likewise, David finds himself in caves for a time, those inner worlds of the earth, unseen hearts of darkness.

There are some new ideas going around today about the Christian life. We might thank our seemingly television-controlled popular culture for this. I'm opining here, but I do not ever remember a time since I've been living when our culture has been so centered on television. Unfortunately, many skewed ideas about Christianity come from various television shows. Perhaps this is where the idea that being a Christian means living a life of continuous mountaintop experiences comes from. The Christian life is not always lived at the crest of the wave or on the top of the mountain. All of us have to go through the valleys or the dark, unpleasant cave experiences of life.

David's heart is in darkness while he is on the run, and he finds himself in some of the cave experiences of life. Just remember, God is getting David ready to be a king, just like He is getting you and me ready to complete our next step for Him, whatever that may be. The Bible says we shall reign with Christ, but the Bible also says we will suffer. Why? Because suffering is something God uses to prepare our hearts for what He has destined for us.

David's Tribulations: The Trials of the Heart in Darkness

Have you ever been truly fearful? David knew about true life-and-death situations. My bet is he would have won the *Survivor* television contest. I believe he is actually afraid because he is living in fear, and he is making unwise decisions. Chapter 21 of 1 Samuel chronicles some of his mistakes.

In the first few verses of this chapter, David has gone to Nob to see Ahimelech, the priest. Nob is a place of worship where many priests live. Ahimelech is the priest in charge. Ahimelech becomes a bit fearful when David appears in Nob because he knows there is open hostility and hatred on Saul's part toward David. When he sees David, he naturally wonders what is up. He finally asks David, "Why are you alone? Why is no one with you?"

David answers him, but he lies. "The king charged me with a certain matter and said to me, 'No one is to know anything about your mission and your instructions'" (v. 2). Interesting. The Bible does not necessarily approve of the behavior of its heroes; it just records their behavior. Remember, David is a man after God's own heart, but he isn't perfect. He is sensitive to God. He is responsive to God. God could easily get David's attention.

David then makes two requests of Ahimilech. First, he asks for some bread (v. 3). Then he asks for a sword (v. 8). The only bread the priest has is the shewbread, or the holy, sanctified, sacred bread. The Lord Jesus makes reference to this experience later in the Bible in the New Testament in Mark 2:25–26. What does it all mean? It illustrates to us that sometimes though the letter of the law may be broken, the spirit of the law is still kept. That's an important concept for us today.

The items David asks for are symbolic. He asks for bread and for a sword. These are two things you really ought to find at the house of worship. At a church, a person should find bread to sustain him or her on the journey and a sword to equip him or her for life's battles. You may think David doesn't deserve bread, especially holy bread. When do we ever deserve what the Lord provides for us? If you and I received what we deserve, we would probably be skeletons. The Lord provides for us not on the basis of how good we are, but on the basis of how good He is. The Lord pours out His blessings upon us not because we deserve them, but because He's that kind of God.

1 Samuel 21:7 the plot thickens. We learn of a new character named Doeg. Doeg is a spy for King Saul. But that's not his day job. During the day, he works as the chief herder for Saul, meaning he takes care of the mules and donkeys. As Saul's James Bond, he makes notes of everything David does, knowing he will be able to share it with Saul later. And he does.

In verse 10 David is still living in fear. He mistakenly runs to a place called Gath. From Nob to Gath. Sounds like a good title for a book David could write. Do you know who came from Gath? Goliath did! There is a king in Gath named Achish. Picture David, God's beloved, running from Saul because fear is dominating his heart. He runs right into Goliath's hometown. He is recognized immediately. Here's the man who killed their big hero. They say to their king in verse 11, "Isn't this David, the king of the land? Isn't he the one they sing about in their dances: 'Saul has slain his thousands, and David his tens of thousands'?" "David took these words to heart and was very much afraid of Achish king of Gath" (v. 12).

It's interesting what happens when believers wind up in enemy territory, out of the will of God. When believers are living in fear, they may behave strangely. Fear is the enemy of faith. Verse 13 says about David, "So he pretended to be insane in their presence; and while he was in their hands he acted like a madman, making marks on the doors of the gate and letting saliva run down his beard." David knows he's in trouble, so he pretends he is crazy. He crawls around slobbering and scrabbling or scribbling on the walls.

King Achish says, "Am I so short of madmen that you have to bring this fellow here to carry on like this in front of me? Must this man come into my house?" (v. 15). In other words, he's basically telling his people he has enough nuts around him already, and he doesn't need another one.

It happens to Christians sometimes, too. They realize they are in enemy territory, and they make unwise decisions. If you're living out of the will of God as a Christian, you may be setting yourself up to make really bad choices. David made a bad decision to go to Gath. Think about it. Christians, including David, often get into trouble when they take refuge in the world instead of in the Lord.

David gets out of Gath and moves to the cave of Adullam, which is approximately twelve to thirteen miles from Bethlehem (1 Sam. 22:1). That's an area of the world with mammoth caves, and many people can hide in them. David is hiding in one of these caves, and his family joins him along with a group of men. The men who come to him are looking for a leader.

As David undergoes these cave experiences in his life, he becomes a different man. His experiences are changing him. The songs he writes are different, showing evidence of his deeper, more focused love for the Lord. The men who join David change as well.

They probably straggled in a few at a time at first, seeking an identity and a place to make a contribution. Yet, they were men frustrated and under pressure. They were restless and in distress. Many were in debt, some even in a state of bankruptcy. They were a discontented band, a motley crew of men seeking a leader. Nevertheless, this strange mixture of people decided to center their lives on David. They counted on David to provide for their needs in exchange for their loyalty and their fighting skills. David becomes their focus, just as Jesus should become ours.

These men become the nucleus of David's fighting force. He trains them, and eventually they will become leaders in his kingdom. David's situation paints a beautiful picture of the kind of people who come to Jesus. Perhaps they are people who are spiritually bankrupt, people who have been through devastating losses, or people who have lived as slaves to various addictions. We don't come to Christ because we are all we ought to be. We come to Christ because of the needs in our lives. Christ and only Christ can meet those needs.

Do you know anyone today in distress? Billy Joel sang a song in the 1980s called "Pressure." To me, the lyrics offer a commentary on the way many of us live today. Part of one verse in the song states you will feel that "loaded guns" as in your face, and "you'll have to deal with pressure." But later he adds, "You'll have to answer to your own pressure." Not exactly a happy song.

I believe we have more pressures in our lives today than at any other time I have witnessed. It's kind of ironic. We have so many labor-saving devices such as microwave ovens, dish-washers, and bread-making machines. We're even able to bank and shop on-line and pay for our gas at the pump. But people seem more irritable, depressed, and tired than ever. We don't ever have enough time and money. Consider our consumer credit card debt in America. It's certainly stressful to be in debt for thousands and thousands of dollars. It's also stressful to be in debt spiritually. Unfortunately, many people are almost dead spiritually.

Are you dissatisfied with your life? Are you restless? Do you feel like something is missing? Jesus Christ, who created you and your heart, knows exactly how to fill and satisfy it. Cast your lot with Him, and focus on Him as your life leader.

In Luke 14:21, Jesus told a parable. He said, "Go out quickly into the streets and alleys of the town and bring in the poor, the crippled, the blind and the lame." It's beautiful to see those who have been brought into the family of Jesus Christ. Not perfect people by any means. But people who know they need a leader, so they're willing to be submissive and to follow the authority of a leader, the authority of the Lord. Likewise, David has a group of ragtag followers who have decided to cast their lot, cave experiences and all, with his.

The rest of chapter 22 of 1 Samuel is tragic. David has to endure many challenges. The scene switches quickly back to Saul in verse 6. Just like in a novel or movie when there is an edit and the scene changes, the Bible is changing scenes here. The focus shifts from the cave of Adullam to the palace of Saul. Lights up on Saul's pity party. He's engaging in the act of feeling sorry for himself. He calls an emergency staff meeting. Do you think he conducted a professional meeting complete with correct office protocol and effective staff management at this time? Yeah, right. He harangues his staff and chews them out. He won't even call them by name. Ever been in a meeting like that?

Saul now harbors so much hatred in his heart for David that he calls him that "son of Jesse." It's still bugging Saul that David can gain such loyalty among the people of Israel. "None of you is concerned about me" (v. 8).

Doeg, Saul's own "007," speaks up. Doeg shares everything he saw happen in Nob. Saul steams and then sends for Ahimelech and the priests (v. 9). He brings them before him, and he challenges them concerning their conduct toward David. Ahimelech makes a beautiful speech. He defends David. Ahimelech inquires, "Who of all your servants is as loyal as David, the king's son-in-law, captain of your bodyguard and highly respected in your household?" (v. 14). Yet none of this soothes Saul's anger toward David.

Saul commands his soldiers, "Turn and kill the priests of the LORD" (v. 17). His power and jealousy mixed lethally here. Saul tells Doeg, "You turn and strike down the priests" (v. 18). That's just what Doeg wanted to hear. Doeg begins the slaughter, and proceeds to kill eighty-five of the priests of God. He doesn't stop there. He goes back to the village of Nob. It says in verse 19 that he smites with the edge of the sword the "men and women, its children and infants, and its cattle, donkeys and sheep." He obliterates the town. It's haunting to realize that the literal name for the village of Nob means "nothing," and that is what it became.

Meanwhile, at the cave of Adullam, David is standing. In the distance, he sees a breathless man running toward him. As the man approaches, David recognizes him as the young man Abiathar, the son of Ahimelech. He tells David everything that has happened. David realizes his responsibility in causing the deaths of the people in Nob. David's mistakes have cost a high and tragic price.

The books of 1 and 2 Samuel display David's external circumstances—the historical data, the places and locations, and the names of the characters as they move in and out of the scenes. But remember, David was a poet, a composer, and a songwriter as well. He wrote many of the psalms in your Bible, and many of them depict David's internal circumstances during his cave experiences. Sometimes it's easy to think we won't learn much about God if we aren't on the mountaintop. But in reality, we probably learn more about God in the caves than anywhere else in life. Cave experiences are definitely times of trial and tribulation. But as chapter 23 points out, they are also times of training.

David's Training: The Training of the Heart in Darkness

God gives us trials to experience in the caves of life, but He also trains us while we're in those caves, especially in what prayer is all about.

The action now shifts to a place called Keilah. The Philistines attack the people there. Basically, David and his crew go help the people in Keilah, and they win. God is training and teaching David some of the lessons that will serve him well when he's on the throne of Israel.

One lesson David learns is the importance of prayer and the Word of God. Verse 2 of chapter 23 says that David "inquired of the LORD." This time David turns in the right direction, and he seeks God's wisdom. He may have realized his need to seek the Lord and to stay in fellowship with the Lord. This is something each of us needs to realize as well. David simply asks the Lord, "Shall I go and attack these Philistines?"

The Lord says to David, "Go."

David's men tell David they are afraid. So David inquires of the Lord again (vv. 3–4). He's learning to seek Him first. He prays and prays. Sometimes we pray about something and then we pray again. Don't give up. Don't quit praying. Some of you have been praying for people's salvation for a long time, and nothing has happened yet. Don't give up.

Years ago I served a church that had what you might call an "old-timey" arrangement. Maybe you were brought up in a church like that. On each side of the pulpit were pews—the amen corners. On one side sat the ladies. On the other side sat the men. We would have testimony meetings. One sister's husband was sitting in the men's amen corner. He was actually a judge in our county. She was a very godly woman. Sometimes she would get up during our testimony meeting and point to her husband and say, "I prayed twenty years for that man over there to get saved." I've thought about her and her husband often. What if she had prayed ten years and stopped? What if she stopped after sixteen years, feeling sure it would never happen? Don't ever give up. Keep praying. He will answer you. God does hear your prayers.

When Abiathar fled, he came down with an ephod (v. 6). An ephod was part of the clothing a priest wore, so it's significant because it's symbolic. Inside the ephod a priest had the urim and the thummim. Apparently, these were stones the priest used to figure out the will of God. The urim meant light, and the thummim meant perfection. They were placed in the breastplate of the priest. We don't use stones today to determine God's will. We have God's Word instead. If you want to know His will for you, thumb through His Word and pray. These two things go together.

David's best friend Jonathan reappears: "And Saul's son Jonathan went to David at Horesh and helped him find strength in God" (v. 16). That's a beautiful thought. Jonathan is a real friend. When you are going through the cave experiences of life, you may realize that God has people all along the way. In those times of testing, God will send someone your way to encourage and strengthen you. Jonathan took David's hand and put it in God's hand. That's the best thing a friend can do for you. If you know someone who is going through a cave experience, the best thing you can do is to remind that person of God's promises.

Jonathan and David then renew their covenant. This is actually the last time they will ever see each other. I had a best friend one time. He came by my house and told me his dad had a new job in another town and he would be moving. He said he'd be back, and he'd see me again. I was maybe seven or eight years old. He moved, and I never saw him again. Sometimes friends leave us. David never saw his friend physically again, but God gave David the sweet experience of a valued friendship as he endured cave experiences.

But let's not forget about Saul. He's still on David's trail. In verses 19 through 28, you can almost hear the bloodhounds baying as they lead the men closer and closer to David. The climax of the chapter comes down to two men on two sides of the same mountain. David is on one side. Saul is on the other. "Saul and his forces were closing in on David and his men to capture them" (v. 26). David is surrounded. Saul is virtually breathing down his neck waiting for the perfect moment to attack.

"A messenger came to Saul, saying, 'Come quickly! The Philistines are raiding the land'" (v. 27). Now that's a climax. He is just about to find what he has been seeking so long and then he is called to protect the homeland. This really teaches us about the providence of God. You think you're going under. You think you will definitely be attacked. And then something happens out of the clear blue, and you are delivered. Definitely a God thing!

When Janet and I were in seminary, we were as poor as Tom's turkey. No, I don't know how poor Tom's turkey was, but it must have been pretty poverty-stricken. We didn't have anything—seriously. Sunday dinner might consist of banana sandwiches—and if we had a little extra, we'd get to smear peanut butter on them. I'll never forget what happened during that time. There were school bills and other obligations that I needed to pay. I didn't have anything in the world to pay with. While I was studying the Scripture, I ran across Psalm 37:3: "Trust in the LORD and do good; dwell in the land and enjoy safe pasture."

I told the Lord as best I knew I was trusting in Him. I was studying there at the seminary to prepare to preach for Him. I told Him I thought I was doing the good He wanted me to do. The Lord's promise was that I would dwell in the land and be fed. I claimed that promise.

The next morning I went to our mailbox at the school. A sweet Christian layman in Bremen, Georgia, who was the general manager of Sewell Clothing Company, had written me a letter to say, "The Lord just laid it on my heart to help you a little bit." He sent me a check. It was enough to pay for every financial obligation I had and to take Janet out to dinner.

That was one of my early cave experiences, and I felt it was a trial. Now I realize it was also a time of training. David had many cave experiences, and his were times of trial, training, and triumph.

David's Triumph:
The Triumph of the Heart in Darkness

What if someone asked you, "What's the greatest victory David ever won?"

You might reply, "Definitely the valley of Elah, where David defeated the giant Goliath."

That was certainly a great victory, but I would answer that question differently. I believe the greatest victory David ever won was in the cave of En Gedi. In chapter 24, David's victory over himself, over Saul, and over sin is recorded.

Verse 1 describes him in the wilderness of En Gedi. En Gedi literally means "spring of the wild goat." It's a beautiful place on the western banks of the Dead Sea, which marks the lowest spot on the earth. Speaking both literally and figuratively, David is about as low as he can go. His heart is going into deeper and deeper darkness. He's about to bottom out in his life while he is hiding out in caves. Some of the caves in this area are as large as luxury hotel lobbies. You could put a full basketball court in some of them. Some can easily hold 300,000 people.

Here David and his men hide. Saul and his men come near still pursuing David with three thousand men. Saul feels the call of nature and goes into the cave. The Bible says he relieves himself. David and his men are hiding in the dark recesses of the cave. All of a sudden, David's men see a large shadow fill up the mouth of the cave. It's Saul. Picture the scene. The desert sun is so bright, Saul cannot see anything when he walks into the dark cave. David's men realize they're about to hit the bulls-eye. They say, "This is the day the LORD spoke of when he said to you, 'I will give your enemy into your hands for you to deal with as you wish'" (v. 4). If you consider appearances only, David's men are right. It does seem to be the perfect time for an attack.

It's easy to make the mistake of thinking that outward appearances or favorable circumstances are always indications that God is in a matter. But it's better not to assume. David's men are telling him to kill Saul. They remind him that Saul threw a javelin at him twice in attempts to kill him. They also remind him that Saul is the man who lies about him. Here is the man who has chased David in and out of caves all over the land. Here is the man keeping David from the kingdom that God has promised. You can almost hear David's men encouraging him to do the dirty deed.

If you think about it, the true test of a Christian comes when his or her enemy is in a vulnerable position. It's all about character. What will you do when you have a chance to exact revenge on your enemies and show your true colors?

David refuses to seek revenge. His opportunity for revenge actually becomes a time to exercise restraint. David knows he is God's anointed one, and he knows he can wait for God's timing. It would be better for David to be dead than to live on Saul's level, which makes rules by hatred and makes kings go insane. Saul is a man after the devil's heart, but David is a man after God's heart. Imagine what David's men must think as they see their leader let his chance for revenge slip by. Yet, David's actions witness clearer than any bloody killing could.

David does sneak up behind Saul, however, and he cuts off a piece of his clothing. When Saul leaves the cave, David follows him. David calls out, "My lord the king!"

Saul hears the voice and slowly turns around. The hair rises on his neck. He looks up and sees David's hand holding a piece of his robe, which flaps violently in the hot desert wind. Saul's heart does a free fall. The realization hits Saul. That could be his heart swinging in the wind.

It's a long story, but basically David demonstrates here that he will not live according to the retaliatory ways of this world. Instead, he will live according to the ways of God. David decides to let God put him on the throne, not himself. That's a good lesson for all of us to apply to our lives. Think of Jesus. He faced temptation in the wilderness as He was offered the "kingdoms of the world" (Matt. 4:8). That temptation was a shortcut, a cheap and quick imitation of the true kingdom to come. Don't let the shortcut to fame or fortune tempt you. God gives us His kingdom on the long, hard road of sanctification.

David's story at this point also illustrates his respect for his authority, which I feel many people have lost today. David considers himself a nobody. You see, David was Saul's enemy, but Saul was never David's enemy. The fact is Saul is still on the throne. Maybe he's not the king he needs to be, but he is David's king. As long as the king lives, David has no right under God to harm him.

Are you humble enough to submit to your authorities? It's a good self-test for all of us. Authorities are with us throughout our lives on the job or at the church or in the office where we pay our taxes. I'm going to level with you. If you have trouble with authority, then you are in rebellion against God. David did the right thing, even though he was encouraged to kill his king in the cave.

There are incredible moments in the Bible. Moments where we the reader can almost see the actions and expressions of the people on a large movie screen. Verse 8 portrays such a scene to me. David calls to Saul as he holds up the piece of his robe. David calls him, "My lord the king." Can you picture that moment? Saul probably felt goose bumps rise on his flesh. Saul's immediate realization that he could be dead combined with David's sincerity in calling to his king must have stunned Saul. In fact, it is David's sincerity that convicts Saul. We know this because the Bible says he is stricken, and he weeps.

I've talked quite a bit about plot and climax in this chapter, comparing what's happening in David's life to a compelling story line. Well, no story line would be complete without a resolution. When Saul acknowledges that David will one day be king, he then asks him to be kind to his family. As David promises this to Saul, a beautiful resolution of the story so far occurs. After that, Saul goes home, and David returns to a cave.

In Romans 12:17–21, the New Testament recounts how David lived in the cave of En Gedi. "Do not repay anyone evil for evil. Be careful to do what is right in the eyes of everybody. If it is possible, as far as it depends on you, live at peace with everyone. Do not take revenge, my friends, but leave room for God's wrath, for it is written: 'It is mine to avenge; I will repay,' says the Lord. On the contrary: 'If your enemy is hungry, feed him; if he is thirsty, give him something to drink. In doing this, you will heap burning coals on his head.' Do not be overcome by evil, but overcome evil with good."

It all boils down to each one of us and the level of life on which we choose to live. We can live on the satanic level, rendering evil for good. We can live on the merely human level, rendering evil for evil. Or, we can live on the divine level, rendering good for evil.

In the caves, David wrote some of the best psalms in the Bible. For example, consider Psalms 34, 57, and 142. In these psalms, David often mentions "refuge." Did you know that this is what the Cave of Adullum means? That word *refuge* means a place to run and hide geographically, but it also means God, our refuge.

Through David's cave experiences while his heart is in darkness, he learns that his only true refuge is God. Because we're human, most of us don't start with God when we have a cave experience. If the car won't start or if our child is sick and fussy, we focus on the problem. Yet, it's often in these cave experiences that we realize God is our refuge.

Marlow finally finds Kurtz in the heart of Africa in Conrad's novel *Heart of Darkness*. But he doesn't like what he discovers because he sees how the evil of Kurtz's heart has manifested itself. Unfortunately, that evilness lurks in all human hearts without God. We all have hearts of darkness in need of God's redemption through Jesus Christ.

David was a man after God's own heart. For a time in his life, though, his heart lived in darkness as he was on the run from cave to cave. Our hearts don't have to be hearts *in* darkness or hearts *of* darkness because we have a redeemer named Jesus Christ. Be a man or woman after God's own heart as David, our Braveheart, was—and enjoy a heart and a life that lives in the light, not the darkness.

CHAPTER 5

Enemy Matters, or Desperately Seeking David

"You have heard that it was said, 'Love your neighbor and hate your enemy.' But I tell you: Love your enemies and pray for those who persecute you."
MATTHEW 5:43–44

1 SAMUEL 24   Darth Vader and Luke Skywalker. Bugs Bunny versus Elmer Fudd. Sherlock Holmes and Professor Moriarty. James Bond and his nemesis, Ernst Blofeld. Batman and The Joker. What do all these people have in common? They're enemies, of course.

Since the beginning of mankind, there have been stories of one person plotting evil against his or her enemy. The list of enemies in our current culture and past history is seemingly endless.

As Saul is desperately seeking David in the Middle Eastern wilderness, we see another enemy relationship. Saul has made David his enemy by seeking his death and demise. But David has not made an enemy of Saul.

Just what is an enemy? *The American Heritage Dictionary* defines enemy as "one who manifests malice or hostility toward, or opposes the purposes or interests of, another; a foe, an opponent." An enemy is someone who means another harm. King Saul fits the definition perfectly because he shows increasing ill will and hostility toward David.

Consider the field of literature and some enemy relationships portrayed there. One diabolical foe I remember is Iago from Shakespeare's tragic play, *Othello*. Iago determines to destroy his general, Othello, whom Iago has made his enemy. This corrupt and vile character plants the idea in Othello's head that his wife, Desdemona, is committing adultery. Why? Because Iago is jealous of a guy named Cassio when he is appointed as Othello's chief lieutenant. Iago wants that job. Remember, an enemy is a person who seeks to bring another person down. All the way down. Iago plots Othello's downfall by falsely implicating Desdemona and Cassio in a love affair. Tragically, Othello believes the false accusations and is overcome with jealousy. He kills his wife in a fit of passion, only to learn later she was innocent. The tragedy does not end there, however, because Othello then kills himself.

Iago's character illustrates to me just how evil one human can be to another. He is driven to destroy the man he has made his enemy. In one memorable passage from the play, Iago says, "The thought [of revenge] . . . doth, like a poisonous mineral, gnaw my inwards; and nothing can or shall content my soul till I am evened with him, wife for wife; or failing so, yet that I put the Moor [Othello] into a jealousy so strong that judgement cannot cure."[2]

In addition to creating villainous enemies, Shakespeare writes works with tight plot lines. In recent years, many of his plays have been remade into movies to cater to a young audience. I'm reminded of the 1996 movie version of *Romeo and Juliet,* in which the story of Romeo and Juliet is told in what movie critic Leonard Maltin calls a "postmodern MTV style through the perspective of rival gangs."

I recently noticed that another of Shakespeare's stories has morphed into a movie. It's entitled *O* and is based on Shakespeare's play *Othello*. Again, I believe it confirms just how universal a story is if it can evolve into new forms for new audiences.

Of course, the movie is very different than the original Shakespeare play. For example, according to a plot summary found on Internet Movie Database (www.imdb.org), the film's setting takes place at "an elite private high school in the American South," not in Italy. The characters are teenagers, not soldiers and gentlemen as they are in Shakespeare's play. Finally, the conflict in the movie does not center on war or the threat of war, as it does in the play. In the movie, the conflict occurs on the basketball court.

Nevertheless, the release of this movie confirms that people often seek good stories as entertainment, and Shakespeare was on to an interesting plot line pitting evil against good when he penned his play *Othello*.

The plot summary characterizes *Othello* as a draw for today's young people: "This tale of treachery, jealousy, and mistrust will introduce a new audience to the genius of William Shakespeare and some of his most intriguing and intelligent characters . . . The film thoroughly examines the emotions of its characters. Through jealousy, favoritism, trust, and envy, to popularity, conformity, and the extreme measure some will take to fulfill their feelings, *O* looks into the heart of darkness, not through a sadistic serial killer or demonic monster, but through one of the most dangerous figures of all, a friend with ulterior motives."

While the story of David and Saul does not have the type of tragic ending Shakespeare's *Othello* does, there is an obvious similarity in the motivations of the characters and in the themes of both stories. Both Iago and Saul allow jealousy to cloud their judgment. Both villains let their passionate hatred of their enemies outweigh logic when making decisions. Both men are insecure in their positions and seek to bring others down. One might even argue that they are dissatisfied with their lives. That's a dangerous state in which to live.

Often, the theme of a good story is good versus evil, and we all love a good story. Many view the Christian faith as a fight between good and evil. But with David and Saul it's different.

Their story is reversed. It's really about evil versus good. Saul, the king, is letting his jealousy of David rule his thinking, and therefore, he seeks to do harm to David, our Braveheart.

What does David do? Does he always react on a human level, as we would probably do? During this treacherous time, David shows a faith, fortitude, and form we can follow today when we're facing our enemies.

David's Faith

For approximately ten years, David is a fugitive running from Saul, who seeks to murder him. Remember, David is the one whom God has selected to be Saul's successor, and God has rejected Saul because of his disobedience. Even so, David is living as a victim of Saul's vicious antagonism and hatred. In reality, Saul knows it's all over for him. He knows the Lord has rejected him because of his own unwise decisions, yet he is trying to prevent the inevitable and deny the sovereign will and plan of God. Saul, like Iago, is a man who has allowed jealousy to control his life.

David is on the run, hiding mostly in nearby caves. Picture David in the cave at En Gedi, which is in the southern part of the land of Israel, near the Dead Sea. In a figurative sense, David is at a low point in his life because he is living in fear for his life. He's also at a low point geographically, since he's at the Dead Sea. He knows he has been chosen by God to be king, but what is he doing? He's trying to escape his spear-throwing king. It seems there is simply no refuge for him. He seeks caves for their protection and shelter. Yet, everywhere he turns he encounters Saul stalking him. If ever there was a time for his faith to be tested, this was it.

For the first time, David realizes what it means to have an enemy in life. Do you have an enemy? When I was sixteen years old, I started preaching. By the time I was eighteen, I was a pastor at my first church. I heard that somebody in the church was criticizing me. I knew this person and thought of him as a friend. The person verbally attacked me. Now get this. I was just a young, single guy at the time. When I heard what had been said, I went home, went into my room, fell across the bed, and cried. It shocked me that anyone would be so unkind. I'm older and wiser now, and I have found that most of us will encounter people who are enemies who mean to do us harm. Believe it. It just is not possible in this world to always "live at peace with everyone" as Romans 12:18 suggests.

Three thousand soldiers are with King Saul as he pursues David near the cave of En Gedi. First Samuel 24:3 details Saul's journey into that cave to relieve himself. Saul cannot see all the vigilant eyes focused on him—eyes of men hoping David will seize this opportunity to kill Saul.

Verse 4 expands on just what an opportunity David has to get rid of his pursuer. David's men say to him, "This is the day the LORD spoke of when he said to you, 'I will give your enemy into your hands for you to deal with as you wish'" (v. 4). The men see a God-given opportunity to do away with Saul who is preventing David from stepping to the throne God has selected for him. They are basically rationalizing the decision for David by reminding him that God said he would deliver his enemy into his hand. In reality, an easy way out has just presented itself to David.

The real application for us occurs when we ask ourselves what we would do if we had a similar opportunity. Would we have enough faith to believe that vengeance is to be left to the Lord? Would we trust that God evens the score? The lesson here is a hard one. We should never decide the will of God on the basis of outward circumstances. Just because a situation to exact revenge presents itself to us does not mean God is leading us to do it. It takes faith to see a situation like that in those terms. David had faith. The challenge is, Do we?

The idea of making decisions based on outward circumstances reminds me of Jonah (see Jonah 1:1–3). No question about it, Jonah was a man living out of God's will. God specifically told him to go to Nineveh. But Jonah did not want to go. Jonah knew if he preached what God wanted him to preach and if people repented, God would save them. In effect, Jonah didn't want them to be saved. He wanted God to judge them. Actually, he wanted God to kill them, and he felt he was right. God told Jonah to go to Nineveh, and Jonah chose to go in the opposite direction. He went to Joppa where the ships were embarking, and he found a ship going exactly where he wanted to go. He even had enough money to pay the price of the voyage. He thought he was doing just what God wanted him to do.

Jonah considered all the circumstances to be lining up for him according to God's will for his life. Yet, he was deliberately disobeying God. Jonah's circumstances weren't the will of God at all. His opportunity in and of itself was not evidence that this was what God wanted him to do. In fact, it was not at all what God wanted him to do.

Sometimes we are able to manipulate opportunities. Maybe we think we can throw the Lord a hint or two. We try to arrange and construct circumstances ourselves, and then we think we've got a "God thing" going on. In reality, we've just put God off.

David has an opportunity at the mouth of the cave to cause some serious harm to his nemesis. What do you do when you have an opportunity for revenge? Do you have enough faith to let God take care of your enemy situation for you? David wasn't suckered into using this opportunity for revenge. Instead, he used it as an opportunity for restraint. So what does David do? He cuts off a piece of Saul's robe. David was a man after God's own heart. He wanted to be like God.

In the Gospel of Matthew, Jesus talks about our relationship with our enemies. Jesus says, "You have heard that it was said, 'Love your neighbor and hate your enemy.' But I tell you: Love your enemies and pray for those who persecute you" (Matt. 5:43–44). That's the Lord's way to deal with our enemies.

There are three ways we can respond to those who do us wrong.

First, there's the human level, which returns evil for evil or good for good. If somebody hits you, then you hit him back. If somebody does a good turn for you, then you do a good turn for him. It's really scorekeeping. This is the way most people live.

The second response level is the satanic level, which returns evil for good. Picture two first graders. Cindy asks Aimee for a pencil, and Aimee generously gives Cindy one of her own to use. Cindy then takes Aimee's pencil and breaks it in a game of "pencil-breaks" with Chad who sits behind her.

Finally, there is the divine level that returns good for evil. That's the Jesus level, and it is the level David chooses in this situation.

God has told David that he is going to be king, and David has the faith to believe God. He decides he is not going to take any shortcuts to the throne. He doesn't have to. The Lord Jesus had a shortcut offer made to him by the devil. When Satan was tempting Jesus in the wilderness, not far from this same cave, by the way, Satan says, "All this [kingdoms of the world] I will give you if you will bow down and worship me" (Matt. 4:9).

The devil was offering Jesus all the kingdoms of the world. Funny thing is, God the Father had already decreed that these kingdoms would ultimately be His. But the devil is saying, "Oh, come on. Take this shortcut and get it now." Many people today may take the devil up on his offers. It seems that instant gratification is the name of the game in America today. We don't like to wait for anything. I remember when waiting forty-five seconds to get my computer on-line was lightning speed. Now that's as slow as rush-hour traffic on the expressway.

The devil wants us to take the shortcuts because it makes us rely less on our faith in God. But God's way is the way of sanctification, which is the process of being made holy or set apart for God's purposes. So God allows us to go through cave experiences in life. Have faith and let God do what He wants to do in your life, as He gets you ready for where He wants you to be.

First Samuel 24:5 gives another insight into David and into his true character: "Afterward, David was conscience-stricken for having cut off a corner of his robe." That speaks volumes about David. You will know just how committed you are to the Lord by your reaction to the little inconsistencies and happenings in human life. For example, if a person receives too much change from a sales clerk, what does he or she do? Does this little thing trouble the person, or does the person just let it slide, figuring he or she needs the extra cash more than the store does. When you reach the point that even the little things trouble you, you know you are getting closer to where God wants you to be.

David's Fortitude

There have been many movies released in the past twenty years presenting characters who have guts. These men show bravery and a strong will to right wrongs. Rambo comes to mind as one such character.

In this encounter with Saul at the cave, David shows an incredible amount of fortitude, or strength of mind and will. His faith in God's purpose for him is his foundation, and his fortitude allows him to have the courage he needs.

David is also a humble man. We've actually lost the concept of that word today in this "me first" culture. I'm reminded of another literary character, one who pretends to be a humble man. Uriah Heep in *David Copperfield* by Charles Dickens is yet another character who allows jealousy to obscure his judgment. Dickens's character is also a person who pretends to be humble, but in reality is quite egotistical and selfish.

Because of his fortitude, David is sure of himself and his decision. David says to his men who were probably looking at him with dubious expressions on their faces, "The LORD forbid that I should do such a thing to my master" (v. 6). Notice that David calls Saul "my master." He also calls him "the LORD's anointed." In verse 8, David calls him "my lord the king." In verse 11, he calls him "my father." David obviously respects Saul as his king.

David asks, "Against whom has the king of Israel come out? Whom are you pursuing? A dead dog? A flea?" (v. 14). David is basically acknowledging that compared to the king of Israel, he's a nobody. He's tremendously humble.

David calls out to Saul, "My lord the king" (v. 8). Saul probably realized the implications immediately. He probably thought, *I could be dead meat right now.* Verse 8 continues, "When Saul looked behind him, David bowed down and prostrated himself with his face to the ground." David is saying in word and deed that he does not think of himself as important. Why is David so humble in the presence of a man who is so obviously out of the will of God?

The key to David's humility can be found in the phrases he uses to refer to Saul, his authority. He calls Saul "the Lord's anointed," yet we know that Saul is out of the will of God. God has rejected him. But David recognizes that Saul is still the Lord's anointed ruler for Israel. And indeed Saul was. Do you remember back in the earlier chapters of 1 Samuel? God had anointed Saul to be the king. He was God's chosen man for that particular period of time. Even though Saul was not living for God and had ruthlessly chased David with the intent to kill him, David still had respect for Saul's authority.

In Psalm 105, a principle is given that David illustrates with his actions at the cave with Saul. The psalmist says, "He allowed no one to oppress them; for their sake he rebuked kings: 'Do not touch my anointed ones; do my prophets no harm'" (vv. 14–15). God doesn't want us to do wrong or to feel ill will toward those He puts in authority. Saul was God's anointed, and David was submissive to the principle of authority.

Your view of the authorities in your life can say quite a bit about you. Are you humble enough, as David was, to submit to authority? Maybe those in authority over you aren't what they should be. Nevertheless, as Christians we are commanded to respect them. David had no right to harm his king because Saul was in authority over David.

One of the root problems America faces today is our rebellion against authority. As a nation, we have little or no respect for authority. Many causes of this disrespect can be traced back to the 1960s. The hippie movement and rock culture in America may be considered nostalgic visits to the past now. But if you study their beginnings carefully, you realize that at the very root of much of the music is rebellion against authority. Many popular lyrics attack areas of human authority such as government, the church, and the family. And lack of authority and respect for authority causes chaos.

David was a humble man and a man after God's own heart because he had the fortitude to respect his authority. He refused to touch God's anointed man, even though that man was out of the will of God. David has the guts to refuse to retaliate against this king who has made him an enemy. By doing so, he becomes more like the Lord Jesus. WWJD? WWDD? Just what David did. If you want to know how mature you are as a Christian, notice how you react when your enemy is in your control. David lets God be God when Saul is vulnerable before him.

First Peter 2:21–23 says, "To this you were called, because Christ suffered for you, leaving you an example, that you should follow in his steps. He committed no sin, and no deceit was found in his mouth. When they hurled their insults at him, he did not retaliate; when he suffered, he made no threats. Instead, he entrusted himself to him who judges justly." David refused to seek revenge.

As Saul leaves the cave, he hears David call out to him in great humility. David has made it clear that he will not touch the Lord's anointed, and by so doing provides a beautiful witness for the Lord. We can learn quite a bit about our own witnessing from David. He says, "This day you have seen with your own eyes how the LORD delivered you into my hands in the cave. Some urged me to kill you, but I spared you; I said, 'I will not lift my hand against my master, because he is the Lord's anointed'" (v. 10).

Then David holds up the scrap of robe. "See, my father, look at this piece of your robe in my hand! I cut off the corner of your robe but did not kill you. Now understand and recognize that I am not guilty of wrongdoing or rebellion. I have not wronged you, but you are hunting me down to take my life" (v. 11).

Imagine Saul at that moment. He's busted. He must have realized immediately that it could have been his heart in David's hand instead of a piece of cloth. And that cloth in David's hand provides visible, tangible proof to Saul that David is not his enemy.

David's Form

The combination of David's faith, his fortitude, and his good form while facing an enemy shows believers today many important truths.

"May the LORD judge between you and me" (v. 12). In other words, David is saying that he's not going to play God or try to do God's job. David knows that God and only God is the judge. We are human, and we don't know everything. We simply don't see the big picture. Let God be God. Judgment belongs to the Lord. It is not our responsibility to hand out judgment. David's actions with Saul at the cave provide an excellent form for us to follow in similar circumstances.

"And may the LORD avenge the wrongs you have done to me, but my hand will not touch you" (v. 12). Do you have an enemy? Do you have someone doing you wrong? God says and David shows us by example that we should put our enemies into the hand of God. God can take care of whatever vengeance may be deserved. This is a hard lesson.

Romans 12 presents the classic passage in the New Testament on the principle of no retaliation: "If it is possible, as far as it depends on you, live at peace with everyone" (v. 18). In other words, as Christians, we are to get along with everyone, if possible. But the indication is that there are times when it's not possible. Still we should try. I know there are people who try to do us in, people who don't like us, and people who try to undercut us and make us look bad.

If this is the case, then look at verse 19–21: "Do not take revenge, my friends, but leave room for God's wrath, for it is written: 'It is mine to avenge; I will repay,' says the Lord." "On the contrary: "If your enemy is hungry, feed him; if he is thirsty, give him something to drink. In doing this, you will heap burning coals on his head. Do not be overcome by evil, but overcome evil with good." God says get on the offensive instead of the defensive. In other words, act—don't react.

In 1 Samuel 24, David proves that his heart is pure toward Saul, and that he's not going to retaliate against him. It moves Saul's heart. According to verse 16, "When David finished saying this, Saul asked, 'Is that your voice, David my son?' And he wept aloud." It touched him. The Bible says a soft answer turns away wrath. Hard-hearted Saul melts, and David shows good form like God wants him to and wants us to through all the cave experiences of life.

Saul says, "You are more righteous than I" (v. 17). Basically, Saul has realized that David is very much like the Lord and he himself is not. He acknowledges to himself that David is more righteous than he is. Saul proves that he knows this because later in the verse he says, "You have treated me well, but I have treated you badly."

This is what God says to do. It's God's command. Saul just says, "When a man finds his enemy, does he let him get away unharmed? May the LORD reward you well for the way you treated me today" (v. 19). Saul now knows that David is not his enemy. David was never Saul's enemy, but Saul was David's enemy.

You can't help it if someone has a bad attitude toward you or if somebody does wrong toward you. But you can choose to have a good attitude toward him or her. And you can choose to respond in a godly way to what he has said or done. Verse 20 wraps up the scene as Saul says, "I know that you will surely be king and that the kingdom of Israel will be established in your hands." Saul had a clue, and he knew what was coming.

Saul says something that proves his attitude toward David has changed: "'Now swear to me by the LORD that you will not cut off my descendants or wipe out my name from my father's family.' So David gave his oath to Saul" (vv. 21–22). David promised that he would do what Saul asked. Then they dispersed. Saul went back home, and David went back into a hiding place.

If you have an enemy and you refuse to retaliate by doing good for evil, your enemy will notice. He or she will see your kindness and your sweetness, and it will make an impact. Your enemy may not apologize or hug your neck. But think about it. Is what your enemy does really the issue here? It's what you do that's important. It's about the form you show to others who are watching your Christian walk. You don't do what is right because your enemies will respond to it. You do what is right because it is right, because it is what God wants you to do.

Some of the greatest psalms David wrote were from his cave years. Psalm 142 is an example. I imagine that David wrote this psalm during this particular cave experience with Saul.

"I cry aloud to the LORD; I lift up my voice to the LORD for mercy. I pour out my complaint before him; before him I tell my trouble. When my spirit grows faint within me, it is you who know my way. In the path where I walk men have hidden a snare for me. Look to my right and see; no one is concerned for me. I have no refuge; no one cares for my life" (vv. 1–4).

When Saul began chasing David, David looked for a place to hide. That's what a refuge is. A cave could be considered a refuge. The troubles you have in life could cause you to seek a hiding place or a cave of sorts. People look for all kinds of hiding places when the pressures of life come their way. An unfaithful mate perhaps. Or a rebellious child. Or a jerk of a boss. Difficult circumstances in life may drive us to caves.

Yet, David makes a crucial discovery during his cave years. He discovers that refuge is not a place. He even says, "I have no refuge; no one cares for my life" (v. 4). But he learned, "I cry to you, O LORD; I say, 'You are my refuge, my portion in the land of the living'" (v. 5). Now he sees it! Refuge is not a place. It's a Person. David realizes the Lord is his refuge because there isn't a cave safe enough. Refuge is not a location to which we run. Refuge is a person in whom we trust. And that refuge is Jesus.

CHAPTER 6

Foolish Matters,
or Everybody Plays
the Fool Some Time

Everybody plays the fool sometime;
There's no exception to the rule.
POPULAR LYRIC

1 SAMUEL 25–27   These words come from a 1970s soul
song entitled "Everybody Plays the Fool"
by a group called The Main Ingredient. Interesting how those
lyrics apply to all of us as humans. I must admit it's true. I have
played the fool. You may have. David did also.

The word *fool* has an interesting etymology. It comes from
the Latin word *follies,* meaning "bellows" or "windbag." Maybe
you've known someone you consider a windbag—a talkative
person who communicates nothing of substance or interest.

There's also the idea of the fool as a court jester, the comic
entertainer whose real or pretended madness made him a
source of entertainment for kings and noblemen and gave him
license to poke fun at everything and everyone around him.
Even William Shakespeare got in on the game by creating memorable fools in his plays. One of them is Touchstone in *As You
Like It.* Another is the fool in *King Lear.*

I came dangerously close to playing the fool back when
Janet and I were in seminary. We had just been married. She

worked for one of the professors at the school. He made a risqué comment to her one day. She came home torn up. She told me about it, and I was torn up. Yes, I had a temper. No, I'm not proud of it. The Lord has certainly helped me work on that through the years. Remember, we were just married. I was in my twenties, and I was hot under the collar. I decided I would go to his office, and we would duke it out on the campus. I was falling right into the role of the fool, and the show was ready to begin.

As I approached the professor's office, I saw one of my best friends who is now a pastor in Alabama. He stopped me and said, "Now wait a minute, Jerry. You are going to get kicked out of seminary. How many churches would want to call a pastor who got kicked out of seminary? We need to go to the school's business manager and let him handle it."

That's what we did, and the situation was resolved. But I will never forget how close I came to playing the fool in my own life and how close I came to making extremely foolish decisions for my family.

David, our Braveheart, also played the fool during the time in life chronicled in 1 Samuel 25–27. He's a man on the run. A fugitive. He is God's choice to be the next king of Israel, yet he's constantly searching for a better hiding place. Why? Because David is still in his time of preparation. God wants to prepare us for what he has prepared for us. Remember the Boy Scout motto, "Be prepared"? That's what God asks of David here and what He asks of you and me in our lives. God knows what He is doing in your life, even if it seems hard, and He is moving you in the direction of His perfect plan for your life.

When Samuel anoints David with oil, it signifies an event for David. The Bible says when David was anointed, the Spirit of the Lord came upon David from that day forward. So David was always a Spirit-filled man, right? Not exactly. He was a man after God's own heart. The Spirit of God came upon David from that day forward, but this does not mean David was always

in God's will. It doesn't mean David was Spirit-fille[
and in every situation in his life.

It's the same for you and me today. When you an   ...c
to know the Lord as our Savior, our hearts are indwelt by the
Holy Spirit. This is how it is supposed to work for Christians.
The Bible teaches that it is possible for believers to walk in the
Spirit, but it is also possible for believers to walk in the flesh. We
are not always what we should be. We do not always live under
the control of the Holy Spirit.

Here's another reason why it's valuable for Christians to
study the life of David. His life is an effective illustration of this
truth.

It's also important for us to study David's life because he is
not a perfect human being, just as we're not perfect. He has ups
and downs, good days and bad days. His life is lived in episodes,
just like a sitcom or a TV drama. So let's examine David's life
through a series of episodes in these chapters and learn how we
can live as men and women after God's own heart instead of
playing the fool.

David's Dangerous Episode

Chapter 25 of 1 Samuel exhibits a dangerous episode in
David's life. First of all, Samuel dies. Every earthly source of
comfort is being taken away from David now. David's great
mentor, Samuel, is dead. He is still running from Saul, and he
heads into the wilderness of Paran.

Do you remember any characters from literature or from
childhood stories? I do. Scrooge is a mean character from
Dickens's *A Christmas Carol*. Another character I remember is
Atticus Finch from *To Kill a Mockingbird*. Atticus is a noble
character. To me, David's life reads like a great novel, especially
with all the interesting characters he meets. These different
characters teach us lessons, even now. Two characters we meet
through David in this chapter are Nabal and Abigail, a married
couple.

According to the King James Version, Nabal was "churlish." Not really a word we use too much today. It means "surly." Think of Nabal as gruff—and you'll get the picture. He was churlish and evil. He was mean. It was probably impossible to get along with him. He was nasty and hard and cruel and vicious.

By contrast, we are told that Abigail was a woman of good understanding and of a beautiful countenance. In other words, she was intelligent and attractive. She had good sense, and she had good looks. It's amazing these two people ever got together. Sometimes the most unlikely people marry. Have you ever wondered why some women marry the men they do? According to the customs of that day, Abigail didn't have much choice in the matter. Yet, they were a couple and David is about to enter their lives.

Picture sheep-shearing season in rural Israel. David hears that Nabal is shearing his sheep, so he sends about ten young men out to Nabal (1 Sam. 25:4–5). David tells the young men to say, "Long life to you! Good health to you and your household! And good health to all that is yours! Now I hear that it is sheep-shearing time. When your shepherds were with us, we did not mistreat them, and the whole time they were at Carmel nothing of theirs was missing" (vv. 6–7).

In other words, David is telling his young men to go to Nabal and to tell him that while his shepherds were out in the fields with these sheep, they just kind of took care of them. David's men guarded them. In reality, that particular area was a high crime district, and there was no police department to call for help. David provided a security service.

Even Nabal's men later acknowledge that this is true. Nabal's men say, "Yet these men were very good to us. They did not mistreat us, and the whole time we were out in the fields near them nothing was missing. Night and day they were a wall around us all the time we were herding our sheep near them" (vv. 15–16).

Since David's men had served as security for Nabal's shepherds, it was the custom for them to expect to be rewarded. According to the customs of the day, refreshments and supplies could be expected. It was considered proper etiquette. Miss Manners would approve.

Verse 10 shows us just how mean Nabal is. "Nabal answered David's servants, 'Who is this David? Who is this son of Jesse? Many servants are breaking away from their masters these days.'"

Doesn't sound too hospitable, does it? Nabal must not have been a Southerner! His response is simply hateful and ugly. Nabal is basically asking just who David thinks he is. He lumps or categorizes David in a class of criminals. David? The man who would be king? Yes. Nabal labels him a no good, runaway slave. Have you ever been lumped into a certain class by someone? Maybe your boss categorizes you a certain way. Maybe your relatives do. That kind of categorizing reveals far more about the person who puts people into categories then it does about the people he labels. And that's just what Nabal does here. By reacting the way he does to David, he reveals his true character: "Why should I take my bread and water, and the meat I have slaughtered for my shearers, and give it to men coming from who knows where?" (v. 11).

Talk about playing the fool! Nabal here exemplifies a full-length, three-dimensional portrait of a fool. Jesus, in the New Testament, gives us a portrait of a fool also. In Luke 12:18–19, the story of the rich fool is given. The Scripture says, "This is what I'll do. I will tear down my barns and build bigger ones, and there I will store all my grain and my goods. And I'll say to myself, 'You have plenty of good things laid up for many years.'" Notice any similarities? How about that word *my*? Nabal used it, too. Nabal is just like the rich young fool in the New Testament. Material things come first in his life. He is more interested in keeping what belongs to him than in how what he has could bless other people. He's a fool.

The plot at this point has many problems or complications needing resolution. It's a recipe for disaster. Remember the setting. Sheep-shearing time was full of tension. It was carried on in extremely hot weather. The men were stripped down to the waist, and they were handling stubborn sheep that did not want to be sheared. Picture the sheep stiffening up and struggling against the shearers. Picture the wool with ticks and dung in it. Smell the nauseating, hot odors. Kind of paints an interesting picture, doesn't it? Many times we humans are compared to sheep in the Bible. Are we ever stubborn and stiff against God, who is trying to shear us in some way?

David's timing is off. He doesn't choose the best time to go to Nabal. In fact, Nabal is having a party, really a fall festival. David's actions were proper. His timing was just all wrong because he walks into a very explosive situation and makes a request of a man who is an absolute hothead.

Have you ever met anybody like that? There's just no way to get along with him or her. You can try to show him the love of Jesus, but it only raises his hackles. David's men come back and tell David what has gone on with Nabal. Keep in mind that David was redheaded and a little hotheaded himself. David says to his men, "Put on your swords!" (1 Sam. 25:13). The adrenaline is pumping into his bloodstream. My mother always told me to "act, not react." It's an important concept and one it takes years to fully appreciate. So David chooses to react here, and he decides to play the fool as well.

Verse 21 says, "David had just said, 'It's been useless—all my watching over this fellow's property in the desert so that nothing of his was missing. He has paid me back evil for good.'" He goes on to say that he's going to wipe out the whole crowd at Nabal's fall festival. David loses it. He basically tells his men to get their swords because they're going to wipe Nabal off the face of the earth.

You may be wondering why David watched Nabal's lands in the first place, especially since Nabal never asked him to do so.

Part of it is ancient Israelite custom, and the other part con cerns God's preparations for David. We often learn much about ourselves when we lose our temper or play the fool. We're able to see ourselves the way others see us. I know I have learned much about myself in this way.

David is furious. Isn't this a man after God's own heart? Yes. The Bible says that the Spirit of the Lord came on David from the time he was anointed. David is in a very dangerous situation. Nabal's name literally means "fool." But the danger here is not that Nabal is a fool. The danger here is that *David* is going to play the fool. David allows his anger to get the best of him. He forgets who he is and where he's headed. He is the heir apparent to the throne. He has been chosen by God to be a king. He's going to sit on the throne of the kingdom of Israel one day. He doesn't need to react. But he does.

When we let our anger get the best of us, we forget who we are, too. We forget that we're also heading for a kingdom. We often choose to let the little details cause us to lose our temper. Anger is really a learned response to frustration. Some people have learned to respond to every frustrating experience with anger. Life today is frustrating. Traffic, airport security, bills and taxes, soccer tournaments on the weekends, and on and on. But is blowing it really the best solution? Anger is really a form of insanity. When people choose to let anger take over their lives, they are to some extent out of their minds.

David overreacts to this man, Nabal, who is not even worth the time. He's trying to shoot roaches with a shotgun. He's trying to drive thumbtacks with a sledge hammer. He's boiling over with anger. We all do that sometimes. You can pretty much tell the size of a person by what it takes to make him angry. Most of the time we handle the big things well, and we don't blow our stack. We normally do well in an accident, and we keep our heads. Then, the washing machine breaks down—yowza! It's over. Houston, we've got a problem! We get all out of joint and huff and puff and blow and stomp.

That's what has happened to David here. Maybe it's the stress of being on the run for years. Maybe it's about learning patience to wait for God to bring about His purposes. In any case, David's life during this time teaches us to act and not react and to try not to fall into the trap of playing the fool.

In verse 14, one of Nabal's men realizes the potential for absolute disaster. So he tells Nabal's wife Abigail what has taken place. Abigail immediately knows that this is an emergency. Verse 18 says, "Abigail lost no time." She gets on top of the situation immediately. She prepares food and supplies for David's men. She doesn't tell Nabal about it, and she goes out to meet with David.

Get the picture? David is still fuming. His anger is burning hot, but low like coals in a fire. His eyes are daggers. He's heading toward Nabal's home practically licking his chops like a dog. He's got complete obliteration on his mind. Then Abigail appears. When she approaches David, she falls down before him and bows toward the ground. If you'll read the speech she makes, she refers to him as "my master" six times. She also refers to herself as "your servant" about six times. Abigail pleads with David to not let his anger toward Nabal cause him to react foolishly.

She says in verse 25, "May my lord pay no attention to that wicked man Nabal." She's talking about her own husband. She basically asks David to ignore him. "He is just like his name." She knows his name means "fool." "His name is Fool, and folly goes with him." She's asking David not to pay any attention to Nabal, because he's not worth it. She tells him Nabal is an idiot.

Abigail says, "The LORD has kept you, my master, from bloodshed and from avenging yourself with your own hands" (v. 26). She is again pleading with David not to attack Nabal.

"And let this gift, which your servant has brought to my master, be given to the men who follow you" (v. 27).

"Please forgive your servant's offense" (v. 27). She takes the guilt on herself. She says, "For the LORD will certainly make a lasting dynasty for my master." She knows David is headed for the kingdom. She knows this because she knows David is fighting the battles of the Lord. It's amazing how women can calm men when they're angry. At this point, Abigail is able to calm David and to help him see reason. They say that behind every great man there is an even greater woman. She reminds David of his noble cause, and she pleads with him not to stoop to the level of fighting grudge matches. She reminds him that he is God's man.

"Even though someone is pursuing you to take your life" (v. 29). In other words, she knows that he is a fugitive. "The life of my master [David] will be bound securely in the bundle of the living by the LORD your God. But the lives of your enemies he will hurl away as from the pocket of a sling." Was there an experience in David's life when he used a sling? Remember when he met Goliath? He used a sling. She just kind of dropped that in, and David begins to think. I have a feeling that the more David thought about it, the more embarrassed he became. I picture him turning red. He realizes just how foolish he is being.

Nabal, the fool, is not the source of danger in this dangerous episode for David. Instead, the danger is caused by the threat that David might become a fool. Don't let the fools of this world cause you to react foolishly. Just because other people live the way they live does not mean you have to get down on their level. Act—don't react.

Aren't you glad God uses stop signs like Abigail along the way to keep us from making bad mistakes? If David had gone to war and killed many people, he would have had a black mark on his reign as king all the rest of his days. God has a way of putting some Abigails in your way and in my way to keep us close to Him during dangerous episodes.

David says to Abigail, "Praise be to the LORD, the God of Israel, who has sent you today to meet me. May you be blessed for your good judgment and for keeping me from bloodshed this day and from avenging myself with my own hands" (vv. 32–33). He is thanking Abigail for stopping him.

It's a great man who can be thankful when God puts a road-block in his way to keep him from doing something stupid and foolish. Has God ever put something beautiful in your way to keep you from doing something stupid and foolish? Maybe it's a little child, maybe your wife, maybe a friend.

Abigail goes home. She doesn't even tell her husband what has happened because he is dog-drunk. Verse 36 tells us she gets back, and he's having a drinking party. I may sound harsh, but in my opinion, if you talk to a drunk, you are wasting your time. I spent twenty years of my early ministry chasing drunks and trying to win them to the Lord. Every drunk gets religious. They will talk about their dear old mother. "If only I could hear my mother pray again," one might say. Yes, they get real religious. They'll even get saved four or five times. But when they sober up, they'll run if they see you coming. You are wasting your time for the most part.

I suspect Abigail knew this, so she doesn't say a thing to him. The next morning, Nabal wakes up with a hangover. His head is pounding and Abigail tells Nabal what almost happened to him. When she does, the Bible says Nabal's heart died within him and became as a stone (v. 37). He probably had a heart attack or a stroke. And ten days later, verse 38 says "he died."

When David heard that Nabal had died, he basically rejoiced (v. 39). Are there some people in this world, who, if they died, we would all rejoice? It would be good news if we went home tonight and on CNN or Fox News we heard that Osama Bin Laden or Saddam Hussein had died. There are some people that this world would be better off without.

So David rejoices in Nabal's death. By the way, do you remember what happened in this first verse of this chapter? Samuel died, and they lamented him. Just the opposite of the reaction Nabal got. Would people be sad or glad if you or I died? We ought to so live that when we come to die, people will be sad. That's another point this foolish time in David's life teaches us today.

The rest of the chapter tells about Abigail and David and their marriage. Girls, it may sound old-fashioned, but it's true. The way to a man's heart is through his stomach. David must have enjoyed the meals Abigail made for him and his men.

Remember that David's dangerous episode has taught us to act, and not to react. David came dangerously close to playing the fool and to making a huge mistake.

David's Glorious Episode

Chapter 26 of 1 Samuel shows that David has yet another opportunity to kill Saul. Saul is still pursuing him, and David is still on the run. Saul's three thousand men are on David's trail. David sends out his spies and locates Saul (v. 4). They have made a camp, and Saul is right in the middle of it where he can be cared for. Abner, the captain of his army, is right there with him. The Lord sends a deep sleep among Saul's men, so they are all asleep (v. 12).

David and Abishai, his nephew, sneak down into Saul's camp. Abishai rejoices at the opportunity (v. 8). He begs David to let him hit Saul first.

Wait a minute. Is this a not-so-instant replay? Didn't David already have this temptation? Yes. David had won the victory over the temptation before. Now he has the same temptation again. And he has this nephew, someone close to him, who is trying to talk him into doing something clearly forbidden by God.

What does David do? He puts God's laws first in his life, just as we should. David resists the temptation. He is thinking this time. He's learned to wait on God. He tells Abishai to go for his jug of water and his spear.

Can you picture Abishai? He's young and hotheaded. He tries to put an end to his uncle's grief, he thinks. And yet, he has to curb his desire to murder the king. So he goes in there and comes back grumbling with the spear and the jug of water.

David calls out, "Aren't you going to answer me, Abner?" (v. 14). When Abner hears his voice, it is like steel darts whizzing by his ears. Saul wakes up and his stomach knots up as he realizes he is hearing David's voice. Saul basically blames Abner for falling down on the job of protecting God's anointed king.

Saul asks if it is indeed David. David replies honestly to him, "'Yes it is, my lord the king.' And he added, 'Why is my lord pursuing his servant? What have I done, and what wrong am I guilty of? Now let my lord the king listen to his servant's words. If the LORD has incited you against me, then may he accept an offering. If, however, men have done it, may they be cursed before the LORD!'" (vv. 17–19).

Saul says, "I have sinned. Come back, David my son. Because you considered my life precious today, I will not try to harm you again. Surely I have acted like a fool and have erred greatly" (v. 21). He confesses, but he doesn't repent. Saul has played the fool. Many people spend a lot of time confessing, but they never change their behavior. Saul is one of them. Saul is confessing a lot and admitting a lot. He is owning up to his foolishness, but he doesn't commit to do anything to change his ways. David realizes this, and so in verse 24, he just puts the whole situation into God's hands.

"As surely as I valued your life today." In other words, David is telling Saul he had him in the crosshairs. David says, "So may the LORD value my life and deliver me from all trouble." David is again professing his faith in God by saying he will trust God with his life. This should be our attitude today. You'll always do well when you put your life in the hands of the Lord and let God take care of it. It's a challenge to do this because we think we're best in control. Yet, think of David and his willingness to let God take control. It's a useful lesson for each of us in life.

This is a glorious episode for David. He's exemplifying what it means to walk after the Spirit by showing humility, patience, and trust in the Lord. No question about it. He gives evidence that the Spirit of God is working in his life. Verse 25 says that David went on his way and Saul returned to his place. Saul has played the fool here, yet David is trusting more and more in God.

David's Atrocious Episode

David had it made. The Spirit of God is upon him. He's on top now. He'll never make another mistake again, right? He's human isn't he? All of a sudden, everything spins out of control. Chapter 27 of 1 Samuel displays an atrocious episode in David's life.

"But David thought to himself, 'One of these days I will be destroyed by the hand of Saul. The best thing I can do is to escape to the land of the Philistines'" (v. 1). He is talking to himself. I talk to myself sometimes, don't you? I enjoy intelligent conversation! I've heard it's a sign of genius. Well, maybe. We all soul-talk. But the problem here is that David is talking to himself, not to the Lord. He makes a major blunder. He runs right into the hands of the enemy. In verse 2, he runs to the king of Gath, a man named Achish. He decides to live in the land of the enemy. He is doing what many Christians decide to do with their lives. It seems successful at first.

Saul was told that David was in Gath. So Saul just stopped seeking David (v. 4). That part of this episode was a success. But it could be deceptive. Don't ever assume that just because things seem to be working out, everything is all right. Just because pressures let up doesnt mean God is pleased with what you're doing. It may seem like things are fine, but if you know in your deepest heart of hearts that you're going against what God says is best, you can be sure that God is not happy.

David says to the king, "If I have found favor in your eyes, let a place be assigned to me in one of the country towns, that

I may live there" (v. 5). Achish gives him Ziklag. He just moves into one of the enemy's towns. In effect, he begins living a lie, living a fiction. That's like Christians today who cave in to the culture. Many Christians today live in Ziklag. They have compromised their testimonies. They are living in places of compromise. They may be working deals on the job that are displeasing to the Lord, yet they stay in their Ziklag. Perhaps they married a nonbeliever while they were out of the will of God, and that person hates the name of Jesus. They are in Ziklag. Unfortunately, there are many Christians who find themselves in a compromised position. Their true beliefs become diluted in their own Ziklag (v. 6).

I have a feeling David probably thought he wouldn't stay there very long. Yet he stayed much longer than he thought he would. He stayed there a whole year and four months—sixteen months (v. 7). What happens to him? He becomes a murderous cutthroat. The Bible is not condoning his behavior. The Bible is simply reporting his behavior. The Bible here takes a tone similar to that of Hemingway in his novel *The Old Man and the Sea*. He writes as an observer. That's what the Bible is doing here.

David was up on the mountain of glory when he won the victory in the situation with Saul. Now he's in an atrocious episode in his life. Don't ever think you have arrived as a Christian. The very moment you think you have arrived and that you are some kind of spiritual super saint, you may be the most susceptible to doing something atrocious.

WWDD? What does David do? He starts a series of murderous raids. He goes down to the Gaza Strip area and invades and plunders those cities (v. 8). He kills everybody there. Men, women, and children. He slaughters them. It's atrocious!

After he murders the people of the Gaza area, the king asks him where he had been. He lies (v. 10). On the inside David is an Israelite, but on the outside he's acting like a Philistine. His life is symbolic here, and it has a contemporary application.

Some Christians today are that way. The key to this chapter is that there is no mention of God in it. David's voice is silent when it comes to singing songs. There is no evidence of the playing of the harp. No psalms are written. No promises are claimed. No prayers are offered.

Here's some good news, though. If you find yourself in an atrocious episode in your life or some Ziklag of compromise, the good news is that God will forgive you. If you find yourself playing the fool in your life, God can bring you out. God can turn your life around. He did it for David. He'll do it for you.

CHAPTER 7

Occult Matters, or the Road Not Taken

I took the road less traveled by . . .
ROBERT FROST

1 SAMUEL 28

Americans today are really into choices. At the grocery store, we want to know we have choices before we buy that can of coffee. Columbian or Hawaiian? When we pay for gasoline for our cars, we want the choice of either paying at the pump with cash, paying at the pump with credit, or paying inside with cash or credit. Even in our church services, we want choices. Maybe you like early services, and your friend likes later services.

The expectation of choices goes deeper, though. Think of the abortion debate and the current discussion over stem cell research. People feel that they deserve choices or that it is their right to have choices.

Robert Frost's poem "The Road Not Taken" describes choosing between two roads that "diverged in a yellow wood." After considering his choice, he "took the road less traveled by," and add, "that has made all the difference."

To me, Robert Frost's poem "The Road Not Taken" is all about choices. His poem states a common human dilemma. Did your mother ever tell you, "You can't have your cake and eat it too"?

Think back to high school prom days. A guy really wants to ask a certain girl out, but he's not sure she'll say yes. So he asks another girl to go just in case the first girl says no. Then it turns out the first girl can't go and the second girl can't go. That's a case of not being able to have your cake and eat it, too.

The road we choose in life takes us down a path and provides for us various experiences, problems, and solutions to those problems. Yet, no matter which road we choose, there is always another road we could have chosen. And that "road not taken" may haunt us for the rest of our lives.

In 1 Samuel 28, both David and Saul are living through repercussions of their earlier choices. Both men are in precarious situations in this chapter. David is working for a pagan, enemy king, and Saul is consulting a witch for advice. Both men have chosen their roads. For both men, "the road not taken" may have been the better choice. Do you remember the slogan for Greyhound buses, "Leave the driving to us"? Well, God in His sovereignty always leaves the decision-making up to us.

First Samuel 28 narrates bizarre events in the lives of both Saul and David. But perhaps what God is really trying to teach us in this chapter is that He is always available to help us choose the right road. God does not want us to regret "the road not taken." One "road" I've never traveled is the road to the occult. It used to be that sneaking a look at your horoscope in the morning newspaper was considered taboo. If you chose to do it, you certainly did not want to be caught. Checking a horoscope was considered silly and unnecessary, especially because some people at least knew of God's warning against supernatural powers.

Life is different today. In fact, an Associated Press news story proving just how different life is showed up in many newspapers around the country on August 28, 2001. The story tells of a new astrology school that is believed to be the first of its kind to be accredited. The Astrological Institute, founded by Joyce Jensen, offers a diploma in astrology and psychology. The article states that courses at the institute "include a 'master class on the asteroid goddess' and 'how to write an astrological column.'" Horoscopes, psychics, witches, spells, séances, palm reading—we're in a cultural mix these days. Whatever you believe is OK. It doesn't matter if you believe in the goddess, while someone else believes in the one true God. It also seems today that if we're not completely accepting of one another's beliefs, there's a threat of being labeled "intolerant."

Sometimes I wonder if tolerance is actually the issue. Now get this, I am not advocating intolerance in any way, shape, or form. Yet in today's world, it seems as though we're wading through a muddy mixture of beliefs. People want choices in their lives, including their religion. They want religion to serve their needs rather than becoming what the specific religion asks them to strive to become.

Even with all of our "enlightened" thinking and conscious-ness-raising about religion and about respecting one another's beliefs, it is Christianity that seems to take the most hits. Could it be because Christianity asks believers to live by a biblical standard? When those who believe in the muddy mix mentioned above come up against true Christians, there is a mighty clash. It's almost as if one of those car alarms that sounds like a siren goes off, and everyone around stops, looks, and listens. I think all of this is most telling with the youngest and most impressionable members of society: our teens.

I recently read another Associated Press report about a teenager. It is a disturbing story. According to the AP story dated February 10, 2002, a teenager in Virginia "confessed to the sword slaying of a prominent scientist, saying fantasy creatures gave him permission to kill the man in order to protect a friend." Apparently, the teenager was a friend of the scientist's daughter and felt that she was in danger from her father. According to the story, "the teenager said vampires and creatures names Ordog, Sabba and Nicodemus then gave him permission for the Dec. 8, 2001, slaying to protect [the girl]." The teen stabbed the scientist with a 27-inch sword, drank his blood and then went "into a frenzy."

The teen is awaiting first-degree murder charges with three other young people. To me, the most telling part of the article alludes to the occult. It says that the four young people "have told police they shared a devotion to fantasy realms dominated by vampires and witchcraft."

I know it's not popular to take a stand these days. But, I have never been so aware of satanic and occultic influences on young people as I am today. From television shows such as "Charmed" and "Buffy, the Vampire Slayer" to books written for young adults such as *Girl Goddess #9* by Francesca Lia Block, teens are taught to accept the occult.

But it's not just teenagers who have been influenced by the occult. Many notable people in history have also been involved. The most recent book I've read on the subject is entitled *Degenerate Moderns*. It is documented there that the father of modern psychology, Sigmund Freud, and his heir apparent, Carl Jung, were both deeply involved in the occult. Jung claimed to have a spirit medium named Philemon, who was an old man with the horns of a bull. Jung supposedly made contact with this spirit medium.

Just what is the occult? *The American Heritage Dictionary* defines *occult* with two general definitions. The first says, "Of, pertaining to, dealing with, or knowledgeable in supernatural influences, agencies, or phenomena." The second says, "Beyond the realm of human comprehension; mysterious; inscrutable." Both definitions apply in this chapter.

The information we learn about the occult in this puzzling chapter of 1 Samuel is not given anywhere else in the Bible. This chapter also spotlights human choices. David's life continues to show us that God always gives us choices in our own lives. God provides the direction if we choose to follow it, but He does not make any choices for us.

Remember, David has been selected by the Lord to be the second king of Israel. The Lord has rejected Saul, the first king, and David is God's chosen successor. Saul is very jealous of David. He has seen the handwriting on the wall. He knows that he is on his way out, and David is on his way up. Saul is discontented and unhappy. He knows what is going to happen; yet he is trying to prevent the providence of God.

For approximately ten years, David has been on the run. He's been on mountains, in caves, and in forests. When the chapter opens, he is still over in Ziklag, which is Israel's enemy territory.

It looks like the chapter will be all about David (v. 1). The Philistines have gathered their army together for war with the nation of Israel. They are determined to stamp out Saul and his army. David is in Ziklag because he has lied about his situation and compromised his principles. Just because the Bible says David is a man after God's own heart doesn't mean David was a perfect man. He wasn't. His life shows us he was flawed. His Ziklag experience, for example, is one of these situations. Maybe this is why David's life speaks to us today. He struggled with making the right and wrong decisions his entire life, just as we do.

David is facing the possibility of having to go to battle to fight against his own people. Why? Because of lies he has told and because at this point in his life, he is out of the will of God. He's chosen his "road," and he's taking it. So the king of Gath, Achish, comes to David and tells him that he wants David to help him defeaat the Israelites. David probably put on a confident, manly front, even though he is hearing an enemy king planning to fight his own people. What does David do? He basically communicates to the king that he is ready to fight.

Then the king of Gath tells David that his new job is to be his own personal bodyguard. Interesting. Here is a man who has been selected by God to be the king over all Israel, and yet he is now reduced to being the bodyguard of a pagan king. Is this David's other road? Is his new position a result of choices he made?

That's how the chapter opens. Then there's a quick edit, a cut, and we see Saul's demise. David is off the scene for the rest of this chapter, which basically chronicles Saul's journey to the end of his life.

Isaiah 55:6 says, "Seek the LORD while he may be found; call on him while he is near." Saul had many opportunities to call on the Lord during his reign. He could have received the guidance, direction, and leadership of the Lord, but he refused to do so. Now he comes to another fork in the road of his life. He chooses a path. Perhaps he chooses "the road not taken." The road Saul chooses certainly does make "all the difference" in his life. Saul actually has only two choices. He can either turn to David and acknowledge that David is God's choice to be the next king, or he can turn to the demonic world, the occult world to help him figure out why he is so miserable. The road he chooses is the road of the occult.

Desperately Seeking

Saul is a desperate man. The prophet Samuel, who could have been a real help to Saul, is dead. He is off the scene. Saul had put away mediums and spiritists out of the land (v. 3). In other words, witches and people associated with the occult were not allowed in Israel. God had commanded the people of Israel to have nothing to do with the fallen spirit-world. They were commanded to have no contact with mediums who contact spiritual entities or make contact with demonic forces. Today, we call them wizards, witches, or psychics. God takes no prisoners in His communication on this topic.

For example, in Leviticus 19:31, God talks to Israel: "Do not turn to mediums or seek out spiritists, for you will be defiled by them." In other words, don't pay any attention to mediums who have spirit guides or entities. "I am the LORD your God." He is telling the Israelites that they had Him. "I am

God. I am enough. You don't need anything the demonic side offers."

Leviticus 20:6 says, "I will set my face against the person who turns to mediums and spiritists to prostitute himself by following them, and I will cut him off from his people." God makes it clear. He commands us to ban them from our midst. It's interesting to note that Saul had banned them from the land of Israel.

Deuteronomy 18:9 says, "When you enter the land the LORD your God is giving you, do not learn to imitate the detestable ways of the nations there." God is saying, "You are different. You are my people. God's people. You should be different from the people of the world." This is the same message to Christians in our culture today. There may be very few people, even Christian people, listening and obeying God today, but that doesn't mean God has changed. It means our society has changed.

"Let no one be found among you who sacrifices his son or daughter in the fire, who practices divination or sorcery, interprets omens, engages in witchcraft, or casts spells, or who is a medium or spiritist or who consults the dead. Anyone who does these things is detestable to the LORD" (vv. 10–12).

First Samuel 28 shows us that Saul becomes "an abomination." He's a desperate man in a desperate situation. Deep in his psyche, he knows it's all over for him. It's obvious that God has selected David to be the next king and that God has rejected Saul. It's just a matter of time, and Saul knows it. What does he do? He makes unwise choices like many of us do when we're up against a wall. Saul tries to fight almighty God. He attempts to resist the sovereign will of God. Saul versus God. Not a tough fight to call. You can't fight God and win.

First Samuel 28:4 shows the preparations both armies are making for war. The Philistines pitch their camp in Shunem. That's about sixteen miles southwest of the Sea of Galilee. Saul's armies are in Gilboa. That's about five miles south of

Shunem. "When Saul saw the Philistine army, he was afraid; terror filled his heart" (v. 5). He is a desperate man. He does what a lot of people do in times of desperation, which he has been unwilling to do during his entire reign. He turns to God.

Saul "inquired of the LORD" (v. 6). He sought direction from the Lord, yet he doesn't receive it. The Lord did not answer him. Hard to believe. How can God not answer a person who is calling upon Him? The Bible says it can happen.

"Then they will call to me but I will not answer" (Prov. 1:28). God appeals to some people over and over by calling on them and calling on them. Some people choose to ignore God every time He calls on them. Too much time can pass, though. A point can be reached where God won't answer.

Talk about taking the road that has made "all the difference." Imagine choosing a road away from God.

It's terrible to realize that a person can get to the point where it's too late to pray or to seek the Lord. Saul did. He couldn't get an answer. He tried dreams, the Urim, and prophets. But he received no reply. In the Old Testament, people used those three methods to find direction from the Lord. Sometimes God revealed Himself in dreams. No dreams for Saul. Today we have the Lord Jesus Christ, so we don't need dreams. Urim was one of the two stones put in the breastplate of the priests. The other stone was the thummin. There weren't any priests around Saul. They were all over on David's side. Priests were not an option. Finally, Saul couldn't get any information from prophets because none of the prophets were with him. They were all with David. In fact, both Gad and Nathan were with David, not Saul.

At this point, heaven is closed to Saul. There is no answer there for him. His desperation is absolute. Because of his desperation, Saul seeks what he had banned in his land earlier (v. 7). He seeks direction from the occult world. He freaked. What makes someone this desperate? Honestly, I think it comes from living outside the will of God. This is why people consult astrologers or frantically find their horoscope in the newspaper each morning. This is why people go to witches and palm readers, hoping to hear how a problem will be resolved. They are desperately seeking direction for their lives that can come only from the Lord.

When I was a boy, there was a witch in our area of Georgia. She lived in Heard County, and her name was Mahaley Lancaster. At one time, her father had served on the Georgia supreme court. She was a smart woman. Mahaley Lancaster had a law degree and was a member of the Georgia bar. Legend has it that she sold her soul to the devil in exchange for psychic powers. Sounds like the story of Faust, doesn't it? On Sundays, people used to travel down into that rural county to seek Mahaley's guidance. Sometimes the roads would be lined with people hoping for a chance to ask her to contact the spirit world for them. That's one road I never took.

People are the same today. They will do unimaginable things when they are out of the will of God. Saul had knocked on the door of heaven and there was no answer. Now he decides to knock on the door of hell. He makes a choice, and he commands his men to find him a witch.

His men tell him there is a witch at Endor, which is about two or three miles northeast of Shunem on Mount Tabor. This is an interesting situation, because it means that if Saul wants to consult her, he must skirt dangerous enemy territory in order to reach her.

Saul disguises himself. Actually, he reveals himself because he shows the darkness of his own heart and soul. He puts on common clothes so he won't look like a king. Two of his men are with him. It's the dark of night. They come into the cave of the witch of Endor, and Saul says to her, "Consult a spirit for me and bring up for me the one I name" (v. 8). How weird is that? Well, that's what folks did who went to witches in those days. The witches claimed that they had spirit guides who could put them in contact with dead people.

Saul's asking the witch at Endor to communicate with the dead for him. He's desperately seeking guidance because God is not answering him.

Deceptively Seeking

Get the picture? Saul is the king who has outlawed all occultic practices. But he is seeking spiritual guidance from someone who practices the very thing he has banned. Does that sound hypocritical? Saul is deceptive about it all. He doesn't want her to know who he is. Notice that the witch hesitates in verse 9 as she realizes that what he's asking her to do can get her in trouble.

Saul tries to calm her fears: "Saul swore to her by the LORD, 'As surely as the LORD lives, you will not be punished for this'" (v. 10). He swears to her by the Lord. Does that also sound hypocritical? In the name of the Lord who had said there would be punishment for this kind of thing, Saul promises no punishment. Saul has not gotten the messages God has tried to send him. You cannot defy God and expect to get by with it. You are on thin ice when you rebel against the Word of the living God. You may think you are going to break God's Word and get away with it. But you won't break God's Word: God's Word will break you.

We talk about breaking the Ten Commandments. If we do break them, we're really not the ones doing the breaking. If we choose to disobey a commandment, that commandment breaks us. You can violate the Ten Commandments. That is your choice. But by disobeying God, you will be the one who is broken.

Saul has chosen his road. He's following it. Maybe his road is more like a river with rapids. He is in the rapids, and they are speeding up. He's getting closer and closer to the waterfall. Soon he will plunge into the abyss, which in this case is his judgment time. And yet he tells the witch that there will be no punishment for her.

She asks, "Whom shall I bring up for you?" (v. 11). She is getting ready to play her little supernatural game.

He says, "Bring up Samuel."

Samuel! That's interesting. Saul was not interested in what Samuel had to say when he was alive. Now he wants to call him up from death. Saul really shows us our own human nature. We don't appreciate what we have many times until it is gone. Saul is in a desperate situation and is longing for Samuel's advice and counsel. Saul deceptively seeks the guidance he previously spurned. Samuel had prayed for Saul. Saul didn't care. Samuel had sought to advise Saul. Saul didn't care.

Perhaps some of you are like Saul. Your mothers and fathers have tried to help you. You haven't been interested. Pastors, youth workers, and godly Christian friends have tried to help you choose the right road. You aren't interested. When you come closer to the end of the road you've chosen, you may wish you could talk to some of those who tried to help you along the way. But it may be too late. Your Samuel may be dead when you're desperate.

We left Saul saying, "Bring up Samuel" to the witch at Endor. This might make the hair on the back of your neck rise up. We see what happens next in verses 12–14: "When the woman saw Samuel, she cried out at the top of her voice and said to Saul, "Why have you deceived me? You are Saul!"

"The king said to her, 'Don't be afraid. What do you see?' The woman said, 'I see a spirit coming up out of the ground.'"

She's shaking. She's scared. She didn't count on this. It's probably a little too real for her. Kind of like all those reality TV shows that are popular now. Yes, they're popular and they look thrilling, but many times viewers find out they've been edited. This witch probably "edited" all her supernatural stunts before now. But even she is scared and surprised.

Saul says to her, "What does he look like?"

She says, "An old man wearing a robe is coming up." Then "Saul knew it was Samuel, and he bowed down and prostrated himself with his face to the ground."

This really is a pitiful portrait of the human condition. Saul had it all, and yet he ends up like this. It's all about the road down which he chose to travel. He's become God's enemy. Even though it's hard to believe, a human being can find himself in a position where he is fighting God, and God is fighting him.

After reading verses 17 and 18, you might ask what this is all about. Is it real? Did it happen? This is the only place in the Bible that chronicles something of this nature. Does it lend legitimacy to people who try to contact the dead today? Of course, we know that's not right because the principles taught in Leviticus and Deuteronomy make it clear that Christians are not to attempt to make contact with the dead.

We find ourselves at a fork in the road. There are only two directions to go with this situation. The appearance by Samuel either was an impersonation by a demon or it was an experience that really happened. Bible teachers are divided on this. Some say it was just a false impersonation. Sometimes people contact these spirit guides and a demon impersonates someone. To be honest with you, I think it really happened. When the woman saw Samuel, she cried with a loud voice (v. 12). It scared the willies out of her. She didn't expect her magic to work. She was shocked to see Samuel. It wasn't something she was doing as part of her art and craft. I believe the Lord did it, not this witch.

The Lord used this miraculous, supernatural means to finally get a message of judgment to Saul. I believe God allowed this to happen by His power and permission. God did something miraculous and remarkable to communicate a judgment on a king who had turned his back on the Lord. Now the Lord had turned His back on him.

Remember how it all started? Back in 1 Samuel 15, when Saul had just been selected king, he went to a place called

Amalek. God had commanded Saul that the entire place was to be wiped out. Saul disobeyed. Maybe he thought he knew better. When Samuel came on the scene, he asked Saul if he did what God had told him to do. Saul lied and said he did. Then a sheep bleated. Samuel asked what the bleating of the sheep was all about.

The act of obeying our authorities is a beautiful illustration of what the Christian life should be. God can bless us through our obedience to our authorities, even if those authorities are operating in the wrong. Many times, those in authority over an obedient Christian come to see where they've been wrong. The first step away from God is disobedience. It can be simple. You might choose not to tithe one Sunday. You might choose not to attend a meeting when you're off at a convention in another city. Saul was disobedient, even in the little things, and that's why God's judgment came down on him.

"The LORD will hand over both Israel and you to the Philistines" (v. 19). In other words, it's going to be a slaughter and unfortunately, Saul is going to lose big time.

It gets worse. "And tomorrow you and your sons will be with me" (v. 19). There is no mincing of words here. Tomorrow Saul and his sons will be dead. It's one thing to dread the possibility that something will take place. It's another thing to know absolutely that it will take place.

Saul's life is a sad portrait of what could have been. His life is a tragedy of the "almosts" in life. Saul started off head and shoulders above everybody else in Israel. He showed such promise, and he had such opportunities. He could have been used tremendously of God. And where did he end up? Disguised at night in a witch's cave hearing the sad message of his impending death.

Dejectedly Seeking

"O, the grievous shipwrecks of some great ships." Saul's life is nothing but a shipwreck. Right after Saul hears his tragic news, verse 20 says, "Immediately Saul fell full length on the ground." That means he fell flat on the ground. This news struck terror in his heart. It flattened him out on the floor.

I do not like to skip meals. Sometimes if I'm traveling or very busy, it can't be avoided. But generally, I try to eat regularly. We learn that Saul had not had anything to eat all day (v. 22). He had no strength. Imagine hearing the horrific news that Saul heard about his upcoming death and not having eaten anything all day. "When the woman came to Saul and saw that he was greatly shaken, she said, 'Look, your maidservant has obeyed you. I took my life in my hands and did what you told me to do. Now please listen to your servant and let me give you some food so you may eat and have the strength to go on your way'" (vv. 21–22).

Saul refuses to eat. His body collapses. His soul implodes like a tall building falling inward. His spirit dies. But his servants, together with the woman, compel him. So he finally listens to them, and he gets up and sits (v. 23).

We learn that the woman has a calf in the house. She quickly kills it and then kneads flour to bake unleavened bread. She brings the food to Saul for nourishment (v. 24).

Do you remember when the prodigal son came back home from the far country? The father killed the fatted calf, and the prodigal son enjoyed the meal in his father's house. In contrast, Saul eats the fatted calf in the devil's house. It's his last meal. Ironically, it's a meal fit for a king—and here sits Saul right on death row.

One of my worst childhood nightmares involved my being left by my parents. I didn't want to be abandoned. At this point in Saul's life, God abandons him. God leaves him, and Saul knows it and feels it. There is no indication that he had any desire to repent. There is no suggestion that he made any plea to God asking for forgiveness. Nothing shows that Saul wanted to turn his life over to the Lord. It's a terrible tragedy to reject God. It is even worse to be rejected by Him.

In the Old Testament, Amos talks about people who would not hear the Word of God. Amos said there would come a time when people would refuse the Word of God, and there would be a famine of the Word in the land. This chapter of 1 Samuel closes by saying Saul and his men went away "that same night." Isn't it symbolic that the last, dark deeds of Saul's life occurred at night, when the light is absent. Even the light has abandoned Saul.

Think of another last supper. The night before the cross the Lord Jesus gathered His disciples in an upper room. Jesus said to His disciples that one of them would betray Him. Who? Judas, of course. And Jesus told Judas to go ahead with the betrayal.

John 13:30 says, "As soon as Judas had taken the bread, he went out. And it was night." It's always night when you turn away from the Lord. Light cannot follow when you walk into darkness. The light abandons darkness just as God abandoned Saul.

When the Lord Jesus Christ went to the cross of Calvary to die for our sins, Mark 15:33 says, "At the sixth hour darkness came over the whole land until the ninth hour." Jesus went into outer darkness for you and for me. He conquered the darkness so that we don't have to feel abandoned by His light the way Saul did.

How can we apply the message of Saul's life to our lives today? His life and his experience with the witch of Endor warn us not to go too far from God. In other words, Saul chose a "road" that made "all the difference" in his life. You and I have an opportunity to choose God's road and to live in His light and never be abandoned by Him.

A teacher recently shared a humorous story with me. A teacher had her class of eighth graders read Robert Frost's poem, "The Road Not Taken." She asked the students to relate the conflict in the poem to a personal experience. One young man figured it all out. He told her that "the road not taken" was symbolic of all the food on a restaurant menu that you don't choose when you place your order. I totally understand! It goes deeper than that, though. God has given each of us the power to choose our own road. Let's choose to love Him and to serve Him forever.

CHAPTER 8

Restoration Matters, or The Gospel According to Scrooge

"Restore us to yourself,
O Lord, that we may return;
renew our days as of old."
LAMENTATIONS 5:21

1 SAMUEL 29–30   Do you remember Scrooge? What a character he is. The words *stingy, mean,* and *ornery* come to mind when we think of him. He lives a joyless, loveless life until he has a chance for restoration.

A Christmas Carol by Charles Dickens is a tale from classic literature. Most of us have seen or read a version of this story. The protagonist, Ebenezer Scrooge, is presented as the miserly, embittered employer of Bob Crachit. Yet Scrooge's "encounters with four ghosts in a dream bring about a remarkable transformation. Once a 'good-hearted lad,' he has become 'a squeezing, covetous old sinner,' hard and sharp as flint, and 'as self-contained and solitary as an oyster.' His heart is restored to goodness by a combination of terror and pity after his vivid dreams on Christmas Eve, and he becomes a generous benefactor."

Many times in life, we have the tendency to become "as self-contained and solitary as an oyster" just like Ebenezer

Scrooge. Perhaps we cease to have as close a relationship with the Lord as we once had. Maybe we become increasingly self-absorbed, focusing only on our own problems in life. In any case, the story of Scrooge's restoration is one that speaks to generations because of its universality. His heart is touched, and he is restored to goodness.

A few years ago our church's music ministry presented a delightful Christmas musical entitled "The Gospel According to Scrooge." It gave an interesting gospel twist to Dickens's story. At the end Scrooge was restored to God by means of a return to Jesus Christ.

The Bible says, "Above all else, guard your heart, for it is the wellspring of life" (Prov. 4:23). Scrooge's heart is sinful. He is self-centered, amassing wealth only to hoard it. He has issues of the heart. Though not exactly a Scrooge, David also has issues of the heart, and 1 Samuel 29 and 30 show David's restoration. He returns to the Lord after living out of the will of God. His heart is restored.

Chapter 29 picks up the narrative started in chapter 28. The first two verses connect the two chapters together. Saul's tragic consultation with the witch of Endor occurs in the interim.

It is clear that David is in a precarious situation. The Philistines are amassing a great army for an all-out assault and war against Saul and the armies of Israel. David is living with the enemy. The Philistine king, Achish, has made David his personal bodyguard to protect him in battle.

Picture David, the man who has been selected by God to be the king of the Israelites, fighting against his own people. It really happened. Why? Because David has made choices out of God's will. Remember 1 Samuel 27:1 says, "David thought to himself, 'One of these days I will be destroyed by the hand of Saul. The best thing I can do is to escape to the land of the Philistines.'"

The fact that the Bible records an incident does not mean that the Bible approves of the incident. Often the Bible reads like a daily newspaper. The Bible's point of view is many times omniscient. Sometimes the Bible has that "just-the-facts-ma'am" tone. Many say that Ernest Hemingway wrote in an observational and often cold style. In some of his books, he reports the action happening to his characters just as the Bible describes David's life at this time by simply reporting facts.

In fact, David is having a hard time. He's been a fugitive running for his life for about ten years. Maybe all that running has made him a little paranoid. Maybe he relies less on God and more on man. If a king who wanted to kill me were chasing me, I know I wouldn't be normal. The stress of that situation would affect my decision-making skills. It's kind of unfair, actually. We can read David's account and draw conclusions about what he should or shouldn't have done. But if we were in the same situation, we may have made the same choices David did.

We can understand why David did what he did, but that doesn't change the fact that what he did was out of God's perfect will and plan for his life. The point is, David's life can be used to teach us how to live for God today. His situation is a reminder for us to make wise choices in life. Otherwise, we can drift from God's perfect plan and His will for our lives.

David's situation also shows us that a Christian cannot compromise with the enemy and get away with it. You can't hang out with the enemy and expect your life to be normal. There was a movie a few years ago entitled *Sleeping with the Enemy.* I didn't see it, but I read about it. The movie starred Julia Roberts as a young wife married to an abusive husband. After she makes her choice to marry him, she realizes that he is dangerous, and that she has been "sleeping with the enemy." David is also sleeping with the enemy as he stays in Ziklag. David's situation illustrates that even when we are out of the will of God, He will sometimes graciously and mercifully rescue us and restore us in spite of our miserable failures.

Here's the deal. David is on the verge of going to war against his own people. He's about to fight Saul and Jonathan and the very people he will one day serve as king. Kind of a sticky situation. What happens next? First, let's examine God's intervention.

God's Intervention

Picture troops marching to battle. David is in the rear with Achish, the king. The armor-shod feet are stomping to a militant, regular rhythm. Metal shields are gleaming in the sun. Hundreds and thousands of troops walk erect as wave after wave of men march onward. There's David bringing up the rear. At this point, the realization may hit him. He knows he is out of the will of God, and it's all about to come crashing down around him. He is preparing to fight God's people.

Have you ever been in a critical situation like David's? It's definitely what is called a "do-or-die situation." What does David do? This next part shows without a doubt how God often works behind the scenes in the circumstances of our lives. This should give us confidence. "The commanders of the Philistines asked, 'What about these Hebrews?' Achish replied, 'Is this not David, who was an officer of Saul king of Israel? He has already been with me for over a year, and from the day he left Saul until now, I have found no fault in him'" (v. 3).

In other words, the princes or the leaders of the Philistine armies look at David and his men asking why they are there. Why? They know that David doesn't belong there. It's the same question many could ask of Christians sometimes. "What about these Christians?" The secular world often understands better than the Christian world that there is no fellowship between born-again believers and the world. Sometimes Christians need to hear someone ask them what they're doing or why they're in a certain place.

I remember a story about a Christian who was seeking to be a witness for the Lord. He was involved in dancing, and a pastor had told him it was not wise for a Christian to be involved in dancing. The young man said, "I can be a witness for the Lord on the dance floor."

The pastor said, "I would invite you to try."

One night on the dance floor, right in the middle of a dance, he asked a question of his dance partner. He said, "Are you a Christian?"

The girl he was dancing with stopped and said, "No way! Are you?"

He said, "Well, yes."

She said, "Then what are you doing here?"

It's true. Many times, the secular world knows that there are some places where Christians don't belong.

Achish defends David to the Philistine princes. The princes explode with anger. They say, "Send the man back, that he may return to the place you assigned him. He must not go with us into battle, or he will turn against us during the fighting. How better could he regain his master's favor than by taking the heads of our own men?" (v. 4).

The princes are streetwise. They do not want David to go to battle with them because they feel they can't trust him. The princes predict David's true loyalties lie with Saul and with his own people.

The princes are adamant. The king tells them that they can trust David. He tells them that David is his man. The princes don't believe it.

The princes push even further. They remind Achish that people have been singing about how many tens of thousands of people David has killed. He's popular. The princes remind the king that this is the guy who killed their hero and champion, Goliath.

Meanwhile, David is in a quandary. He's in a mess because of his doubt and disobedience. Yet God is still working. God has a way of using even circumstances like this to get Christians out of trouble. Have you ever been in a situation where you knew you were not *where* you ought to be and you were not *what* you ought to be? Many times, God intervenes in situations like this. He intervenes here. God can even make our enemies serve His purposes.

David doesn't mention the Lord much in this chapter. Yet God's presence can be seen and felt all over the chapter. He is working in the circumstances, which prove to be the scissors God uses to cut David free of the net of compromise and disobedience that entangles him.

So the king submits to the princes about the matter. He basically tells David that he's been a good worker, but he can't let him go into battle because the princes are forbidding it. The king says, "Turn back and go in peace; do nothing to displease the Philistine rulers" (v. 7).

Can you imagine David's sigh of relief? It was a close call. But living as a fugitive for ten years has given David a poker face. He puts on a believable front. Maybe his acting job could have been nominated for an Oscar if they had been around in those days. "'But what have I done?' asked David. 'What have you found against your servant from the day I came to you until now? Why can't I go and fight against the enemies of my lord the king?'" (v. 8).

He definitely puts on a good show. Children sometimes put on an act for their parents or their teachers. Usually parents can see right through it. But the king doesn't appear to notice that David is acting.

This all makes me a little nervous. I'm afraid his window of opportunity is going to shut. It reminds me of America's involvement in the space program. The space shuttles and other aircraft we send up have to find the right window in time and space in order to reenter earth's atmosphere safely.

Thankfully, God stepped into the scene to rescue David. He does the same thing for us in our lives today. Has it ever happened to you? If God had not intervened, you may have been in a situation where you would have sinned and that would have been disastrous to the work of the Lord. It would have grieved your own heart and would have been a permanent stain on your testimony. Yet God stepped in and intervened and arranged the circumstances so that you got out of the situation.

God's wonderful intervention means smooth sailing from now on, right? Not exactly. The Christian life doesn't work that way. That's one reason why the Bible includes incidents like David's. They show us that the Bible is true to life and that God works even in life's difficult circumstances.

It's going to get rough for David, even though God does intervene. He keeps David from fighting the very people that he is destined to serve as king. That would have ruined everything. The Israelites would have never accepted David as their king if he fought against them. God intervened, and He delivered him. David is rescued through God's intervention. Yet there is still the devastation sin has caused. What happens next? Suffice it to say that there is no comfort zone for Christians. Now let's examine the devastation caused by sin.

Sin's Devastation

First Samuel 30:1–6 portrays sin's devastation. A Christian cannot sin and get by with it. Even though God forgives and may deliver us from disaster, there is still a devastation that comes from our sin.

Think it's easier for believers? It's not. Don't ever get the idea that God has a different set of consequences for believers and nonbelievers in response to sin. Just because you're saved doesn't mean you can sin and get by with it. God will deal with you and your sin. Our God is an equal-opportunity God. His laws apply equally to nonbelievers and to believers.

What happens as a result of David's sin and his being in a compromising position in the land of the enemy? First Samuel 30:1 says, "David and his men reached Ziklag on the third day." That's the Philistine town where David and his men were living with their wives and children. Remember, David and his men had just marched off to war. They had left their families unguarded and unprotected. Now they are returning. They are praising the Lord because they did not have to fight their own people. As they travel home rejoicing, they see smoke billowing from ashes in Ziklag. Have you ever been in a situation you thought couldn't possibly get worse, but it did? That's what's going on with David here. God is using the enemy, the Amalekites, as a rod to teach David a valuable lesson.

When they arrive, they see their homes engulfed in flames. They make the devastating discovery that their wives and children have been taken prisoner by the Amalekites, enemies of the children of Israel. No joyful homecoming for them. Instead, it's a devastation.

It's the same way with some Christians today. Perhaps they have lived in a backslidden state. Maybe they have wandered away from the Lord for a period of years. In the course of their wandering out of God's will, they have paid a very high price. Perhaps the cost has been their family or their job or their standing in the community. In any case, it's a devastating situation.

When David and his men get to Ziklag, they see what has happened. The city is burned, and their families are taken captive. David and those who were with him lifted up their voices and wept until they had no more strength to weep. They cried until they couldn't cry any more (vv. 3–4). Have you been there? It can happen to a Christian who gets out of the will of God because of sin's devastation on their families and on those who are dear to them. You may choose to leave your family for some other person, but there may come a day when your own children will look in your face and tell you they hate you. You'll cry until you can cry no more. You may think you've mastered the art of the deal, but the time may come when that business will collapse and you'll lose everything. You'll cry until you can weep no more.

We're seeing the worst day in David's life. But in a way, it's the best day of his life. What is happening here just burns away more of the bonds that have been keeping David with the enemy. David's last link with the Philistines has finally been broken.

Some of you have had some devastating, hurtful days that brought tears in your life. But God was at work. God was using those devastating situations to cut you loose from this world and to bring you back to Him. That's what God is doing in the life of David. God is bringing him back.

There is no evidence that David had a relationship with the Lord while he was among the Philistines. Yes, he was still God's chosen man. He continued to be a man after God's own heart. The problem was he wasn't developing that vital relationship with God. He wasn't in fellowship with the Lord.

It gets worse: "David was greatly distressed because the men were talking of stoning him; each one was bitter in spirit because of his sons and daughters" (v. 6). In other words, people were bitter toward him. David's followers return from going to battle, and their own wives and children have been captured by the enemy. They are discontented and murmur that they should kill David. That's human nature, isn't it? Follow someone one day; talk about stoning him the next day. We're fickle people, and we often let circumstances cloud our judgment.

It's interesting to observe how tragedy affects people. Tragedy will bring out either the worst or the best in people. When it brings out the worst in people, they often seek to blame someone. I have seen this through the years of my ministry. Sometimes a real tragedy occurs in a person's life and then bitterness comes into their heart. Honestly, I think it's really all about being angry at the Lord and having a grievance against Him. Most people aren't willing to declare their grievance against the Lord, however, so they may begin to look for somebody else to blame. They may seek someone on whom they can vent their anger.

David's family is gone. His city is burned. The people who were closest to him have turned on him. This is probably the lowest point in David's life until now. Have you ever hit bottom? At least, there's only one direction you can go, which is up. What happens next? Now let's examine the restoration of David.

David's Restoration

David has been kicked out of his enemy's land. His own people have turned on him. He has nowhere left to turn except to God. For the first time in sixteen months, he finally looks up and acknowledges that he needs the Lord. Sometimes in life, there is nothing in our circumstances to encourage us. In times like these, we can always find encouragement in the Lord.

David's life turns around in the middle of verse 6, which marks the climax of the story. After this point, David's life works toward resolution. Why? His fellowship with the Lord is renewed: "David found strength in the LORD his God." He has no other place to receive encouragement. Not in Philistia. Not in his own army. Everything else is gone. He has nowhere else to look except up. Perhaps someone you know needs to follow in David's devastating footsteps. Maybe someone you know needs to reach the point David did. Maybe that someone is you. David finally encouraged and strengthened himself in the Lord.

The question is how did he go about encouraging himself in the Lord. There are several ways he may have reached out for encouragement. David may have looked back at his past to see what God had done for him. Regardless of how any of us might have failed the Lord, we can always look back and see there's never been a time when the Lord let us down. Can you say the Lord has ever let you down? No. He has never failed you. He has always been there.

So look back and see what God has done for you in the past. It will encourage you. Sometimes people keep a list on paper or on the computer of what the Lord has done for them. It's amazing to see that God is faithful in the little and big situations in our lives.

David not only looks to the past to see how God delivered him, but he also looks to the future and reminds himself of the promises God had made to him. Some day, He's going to be a king. When I fail the Lord and when I get down, I certainly find encouragement in the Lord when I remind myself that God has made me some wonderful promises. One day I'll reign with Jesus forever and ever. That's what the Bible says. David encourages himself in the promises of God. In fact, he may even sing a little. Remember, David is a singer and a song writer. Music definitely affects our mood. A song can cheer us up or make us cry. I listen to gospel music in my car and find it to be very encouraging.

David encourages himself. He looks at how God delivered him in the past. He looks to the future and claims God's promises. He reaffirms his personal relationship with the Lord. Notice the wording here. "David found strength in the LORD *his* God." Likewise, in Psalm 23, David wrote, "The LORD is *my* Shepherd." Can you say that about yourself? By saying it, David reaffirms and renews that personal relationship with the Lord. He's being restored. He's coming back to the Lord. What did David do? He got away from compromise. He renewed his relationship with God. And now David has been restored just like Scrooge was at the end of *A Christmas Carol.*

Now David is ready to pray again. "David inquired of the LORD" (v. 8). Back in verse 7, he calls his pastor. At that time, the priest was the one who represented the people before God. David asked the priest to bring the ephod—that was one part of the clothing the high priest wore. An ephod is symbolic. It acts as a reminder to pray and to make contact with God. David asks God for direction: "Shall I pursue this raiding party? Will I overtake them?" (v. 8). And God answers him: "Pursue them. You will certainly overtake them and succeed in the rescue."

Saul inquires of the Lord, too. Remember back in 1 Samuel 28:6, Saul inquires of the Lord and "the LORD did not answer him." Saul has gone so far away from God that He will not hear his prayers. David is different. He is a man after God's own heart. That doesn't mean David is perfect. It simply means he knows how to get in touch with the Lord. David asks a direct question, and he gets a direct answer. The Lord is specific. He says, "Pursue."

David goes after the enemy with six hundred men and a promise from God. He's running with a promise. He's going back to reclaim his family now. Perhaps some of you have paid the price of backsliding with your family. Go after your family if you have lost them. If the devil has taken them captive, go claim them back for Jesus. You may not even know where your kids are. Find them. Reclaim them for the Lord.

In verses 9 and 10, the story gets really interesting. "David and the six hundred men with him came to the Besor Ravine, where some stayed behind, for two hundred men were too exhausted to cross the ravine. But David and four hundred men continued the pursuit." The two hundred men are so exhausted, they have to stay behind. So David assigns them the task of staying with the baggage and guarding the supplies. This is certainly a legitimate part of warfare. Supplies are essential to success. Anyone who understands military strategy knows that keeping the supplies safe is crucial. In World War II, the Merchant Marines were vital because they kept the supplies going to the army.

In the service of the Lord there are always two groups. There are those who go, and there are those who stay. Think of the mission field. There are some who go to the mission field. There are others who stay behind to pray and to give support. Think of a church. God has blessed some of you with strong physical bodies, and you are able to get out and around. You have the strength and energy to be active. You are out there on the firing lines. But there are other people you may not even know in your church. They are shut-ins. Some haven't been to church in a long time. They minister through prayer. Many of these people pray constantly and consistently. Some of God's sweetest saints are behind the scenes guarding the supplies. They offer prayer support and encouragement to keep those on the front lines strong.

At this point, David enjoys good fortune. He and his men run across an Egyptian (v. 11). The man is hungry because he hasn't had anything to eat in three days and three nights. He's actually a servant of one of the Amalekites. This serves as a metaphor for the way the world treats its own. The world always leaves you hungry and unfulfilled. After feeding the Egyptian, David asks him if he can lead his troops to the enemy. The Egyptian says, "Swear to me before God that you will not kill me or hand me over to my master, and I will take you down to them" (v. 15).

David takes no prisoners. He attacks them for twenty-four hours, from twilight until the evening of the next day. He thoroughly routs the Amalekites. They run. David rescues everything that is rightfully his. David gets it all back (vv. 17–20).

Does God ever let us get back what we have lost? Do you think God will let you recover relationships that sin has broken? In a word, yes.

The same is true of the Lord Jesus Himself. Adam lost a lot for us in the Garden of Eden. But when Jesus died on the cross and was buried and rose again, He recovered everything for us. Jesus bought it all back for us.

The only true restoration of humanity can occur through Jesus because sin is in the world, and Jesus is sinless. There have been attempts at telling stories of restoration in our world and in our literature. In fact, stories that use the parable of the prodigal son come to mind. Yet there are some stories in our canon of literature that reverse restoration. George Orwell's novel *1984* is one example. In it, he warns his readers about the dangers of a totalitarian state. He also introduces the reader to his main character named Winston Smith.

According to the *Encyclopedia of Literature,* "The novel is set in an imaginary future world that is dominated by three perpetually warring totalitarian police states. . . . Winston Smith is a minor party functionary in one of these states. His longing for truth and decency leads him to secretly rebel against the government."[3] Eventually, Winston is captured and put in prison, where he is brainwashed into embracing the doctrines of the state. In fact, by the end of his imprisonment, he is no longer an independent thinker. His individuality is obliterated.

Orwell's novel is an example of antirestoration to me. He portrays exactly the opposite of what David finds in his restoration with the Lord. This proves to me that restoration is not a human endeavor. Think of what 2 Corinthians 5:17 says: "Therefore, if anyone is in Christ, he is a new creation; the old has gone, the new has come!" If restoration were a human feat, we would be able to do it more consistently than we do. Restoration is a God thing. We as humans are too weak to restore what once was. We hold too many grudges and too often lack the ability to truly forgive others. When we put David's restoration up against Smith's antirestoration, the contrast is apparent. It makes me grateful to serve a loving, forgiving God who seeks to have a one-on-one relationship with each of His creations.

David and his men enjoy a great victory and then go home. "Then David came to the two hundred men" (v. 21). These are the same 200 who were so exhausted they couldn't fight, so they guarded the supplies. They meet at the Revine Besor. By the way, "Besor" means "good news" or "gospel." This is pure gospel. "They came out to meet David." That reminds me of the day when the Lord comes again and all of God's shut-ins— those people who have been behind the scenes, guarding the supplies—will go forth to meet Jesus. I can see and hear them now shouting and rejoicing. They are hugging their children and their wives and families. They are so happy. Oh, what a day it will be when Jesus comes.

"As David and his men approached, he greeted them" (v. 21). The picture painted here is really a foreshadowing of

Jesus. Imagine the beauty of the Lord's return. He will say to some of the sweet shut-ins, "Well done, good and faithful servant! You have been faithful with a few things; I will put you in charge of many things" (Matt. 25:21).

I wish I didn't have to bring out this next part, but it's here: "All the evil men and troublemakers among David's followers said, 'Because they did not go out with us, we will not share with them the plunder we recovered. However, each man may take his wife and children and go'" (v. 22).Here's another characteristic of human nature. We like to hoard the wealth. Basically, the bad crowd is complaining about the group of two hundred since they didn't go to battle. They reason that they don't deserve any of the victory. Sounds like a bunch of kids, doesn't it?

There are always some people who remind us of the Pharisees in the days of Jesus. There are always people who appear to make themselves gods by proclaiming that some people count more than others. For some reason, these people think that they are judge and jury.

David says, "No, my brothers, you must not do that with what the LORD has given us" (v. 23). In other words, David is telling them if they think they are the ones who won the victory, they are sadly mistaken. The Lord "protected us and handed over to us the forces that came against us." He tells them that God gave them the victory. David shows courage and compassion here, just like Jesus. It's true in life today. Any victories are God's victories. We don't deserve any special praise. David is the first to realize that God won the victory.

In verse 24, David says, "Who will listen to what you say?" Here's the important part. "The share of the man who stayed with the supplies is to be the same as that of him who went down to the battle. All will share alike." There's really a larger application here. The truth here means whether you go or whether you stay, whether you are out on the front lines or whether you're behind the scenes on the prayer lines, when Jesus comes, you'll all share alike.

"David made this a statute and ordinance for Israel from that day to this" (v. 25). David is now well on his way to becoming king. But the standard he sets up is God's standard, too. Everybody shares alike. Matthew 10:41 has always meant a great deal to my wife. It says, "Anyone who receives a prophet because he is a prophet will receive a prophet's reward, and anyone who receives a righteous man because he is a righteous man will receive a righteous man's reward." My wife Janet tended to the home front. She has always made it easy for me to preach and serve the Lord. This verse means that she receives the prophet's reward. We both share together.

David had to get out of Ziklag. He was needed elsewhere. You may be in your own Ziklag. You may need to do what David did. Encourage your heart in the Lord and be restored. Don't wait until some Ziklag has to be burned in your life to do what David did. Seek God's restoration, and live in His will so that you can achieve what He has planned for you.

Thanks to his restoration, David is now following the right path. Have you found yourself in a Ziklag? Then do what David did. Look up to God. Turn back to the Lord. God has a wonderful plan for you, and He wants to bless you and use you in ways you never imagined. If you're living a life of compromise in enemy territory, you can't be used fully of God.

Remember Scrooge? His evil, miserly heart wasn't restored to a good heart until he was near the end of his life. You have an opportunity to seek restoration now. David, our Braveheart, did—and we can, too.

CHAPTER 9

God Goes with You, Greatheart

1 SAMUEL 31–2 SAMUEL 1

Where are you going, Greatheart,
With your eager face and your fiery grace?
Where are you going, Greatheart?
"To fight a fight with all my might,
For Truth and Justice, God and Right,
To grace all Life with His fair Light."
Then God go with you, Greatheart!

Where are you going, Greatheart?
"To beard the Devil in his den;
To smite him with the strength of ten;
To set at large the souls of men."
Then God go with you, Greatheart!

Where are you going, Greatheart?
"To cleanse the earth of noisome things;
To draw from life its poison stings;
To give free play to Freedom's wings."
Then God go with you, Greatheart!

Where are you going, Greatheart?
"To live Today above the Past;
To make Tomorrow sure and fast;
To nail God's colors to the mast."
Then God go with you, Greatheart!

Where are you going, Greatheart?
"To break down old dividing lines;
To carry out my Lord's designs;
To build again His broken shrines."
Then God go with you, Greatheart!

Where are you going, Greatheart?
"To set all burdened peoples free;
To win for all God's liberty;
To 'stablish His sweet sovereignty."
God goeth with you, Greatheart!
—JOHN OXENHAM

Up until now, we have called David our Braveheart. David may earn another name based on his reaction to Saul's death. His heart is certainly brave, but after his king's death, it proves to be great.

At this point in the story, David learns of the deaths of Saul and Jonathan. David's reaction to Saul's death may surprise people. Even though Saul had made David his enemy, David never made Saul his. Therefore, one might expect David to react joyfully. Instead, when David learns of Saul's death, he shows honor, respect, and tribute to his king.

Honor and respect for authority are rare in today's culture. Perhaps this is because of the disrespectful attitudes people see modeled in popular entertainment. Perhaps it is just the fallout of prosperous times. David's response to Saul's death is in stark contrast to what might be expected. His heart harbors no ill will toward his king.

Death is not easy, but it places a reality on life. In a way, death defines life. Death is the punctuation mark at the end of the sentence of life. It is not easy for us to deal with death because our culture does not handle death and tragedy well. In American life, there is little time for anything, especially grieving.

Just like so many other components of modern human life, death is featured on the news, discussed by reporters, and analyzed. Experts give their opinions about the grieving process. Colleges teach classes on death and dying. Oprah devotes episodes of her show to beliefs about the hereafter. Why? Perhaps so we think we can handle death. I wonder if all we are really doing is trivializing it. Nevertheless, when all is said and done, none of us can stop death. It still comes. As American poet Emily Dickinson so aptly puts it, "Because I could not stop for death, he kindly stopped for me."

There is a famous quote about death by English poet John Donne. It says, "Any man's death diminishes me, because I am involved in mankind; and therefore never send to know for whom the bell tolls; it tolls for thee." The bell has tolled for Saul. His death, however, does not thrill David; it diminishes him. The honor, respect, and tribute David portrays regarding Saul's death teach us about our relationship to God.

David shows honor to his slain king.

The Death: Greatheart's Honor

Samuel tells Saul through the witch at Endor that he will die. In 1 Samuel 28:19, Samuel says to Saul. "The LORD will hand over both Israel and you to the Philistines, and tomorrow you and your sons will be with me." Imagine Saul's anguish and fear as the words of Samuel torture him the night before his death.

When Saul dies, others die, too. The Bible teaches that his sons also died and among them Jonathan, who was the best friend of David. It is sad but true. The innocent often suffer because of the sins of the guilty. Many children have paid the price of their parents' sins. Jonathan does.

The same is true of the human race. When Adam sinned in the Garden of Eden, the whole human race fell into sin. Romans 5:12 says, "Therefore, just as sin entered the world through one man, and death through sin, and in this way death came to all men, because all sinned." Of course, humans have a choice in the matter. Yet because of Adam's choice, we are all born into sin.

In 1 Samuel 31:3, the archers wound Saul. They pull their bows and let their arrows go. The arrows pierce Saul's body. Saul knows he is close to death. Saul says to his armor-bearer, "Run me through, or these uncircumcised fellows will come and run me through and abuse me" (v. 4). Saul knows the rules of war. In those days, the victorious warriors would mutilate the bodies of their defeated dead. It was the custom to remove the dead person's sexual organs and to decapitate him. So Saul dreads his death even more because he is aware of the custom. Strangely, Saul seems more concerned about what his enemies will do with his body after his death than about his soul's relationship with God.

Each one of us is not only a body but also a soul. Mark 8:36 says, "What good is it for a man to gain the whole world, yet forfeit his soul?" Saul shows little interest in eternity. He does not pray or plead to God in repentance. As a preacher, I've seen many people get right with God on their deathbeds. Saul doesn't.

There were two thieves who died when Jesus was on the cross. In his dying moments, one thief says, "Jesus, remember me when you come into your kingdom" (Luke 23:42). The Lord replies to him, "Today you will be with me in paradise" (v. 43). There was another thief on the other side of Jesus who died in sin and went to hell. None of us can ever presume a deathbed repentance opportunity. It may not happen.

Saul's death paints a pathetic picture of the human condition. He shows what happens when mankind dies without God. His sons die beside him because of his pitiful legacy. And yet, why?

Back in 1 Samuel 26:9–10, David addresses Saul's death. It's almost as if David is foreshadowing the end of Saul's life. At this point in time, some men are trying to talk David into killing Saul. But David refuses to take matters into his own hands. He says, "As surely as the LORD lives, the LORD himself will strike him; either his time will come and he will die, or he will go into battle and perish" (v. 10). Saul does perish in battle on the mountain of Gilboa.

There are three reasons why Saul dies in battle. They are mentioned in 1 Chronicles 10:13–14. The Bible says, "Saul died because he was unfaithful to the LORD; he did not keep the word of the LORD and even consulted a medium for guidance, and did not inquire of the LORD. So the LORD put him to death and turned the kingdom over to David son of Jesse." Saul actually does inquire of the Lord, but he does it too late. God does not answer him. Saul did not call on the Lord while there was still an opportunity to be heard.

There is a passage in the Book of Proverbs that talks about how the Lord calls some people, but they refuse to answer. The Lord pleads with people sometimes, and they do not respond. Then, the Lord says, "Then they will call to me but I will not answer." Because Saul did not inquire in time, God dealt with him.

Saul's death is a reminder that sin and death go together. Romans 6:23 says, "The wages of sin is death." Sin kills mentally, physically, and emotionally. Saul is a mental wreck after he consults the witch, and he waits for his own impending death. In Saul's case, sin also kills his family and his testimony. This is true today as well.

When David finds out that the Lord's anointed, his king, has been slain, he honors Saul for his life and in his death. David, our Greatheart, "lifts today above the past" just like the Greatheart in the poem. David holds no grudges against the man who sought to kill him. Instead, he honors his authority figure, the king.

David also shows respect to his slain king.

Saul's Disgrace and Greatheart's Respect

First Samuel 31:7 says, "When the Israelites along the valley and those across the Jordan saw that the Israelite army had fled and that Saul and his sons had died, they abandoned their towns and fled. And the Philistines came and occupied them." In other words, when the men of Israel saw what was happening in battle, they ran away.

The Philistines climb Mount Gilboa and scour the spoils of battle just like human buzzards. They find King Saul and his three sons dead among the mangled bodies strewn all over the mountain. Blood stains the ground. The smell of death fills the air. These Philistines know they have won a great victory. They have slain the armies of Israel, and they have killed the king's sons and the king himself.

Verse 9 paints a gory picture of what the Philistines do to Saul: "They cut off his head, and they stripped off his armor." The parallel account in 1 Chronicles 10:10 says that they eventually take Saul's head and display it in the temple of Dagon, one of their pagan gods. They also take Saul's armor and put it in the temple of Ashtaroth, another Philistine god. Finally, the Philistines fasten his body to the wall of Beth Shan.

The Philistines show Saul no respect. It is a fitting metaphor to say the Philistines are sin here. What they do to Saul is exactly what sin always does to us. The Philistines work the way the devil works. The devil first tries to slay you by your sin. Then he tries to strip you. Perhaps you have seen examples of this. Maybe you have seen a person who has decided to live a life of sin. At some point, there comes a time in his or her life where the wages of sin kill all that is dear to that person.

I've seen examples of this throughout my ministry. I've seen people who wander away from the Lord. Sin kills them spiritually. Sin kills their testimony. Sin kills their families. Then the devil comes and strips those he has slain. He strips away purity of heart and peace of mind. Relief cannot be found anywhere. Guilt eats them up because they don't have peace. There they are like Saul's body—darkened, decapitated, hanging to the wall. His body is covered with maggots as it decomposes, swinging in the night wind. That's what the devil desires for each of us. Saul has been stripped, slain, and disgraced.

Saul's memory is shamed and disgraced. After the Philistines decapitate Saul and before they put his head in its final resting place, they send his head and his armor on a little publicity tour. It's good press for the Philistines.

Perhaps it is part of the human condition to rejoice when enemies fall. It's particularly true when one of God's leaders falls. Then the world rejoices when any Christian, especially a Christian leader, allows sin to get the best of him, he openly disgraces the name of the Lord. He becomes the object of scorn. Think of the Jim Bakker scandal. The devil stripped him, and then the devil's crowd made fun of him. Think of the Jimmy Swaggart scandal. After the devil stripped him of a multimillion dollar television ministry, he was the butt of countless jokes in our culture. Sin has slain and stripped many Christians.

Romans 2:24 says, "God's name is blasphemed among the Gentiles because of you." This is a warning to every one of us. We should be vigilant to make sure the actions in our lives never cause the name of God to be blasphemed among the Gentiles. Christians lose quite a bit of credibility with others because of the foolish actions and comments of other Christians. As Christians, it is our goal to carry out our Lord's designs.

The remainder of 1 Samuel 31 tells about the valiant men of a city called Jabesh Gilead. When these men hear that the body of their King Saul is hanging on the wall of Beth Shan, they take action. The men rescue the body and bring it back into Israeli territory in order to show respect to Saul, God's anointed. Then they burn or cremate his body. Finally, these dutiful men take Saul's bones and bury them under a tree. They honor their king. Later, David will take Saul's bones to the tomb of Kish, Saul's father, to honor Israel's first king.

Saul's disgrace doesn't happen suddenly, and his life did not have to end in shame. It overtakes him day-by-day, decision-by-decision, step-by-step until he hits bottom. A famous Chinese philosopher named Lao-Tzu says, "A journey of a thousand miles must begin with a single step." This quote may be fitting for this situation today. Christians don't dive into the pit of shame; they slide into it inch by inch.

Finally, David shows tribute to his slain king.

Saul's Dirge and Greatheart's Tribute

As 2 Samuel 1 begins, David is still unaware of Saul's death. He is now back in Ziklag, having restored his family and his children. David has been there for two days hearing no updated news. He knows there's a battle going on, but he doesn't have CNN or Fox News. No E-mail. No live battle scenes on his television. His culture's communication system relies on messengers.

On the third day a man comes from Saul's camp. His clothes are torn, and dirt is on his head, which is a sign of mourning. The man approaches David. David asks where he is from, and the man replies that he came out of the camp of Israel. He tells David he has escaped (v. 2). David asks how the battle went. The man tells David the Israelites have lost and Saul and Jonathan are dead. David is wary and seeks to verify the man's report (v. 4). David then asks the man how he knows they are dead (v. 5).

Then in verses 6 through 10, the young man tells his story. He says he came along Mount Gilboa and saw Saul dying. Saul had been mortally wounded, but he wasn't dead. The young man then tells David that Saul told him to fall on him and push the king onto his sword to speed up his inevitable death. The young man says, "I stood over him and killed him" (v. 10).

This young man's version of Saul's death is different from what's given in 1 Samuel 31. Why? Because in chapter 31, God's account of how Saul died is given. In 2 Samuel 1, a young man's lie is given. Perhaps he thought he could take some credit for Saul's death and make David happy. As proof of Saul's death, he gives David Saul's crown and his bracelet. David believes the young man temporarily. To show his grief, he tears his clothes. He then mourns and weeps and fasts until evening. At this point, David asks the young man who he is. It turns out that he is an Amalekite.

You may remember that God told Saul to kill the Amalekites. Saul disobeyed. So Saul's sin killed him. Likewise, the sin we don't kill will kill us. The young man thinks he has impressed David, and he expects to hear compliments from him. Instead, David says, "Why were you not afraid to lift your hand to destroy the LORD's anointed?" (v. 14). David is angered that an Amalekite would touch God's anointed king. So David orders him killed.

David is heartbroken when he realizes both Saul and Jonathan are dead. "David took up this lament concerning Saul and his son Jonathan" (v. 17). It's easy to understand why David would mourn for Jonathan, his best friend. But why would he grieve for Saul? Saul hated him and chased him for years, trying to kill him. Remember, Saul hated David, but David did not hate Saul. You can't keep somebody from hating you, but you can keep yourself from hating someone else.

To express his grief, David, the songwriter and musician, composes a magnificent lamentation—a funeral song or dirge.

"And [David] ordered that the men of Judah be taught this lament of the bow" (v. 18). Literally, this refers to the song of the bow. In fact, that is the title of his lamentation. It is put into the book of Jashar, which was a book of stories of Israel's great heroes.

David's lamentation says, "Your glory, O Israel, lies slain on your heights. How the mighty have fallen!" (v. 19). The mighty King Saul is fallen, and David repeats this line three times in this song. It's the theme of his lamentation. "How the mighty have fallen in battle!" (v. 25). "How the mighty have fallen! The weapons of war have perished!" (v. 27).

David refers to Saul and Jonathan in his dirge. The glory of Israel is Saul. Imagine being able to say your sworn enemy is "the glory of Israel." David always saw Saul as God's anointed.

David says, "Tell it not in Gath, proclaim it not in the streets of Ashkelon, lest the daughters of the Philistines be glad, lest the daughters of the uncircumcised rejoice" (v. 20). David is really saying not to publicize Saul's death in Gath because the coarse Philistine girls would just use the news as one more excuse for a drunken party.

David continues, "O mountains of Gilboa, may you have neither dew nor rain, nor fields that yield offerings of grain. For there the shield of the mighty was defiled, the shield of Saul—no longer rubbed with oil" (v. 21). In other words, the warriors' weapons have been dragged through the mud. Saul's shield has been left on the mountain to tarnish and rust, which is an action not befitting God's anointed.

In the original Hebrew, there are passages of this dirge where no verbs are used. This is because David is choked up. He's crying as he laments Saul and Jonathan. Tears are streaming down his face. His voice quivers. He gasps for breath. David is in mourning.

"Saul and Jonathan—in life they were loved and gracious, and in death they were not parted" (v. 23). David's song acknowledges that Jonathan stood beside his father until the end. He was a loyal son. They were together in life, and they were not divided in death. David's tribute portrays the two of them as swifter than eagles and stronger than lions.

David says, "O daughters of Israel, weep for Saul, who clothed you in scarlet and finery, who adorned your garments with ornaments of gold" (v. 24). David cautions his fellow citizens not to forget all the good Saul did for them. In my opinion, David's lamentation would be a rarity today because it is human nature to curse or to feel ill will toward those in authority. This is not true of David, our Greatheart. David actually praises Saul for all of his achievements.

David mourns his best friend. He says, "I grieve for you, Jonathan my brother" (v. 26). Have you ever lost a friend? It is a hard experience. David continues, "You were very dear to me. Your love for me was wonderful, more wonderful than that of women." David is remembering his friendship with Jonathan, who was his dearest friend. David's heart is broken for his best friend.

David's expression of grief can apply to our lives because David does not refuse to face the reality of death. It is a wise person who faces this truth. "Man is destined to die once" (Heb. 9:27). You are not ready to live until you are ready to die.

David also knew how to forgive people who had wronged him. Remember the poem above. David does "break down old dividing lines." Revenge only causes more pain. Forgiveness is the way to a healthy Christian life. You may think your grudge is hurting the person who is dead, but it isn't. It's killing you. David never allowed unforgiveness to make his life miserable.

Finally, David doesn't say one bad word about Saul. He doesn't grab a chance to take a shot. How many of us would do the same? There's a song the munchkins sing in the 1939 movie classic *The Wizard of Oz*. Once Dorothy pours water on the Wicked Witch of the West, she hears the munchkins sing. They sing gleefully because the witch is dead. "Ding Dong! The witch is dead." David doesn't sing a similar song about Saul, though one might expect him to after all he went through.

Proverbs 24:17 says, "Do not gloat when your enemy falls; when he stumbles, do not let your heart rejoice." David's lamentation exemplifies this verse.

In the New Testament, 1 Peter 4:8 says, "Love covers over a multitude of sins." Love covers. David didn't bring up any of Saul's negative traits. He focused on his king's positives instead. He left everything else in God's hands. We must put everything else into God's hands, too. It is not wrong to grieve. First Thessalonians 4:13 says that believers are not to "grieve like the rest of men, who have no hope." It does not say that believers don't feel sorrow; it simply explains that believers don't mourn the same way as those who have no hope. Becoming a Christian does not dehumanize you. You still have feelings. But the good news is that in the midst of sorrow and grief and lamentations in life, God promises to give His peace, grace, and strength.

Jesus told us to love our enemies. David does. He also models for us correct behavior toward those in authority. David doesn't scrap for the throne either. Some people in his position might have after hearing that the king was dead. David honors Saul in life and in death. Why? Because he is a man after God's own heart and because the Spirit of the Lord was on David from the time he was anointed by Samuel. It truly can be said, "God goes with you, Greatheart!"

CHAPTER 10

Bereavement Matters, or Murder, Bloody Murder!

". . . and the earth was filled with violence."
GENESIS 6:11

2 SAMUEL 2–4   Shakespeare's tragedy *Macbeth* deals with human jealousy, murder, ambition, and pride. In the story, Macbeth, a general for King Duncan of Scotland, and his wife weave a plot for the throne based on a prophecy given to Macbeth by three witches. The first prophecy soon comes true, which leads Macbeth to expect the remaining prophecies to be fulfilled. Lady Macbeth helps him create a plan to kill Duncan when he spends the night in their castle.

Macbeth kills the king, but the murder is discovered. Duncan's sons are then suspected of murdering their father, and Macbeth becomes king. Macbeth begins a reign of strife. At the end of the play, Lady Macbeth commits suicide caused by her own guilt, Macbeth is killed, and one of Duncan's sons is rightfully put on the throne.

Conspiracy and intrigue live healthy lives in any kingdom, government, or corporation. Why? Maybe because power corrupts. There are always those people who seek to be near the real or perceived power to inject their own agendas. Macbeth, like Saul, chooses unwisely to put credence in the advice of witches. Macbeth believes that because part of their prophecy appears to come true, he can expect all of it to come true. He also allows what they say about his becoming king to work on him. Humans are weak like this. We often do not put our faith in God and let Him have control of the circumstances of our lives. Life is hard. We think we can do better than God can. But David put his trust in God, and his example can teach us how to do the same today.

At this point in David's story, God's prophecies come true, and David finally becomes king. It's been years since Samuel anointed him, but God's will has prevailed. David's fugitive years are over because Saul is dead.

Have you ever considered how much can change in a day's time? Think of September 11, 2001. What a tragic, horrific day. We will all remember where we were, and what we were doing when we heard the news that America had been attacked. I'll never forget the indelible image of the first tower and then the second tower collapsing in billows of smoke. Our lives changed that day. The Bible says that we should not boast about tomorrow because we do not know what a day may bring. A job offer perhaps. News of someone's death. A tax bill. A car wreck. A marriage proposal. We don't know, but God does. David's ascension to the throne really happened in just one day.

If I had to pick out a theme for this section of David's story, I would pick 2 Samuel 3:1. It says, "The war between the house of Saul and the house of David lasted a long time. David grew stronger and stronger, while the house of Saul grew weaker and weaker." In other words, the balance of power is shifting from Saul's camp to David's. People sometimes tell me they are surprised by all the bloodshed and violence in the Bible, namely in the Old Testament. Some object to the Bible on that basis. I think there are two reasons why the violence is included in the Bible.

First, the Bible is a real book about real people living real life. Think of all the reality shows on television now. Their aim is to attract viewers to the authenticity and the reality of the human situations presented. *Survivor, Fear Factor,* and *The*

Amazing Race are current examples. Likewise, the Bible reports reality, telling exactly what happens and recording all of man's "decisions and revisions which a minute will reverse," to quote the famous poem *The Love Song of J. Alfred Prufrock* by T. S. Eliot. In reality, there was tremendous bloodshed in the situations presented in the Old Testament, so the Bible reports it. That doesn't mean God approves it. The Bible is a book of authentic history telling exactly what transpired. Today's audiences love this stuff!

Second, there is violence and bloodshed in the Old Testament because in spite of human sin and failure, God is still able to accomplish His purposes through man. Nothing can thwart God. Mankind's attempts to obstruct God's plans and purposes may cause violence, but they will ultimately fail. God's will is done regardless, in spite of their best efforts.

This section of 2 Samuel is indeed violent. In fact, three successive murders are recorded. Like Macbeth's ascension to the throne, David's is not easy and does not happen without intrigue and murder.

Murder One: The Murder of a Brother

By this point in David's life, he has learned his lesson. He knows to ask the Lord for direction before he makes major decisions. It's an important lesson for all of us to learn. In everything we do, we should seek the direction and guidance of the Lord.

David inquires of the Lord, "Shall I go up to one of the towns of Judah?" (v. 1).

The Lord's answer is, "Go up."

Then David asks where he should go. He wants specific guidance as many of us do in so many of life's situations. So the Lord answers him and tells him to go to Hebron. Hebron is a city in the news these days. Actually, I believe Hebron will always be in the news. There is constant violence and political upheaval there. In March 2002, I read a news report about several Israeli citizens celebrating the festival of Purim in Hebron, which "commemorates the saving of the Jews from genocide in ancient Persia, as recounted in the Biblical book of Esther."[4] Many Jews celebrated the festival aware that violence between the Israelis and Palestinians could erupt. In fact, the region around Hebron is known to be violent. Tour groups don't go to Hebron any more.

Nevertheless, Hebron is a city filled with biblical significance. Some of the Bible's great men of God such as Abraham, Isaac, and Jacob and their wives are buried in the cave of Machpelah in Hebron. Today, there's a Moslem mosque over the cave. Hebron is also the place where God told David he would begin his reign.

David and all the men who had been faithful and loyal to him up to this point follow him to Hebron. This reminds me of the people who hold signs and wave for politicians when they're campaigning. When the race is over, those people often seek and receive jobs with the candidate. By this time, David has over one thousand supporters who have been loyal and faithful to him. So they move into Hebron.

In verse 4, David is anointed for the second time. He will be anointed three times in his life. The first anointing occurred when Samuel anointed him privately back in 1 Samuel 16. By pouring the holy, anointed oil on David's head, Samuel symbolically recognized that God had selected David to be the king. The second anointing occurs in Hebron and gives David power to rule Judah, but not the entire kingdom.

David's second anointing in Hebron teaches us a lesson today. Every time God gives us a new job to do, we should seek a new infilling, a new anointing of the power of the Holy Spirit. The psalmist said, "I shall be anointed with fresh oil" (Ps. 92:10 KJV). God wants His power on us for every new responsibility, and we need His power to do His work.

The best definition I have ever heard of anointing is "a fresh touch for a fresh task." Whenever God gives you a new assignment, you ought to seek a new anointing. It would be wise to seek God's power in a new and fresh way.

In 2 Samuel 2:4–7, David learns how the people of Jabesh Gilead revered and cared for the dead body of their slain king, Saul. David realizes their tribute, and he expresses his gratitude and appreciation. It's vital for a leader to know how to be thankful and to show recognition. David says, "The LORD bless you for showing this kindness to Saul your master by burying him. May the LORD now show you kindness and faithfulness, and I too will show you the same favor because you have done this" (v. 5).

David is a new king, but he proves to be a wise king because he thanks these people for their thoughtfulness toward his predecessor. David is beginning to consolidate support for a larger share of the kingdom, and his decision to thank the citizens of Jabesh Gilead begins that process.

Abner, who was the commander of Saul's army, reappears in verse 8. He was also the uncle of Saul. This may be the first case of reverse nepotism in the Bible. It's usually the uncle promoting the nephew, not the other way around. Abner is not satisfied with David, so he decides to run a rival kingdom. Basically, he is an opportunist. Abner decides to organize Saul's remaining forces and to select a king to rival David. He's an army commander, so he's a master strategist. He looks around for someone who is weak and who can be controlled. Jonathan is gone. Saul's other descendant, Mephibosheth, cannot be king because of physical limitation. More about Mephibosheth later.

Abner chose another of Saul's sons. His name is Ish-Bosheth (v. 8). Abner simply "made him king" (v. 9). The name Ish-Bosheth literally means "man of shame." His is certainly an unfortunate name for a leader of a nation.

So Abner places Ish-Bosheth over the northern part of the kingdom, which is Israel. For a period of time, there are rival kingdoms. Verse 11 says, "The length of time David was king in

Hebron over the house of Judah was seven years and six months." David is patient. His fugitive years have taught him to wait on God. He doesn't demand that he be king over the entire kingdom. Instead, he proves he is willing to wait on God. Remember, David is a man after God's own heart.

Now enters the violence. We're talking blood as Joab enters the scene. Joab is the son of Zeruiah. In Old Testament days, human life was cheap. The average life span was short. Abner and Joab go to the pool of Gibeon to watch some war games. This reminds me of the gladiators who fought in ancient Rome. They often did not know who or what they would be fighting until they were in the center of the coliseum in front of a mob of people. It was cheap and gory entertainment. It's the same thing here. Both Abner and Joab select twelve men to fight one another while they watch. Roll tape on those reality TV cameras because the war games turn into violent death games. In fact, all twelve on each side are killed.

That's certainly something we can identify with today. Think of the violence of professional sports in America. I can think of instances in hockey and in football where players and fans have turned extremely violent and innocent people have been hurt. America has bloodthirstiness for that kind of violence. It's a human vice, however, and it's not just American. Shakespeare wrote the same kind of violence into his plays, especially *Macbeth*.

From ultimate fighting to BattleBots, violence is prevalent in our culture. The first time I saw BattleBots on television, I was intrigued. Then I realized that perhaps people were taking out their frustrations with these remote control man-made robots built to fight other robots. David did not have BattleBots for fun in his kingdom; he had men playing violent war games that turned real.

There is a spiritual lesson here. Sometimes God's people begin to play games instead of staying faithful and true to Jesus. Sometimes the games turn real and violent. People might allow their own agenda and selfish pride to take over, which may cause them to take their eyes off Jesus. Unfortunately, many foolish choices are made in similar circumstances.

Verse 18 tells about the three sons of Zeruiah. Zeruiah was David's half-sister, and she had three sons. The first, Joab, was the commander-in-chief of David's army. The second, Abishai, was the young warrior who went with David into the very heart of Saul's camp in the heat of battle. He was a very courageous warrior. The third, Asahel, was described as being as fast as a gazelle. He was the athlete of the family. These three sons of Zeruiah are fiercely loyal to David. They love David, and they fight for David, but they are going to create agony and misery for him later.

Asahel is chasing Abner and his men as they run off after the war games turn into real battles. Picture Asahel, who is really fast, chasing Abner, who is an older man and the commander of the army of Saul. Asahel stays right on his back. Asahel turned "neither to the right nor to the left" while following Abner (v. 19). In other words, he's focused, and he's gaining ground all the time.

Abner is not able to outrun him. They actually carry on a conversation while the chase goes on. To paraphrase a lot of Scripture, Abner basically tells Asahel to back off or else Abner might do something to Asahel that will make big brother Joab mad. But Asahel just keeps on coming. Finally, Abner takes the end of his spear and hits Asahel right under the fifth rib. Asahel dies, murdered by Abner.

Joab and Abishai, the two other brothers, are also on Abner's trail. They don't know what has happened to Asahel (v. 24). Then Abner says to Joab, "Must the sword devour forever?" (v. 26). Abner is asking Joab to stop the fighting between them.

"Joab blew the trumpet, and all the men came to a halt; they no longer pursued Israel, nor did they fight anymore"

(v. 28). So they stop. You and I know something that Joab doesn't know at that time. We know about Asahel. Joab doesn't.

Ah, but the plot thickens. "Then Joab returned from pursuing Abner and assembled all his men. Besides Asahel, nineteen of David's men were found missing" (v. 30). They decide to count heads of the living and the dead. Judah, David's kingdom, has the better day. Verses 30 and 31 explain the body count. There were 360 dead from Abner's rival kingdom and only 20 dead, including Asahel from David's side.

Joab's rage reaches a boiling point as he hears the news of his little brother. Again, you may ask why the Bible mentions all this violence and killing. The Bible is showing raw human nature. It displays what happens when we as humans take our eyes off the Lord and focus them instead on ourselves.

Murder one. Asahel, the athlete of the family of Zeruiah, is murdered in cold blood. David's journey to the throne of the entire nation is a bloody one because of the murder, bloody murder.

Murder Two: The Murder of a Commander

Second Samuel 3:1 discusses again the shift in the balance of power. As the remains of Saul's kingdom dwindle, David's kingdom thrives. The chapter also mentions that David has several sons who were born while he was king in Hebron. Remember, the Bible records the fact that many of these men had more than one wife, but the Bible never approves it. In fact, in Deuteronomy 17:15–17, God specifically says that the kings of Israel were not to have multiple wives. But David disobeyed the Lord. David seems to have had trouble in this area, as we will discover.

It's interesting how much of David's life relates to our lives today. For example, David seemingly becomes intricately involved in the affairs of his kingdom, as many of us do. This can be a positive trait. Yet it appears that David got so busy doing his work that he neglected his family. Few of his family members ever shared his faith in the Lord. That's a sad legacy to leave behind you.

Men, it's really a warning. Women, it's a warning to you, too. Your work is essential, of course. But God has given you a family also. Advancing at work is not worth sacrificing your family. What good is it to sell your soul to your work if you lose your family? Go ahead. Become a millionaire. What have you accomplished if you lose your own sons and daughters? Put Jesus first, your family second, and your work third—and you'll live well. Always keep Jesus first. Don't let your children's growing-up years pass you by.

At this point, David is in those child-rearing years, and he makes some very serious mistakes that will haunt him. Things don't go so well for Abner either. Abner gets in a mess. "During the war between the house of Saul and the house of David, Abner had been strengthening his own position in the house of Saul" (v. 6). Abner is taking over. Remember, he's running a rival kingdom. He's a power behind the throne. He's the commander of the army. Doesn't this sound just like politics today?

Abner and Ish-Bosheth, his puppet, get into it. The king accuses Abner of going to Saul's concubine named Rizpah. In those days, a concubine was considered to be a prostitute, but she was allowed in the kingdom. It really ticks Ish-Bosheth that Abner would visit her. He demands of Abner, "Why did you sleep with my father's concubine?" (v. 7).

"Abner was very angry because of what Ish-Bosheth said and he answered, "Am I a dog's head—on Judah's side?'" (v. 8). In other words, Abner is asking Ish-Bosheth who he thinks he is to have the gall to question him. The bottom line is that the two men have a falling out, and a breath-taking turn of events transpires. Suddenly Abner, who is the commander in chief of the enemy's armies, decides that he will defect to David's side. He sees that a successful future is with David.

Abner requests that David "make an agreement with [him]" (see vv. 12–14). David agrees if certain conditions are met. One of the conditions is that David wants his first wife, Michal, back. Remember she is Saul's daughter, and she loved David. When David had to flee as a fugitive, he lost Michal. David gets her back. He may actually live to regret that decision.

David chooses to make a covenant with Abner and to let him defect from Ish-Bosheth. David is a forgiving man. Think about it, though. Here's the guy who has chased David all over the wilderness for Saul. Abner's goal for years was to murder David. Now the two of them enter a peace treaty. David throws a big banquet for Abner (v. 20). Abner probably had his sights set on some powerful, prestigious job in David's administration. Maybe chief of staff. Maybe secretary of state. Abner obviously doesn't mind switching parties. Perhaps Abner was fickle.

It seems to me that so much of what goes on in politics today is expedience rather than conviction. Politicians may do what they think is going to get them elected or on a cable news network during prime time instead of standing for what is genuine, true conviction in their hearts. That's what Abner does.

Abner leaves David to garner support for him throughout the kingdom (v. 21). But there's a problem named Joab. Joab has murder in his heart. It's his brotherly duty to avenge Asahel's murder. That means Abner is dead meat as far as Joab is concerned.

Joab has been off on a little military excursion. Now Joab is back, and told that Abner has been there (v. 23). He goes ballistic, just like a missile en route to its target. Perhaps Joab feels threatened by Abner's presence since Joab is a commander of David's army. They're competitors. So he stomps into the office of the David and demands, "What have you done?" (v. 24). He's talking to a king. "Why did you let him go?" Joab continues, "You know Abner son of Ner; he came to deceive you and observe your movements and find out everything you are doing" (v. 25). He's basically mad at David for letting Abner leave his sight.

So, hotheaded Joab takes the situation into his own hands. He sends some messengers after Abner. David doesn't know anything about this. Joab causes Abner to be called back to Hebron (v. 26).

What do you think happens next? "Now when Abner returned to Hebron, Joab took him aside into the gateway, as though to speak with him privately. And there, to avenge the blood of his brother Asahel, Joab stabbed him in the stomach, and he died" (v. 27).

Here is murder two. When David realizes that Abner has been murdered, he knows he has a serious crisis on his hands as a king trying to build support. His commander in chief has murdered the commander in chief of the kingdom of Israel, which is the northern portion that he's trying to consolidate into one kingdom. Would you suspect David of being involved in a conspiracy? Some might. What does David do? He simply tells the truth. Remember, he's a man after God's own heart. Wouldn't it be wonderful if leaders just told the truth?

David simply tells the truth about Abner and calls for national mourning for the death of this man who had been his enemy. David shows his enemy respect and honor. He did the same with Saul. David exalts Abner and praises him in death. He calls him a prince and says that a great man has fallen. He even requires that his people fast, and he himself refuses to eat. "All the people took note and were pleased; indeed, everything the king did pleased them" (v. 36). David has now earned the favor of the people for all the right reasons.

It works. David's people understand that it wasn't his intention to have Abner killed. David says, "And today, though I am the anointed king, I am weak, and these sons of Zeruiah are too strong for me" (v. 39). He's talking about his own men, his nephews actually. Joab and Abishai. Yes, they love David, and they fight valiantly for David. But they are a burden to him because he constantly has to stop their quarrels.

Jesus had the same problem. He had twelve disciples. Yet it was Simon Peter who caused most of the messes. He cut off a guy's ear one time, and Jesus had to go behind Simon Peter and heal the guy's ear.

Think of James and John. They were known as "the sons of thunder." They caused Jesus quite a bit of misery. The same things happen today in the church of the Lord. There are people who love Jesus. They'll fight for Him. But in reality, they constantly cause problems. You have the sons of Zeruiah in your Bible class or in the music ministry. They always have their noses out of joint. They're trying to do good deeds perhaps, but they're always causing problems.

Murder two is the murder of a commander. Abner is dead because of Joab and his desire to avenge his brother's murder. David's trip to the throne has indeed been a bloody one because of murder, bloody murder.

Murder Three: The Murder of a Usurper

The fourth chapter of 2 Samuel records yet another murder. It's the murder of the king of shame, Ish-Bosheth. "When Ish-Bosheth son of Saul heard that Abner had died in Hebron, he lost courage, and all Israel became alarmed" (v. 1). Ish-Bosheth lost heart as a rival king. A leader is so important to his or her people because he or she provides guidance and direction. A weak leader can cause a nation to become insecure and vulnerable.

In reality, Ish-Bosheth is a usurper. He takes the throne of Israel while David is, in fact, the rightful king. He responds to Abner's desire to set up a rival kingdom and becomes Abner's puppet. Two of his own captains commit high treason. Ish-Bosheth's murder is narrated (2 Sam. 4). In fact, verse 6 says two men stab him while he is lying on his bed at noon. The two captains, Rechab and Baanah, complete the deed by beheading him, thinking David will be proud of them for killing his enemy. They take Ish-Bosheth's head to David. Promotions are in the bag, they think. They've actually committed high treason. What does David do? He has them killed. In fact, he has their hands and feet cut off and their bodies hung up.

Three bloody murders and Saul's dynasty comes to an end. Well, almost. Mephibosheth is still alive, and he will be heard from again. But the way is clear for David, our Braveheart, to become the king of a unified Israel.

Why does God allow us to encounter people like the sons of Zeruiah who cause us such stress as we continue on our journey? Sometimes God uses them as chisels in our lives. Their actions and reactions chip away flaws in our character that ought not to be there. Why? Because the chipping away helps us become more like Jesus. Sometimes these people are used to drive us to God, and we learn kindness and love and patience. Other times, God allows us to see parts of our selves He wants us to change or give to Him.

Shakespeare's Macbeth had his own stresses with the witches and his wife's ambitions and the prophecy he hears. The bloody series of murders that Macbeth begins simply as a result of ambition may not be equaled in any other work of literature—unless that work of literature is the Bible. The series of murders David lives through is just as violent as those presented in Shakespeare's *Macbeth,* but they are different in two ways. David did not start the series of murders by committing a murder first as Macbeth did. Second, the series of murders David lives through is genuine biblically recorded history whereas Macbeth's series is fiction.

Nevertheless, any record of humanity includes the positives and negatives because of sinful human nature. Macbeth wanted the throne of Scotland after hearing a prophecy given by witches. His desire becomes so strong that he murders the reigning king to make it happen. David didn't do it this way. David waited on God for years. He was just a shepherd boy when God selected him to be king. Now he's a man, a father, and finally a king. He's lived through war and now murder, bloody murder.

CHAPTER 11

Capital Matters,
or A Tale of Two Cities

"It was the best of times, it was the worst of times."
CHARLES DICKENS

2 SAMUEL 5   Perhaps when you were in high school you read Charles Dickens's novel *A Tale of Two Cities*. It is set during the French Revolution in two capital cities, London and Paris. There are many characters and a complex plot as aristocrats and peasants struggle for power. In the end, a character named Sydney Carton sacrifices his own life in order to save the lives and freedom of his friends, Charles Darnay and Lucie Manette.

I mention this work of literature for two reasons. First, it deals with two cities that were at one time the cultural and political centers of the civilized world. Dickens wrote the book in 1859 and set it approximately seventy years earlier during the French Revolution. Second, the opening line of the work is universal. The phrase can be applied to any time in human history. David, our Braveheart, could have said his times were the best and the worst. Today, we can say we are living in the best and the worst of times, especially in light of the attacks on America on September 11, 2001.

There are two other cities that may be considered political centers of the civilized world right now. They are Jerusalem and

Washington, D.C. Both are world capitals. Both are seats of power. George Washington established Washington, D.C., as the capital of the United States. David established Jerusalem as the capital of the nation of Israel. Perhaps the comparisons stop there or perhaps not. Now that the United States and Israel are both involved in war, Washington, D.C., and Jerusalem are wartime capitals.

David is in his prime. His reign begins in Hebron when he's thirty years of age, and he serves as the great king of Israel for forty years. Saul was Israel's first king. David is Israel's second king under whom the golden era in the history of the people of Israel occurs.

One of David's first objectives is to consolidate his kingdom. He's been king in Hebron for seven and one-half years. Now he has the opportunity to bring all of the tribes of Israel together into one nation under his leadership with God's help.

David's Crown

Second Samuel 5:1 says, "All the tribes of Israel came to David at Hebron." In other words, all the tribes support David. Why? Basically because they have known him all of his life. He is one of their own, and they know that he is God's choice to be their king. I remember a song from several years ago entitled "We Are Family." That's what these tribes are telling David.

David is an unusual person, and he's going to be an unusual king. He rarely takes matters into his own hands, which goes against much modern thinking today. He waits on God. "You will shepherd my people Israel, and you will become their ruler [or a prince]" (v. 2). He will be a shepherd king.

In Psalms 78:70–72, we are told about David's reign. It says that the Lord "chose David his servant and took him from the sheep pens." Remember, David was a shepherd boy. "From tending the sheep he brought him to be the shepherd of his people Jacob, of Israel his inheritance. And David shepherded them with integrity of heart; with skillful hands he led them."

David leads and feeds God's people. David was not only a political ruler; but he was also a spiritual ruler.

Studying David's life helps us apply spiritual guidance to our lives today. Sure, his life is historically rich, but it's also spiritually rich. In many ways, David is an Old Testament picture of our Shepherd King who leads and feeds us, the Lord Jesus Christ.

There are many comparisons between King David and the Lord Jesus Christ. For instance, look at 2 Samuel 5:3: "The king made a compact [that is, he went into a covenant] with them at Hebron before the LORD, and they anointed David king over Israel." This is David's third anointing, and this one is done publicly for the entire nation. Each anointing has equipped him to be stronger and to do more for the Lord.

There is a beautiful parallel here between David and his anointing as king and the anointing of our King, the Lord Jesus Christ. Hebrews 1:8–9 declares, "About the Son he says, 'Your throne, O God, will last for ever and ever, and righteousness will be the scepter of your kingdom. You have loved righteousness and hated wickedness; therefore God, your God, has set you above your companions by anointing you with the oil of joy.'" Jesus has been anointed King in heaven. He is God's choice, destined to be the King of heaven, the earth, and the universe. But good is always attacked by evil, and Satan sets up a rival kingdom. This happened to David, too. Remember when Abner set up a rival kingdom with Saul's son, Ish-Bosheth? This proves that the struggle between good and evil has always been with us.

When David was anointed king of Hebron, he was able to rule a partial kingdom. He ruled a small number of people. The same thing is true today. Some of us choose to anoint Christ King of our lives. Some of us have yielded our lives to the Lord Jesus. Right now, Jesus rules a small number of people. Philippians 2:10–11 says, "At the name of Jesus every knee should bow, in heaven and on earth and under the earth, and every tongue confess that Jesus Christ is Lord." Eventually, Christ will rule all. Now it is a matter of personal choice. You can either receive Jesus as your King, or you can reject Jesus as your King. But one day the Lord will return and rule over all.

There was a memorable commercial a few years ago about people who choose to neglect their oil filters. Their car winds up with a mechanic who says, "Pay me now or pay me later." That's really the way it is with the lordship and kingship of Jesus. You will either crown Him now or you will crown Him later. You will either acknowledge His lordship over your life now, or you will do it later. Jesus is destined to be the King of the universe. So like David, He receives a crown.

David's City

David realizes that if he is going to reign effectively, he needs a capital city. A capital is a symbolic and physical seat of political power. Hebron is not a viable option because it is in the southern part of Israel. David knows he needs a more centrally located place as a capital city.

David selects Jerusalem as his capital, the seat of his kingdom. Remember, God had given commandments that there would be a place where His name would live. Jerusalem is that place. In fact, Deuteronomy 12:11 says, "To the place the LORD your God will choose as a dwelling for his Name—there you are to bring everything I command you." Politically, David's selection of Jerusalem is an astute move because it unites all Israel. Geographically, he chooses a centrally located city right on the border between the northern and southern tribes.

Decisions like these are important historically and politically. In fact, there is a branch of science devoted to analyzing political struggles in the world through geography. It is called political geography. Political geography is defined as "the scientific study of the relationship between politics and territorial space."[5] In other words, historical events such as wars or invasions can be analyzed by considering the geographic qualities of a nation or state. Poland, for example, has a history of being invaded. A political geographer might say this is because Poland has few natural barriers such as mountains or bodies of water for protection.

In choosing Jerusalem as his capital, David thinks politically and geographically. Jerusalem is a city with a long, violent history, and yet it is still even today considered a world-class city. Even so, it is a divided and conflicted city. Arabs and Jews live there together, yet they live separate lives. Jews, Muslims, and Christians consider Jerusalem to be the foundation place for their faiths. Unfortunately, there is constant fighting there. David left quite a legacy in naming Jerusalem his capital.

When Washington, D.C., was chosen as the capital of the United States, something similar happened. First New York City was considered because it had served the new nation as a provisional capital. Then the government was temporarily relocated to Philadelphia while northerners and southerners fought over where the capital should be. A student of political geography may be happy with the choice of Washington, D.C., because of its central location. At least it was centrally located when the country had only thirteen colonies. Rather than selecting a city in one of the states, a new area was formed called the District of Columbia. George Washington chose a location just south of the tobacco port of George Town, conveniently situated near his Mount Vernon estate.

"Although the region consisted primarily of undeveloped marshland, it was strategically positioned along the navigable portion of the Potomac River with easy access to the lucrative markets of the west and its rich resources. Furthermore, the area was sufficiently removed from the Atlantic Ocean and was thereby protected from marauding foreign navies."[6]

In a recent newspaper column entitled "Washington Matters Little in Real Lives," David Broder discusses a possible new role that Washington, D.C., is playing since the attacks on America on September 11, 2001. "Washington has become a wartime capital, and its preoccupation with terrorism has widened the gap between its officials and hometown America." Washington has only rarely been considered a "wartime capital," but now it is one. In contrast, Jerusalem has been a wartime capital for years.

David's choice of Jerusalem as his capital is a politically brilliant move. It is also a spiritually important move. God says the city is going to be the place where His name dwells. It's going to be known as the City of God and the City of David. It is true. Jerusalem is known by these names today. Jerusalem has recently celebrated its three-thousandth year since its founding. Think about it. What in our world lasts for three thousand years? Not much. But this city named Jerusalem has.

Since its founding, the City of God has had a remarkable history. It is in Jerusalem that the son of David, Solomon, builds the most elaborate, the most luxurious, the most beautiful temple ever constructed. It is in Jerusalem that battles are fought. Sometimes Jerusalem is destroyed with nothing left but ruins, but still it lives as it is built again. It is in Jerusalem that our Lord Jesus Christ comes and performs many miracles and teaches many lessons. It is outside the gates of Jerusalem that Jesus Christ is nailed on a cross. It is at Jerusalem that Jesus is buried. It is in Jerusalem that Jesus Christ rises again from the dead. It is from the Mount of Olives, just across from Jerusalem, that Jesus ascends to heaven. Zechariah 14 predicts that Jesus Christ will return to Jerusalem and rule and reign on this earth for one thousand years.

Jerusalem is perhaps the most exciting city on earth. The Jewish Talmud says that when God poured forth ten measures of beauty on the earth, nine of the measures fell upon Jerusalem. Jerusalem is indeed the City of God.

Psalm 122:6 says, "Pray for the peace of Jerusalem." Have you prayed lately for the peace of Jerusalem? The city seems to be constantly in need of peace. Interestingly, Jerusalem literally means "city of peace."

When David and his men arrive in Jerusalem, it is under the control of the Jebusites. The Jebusites are a Canaanite tribe who are dwelling in the land before David and Joab conquer them. Remember when the children of Israel come into the promised land, they are unable to conquer this city. It isn't an elaborate place at all. It is really just a steep hill surrounded by three valleys. They are the Kidron Valley, the Trophenian Valley, which is the valley of the cheese makers, and the Valley of Gehenna. So David chooses Jerusalem, which has defied Jewish takeover attempts for over four hundred years. The Jebusites are in control.

David and his army approach. The Jebusites taunt David. In fact, they say, "You will not get in here; even the blind and the lame can ward you off" (v. 6). The Jebusites are arrogant and filled with pride. Peace to them was like the peace one feels when one sees a water moccasin sleeping on a rock on a summer day. Just don't get too close. The Jebusites may think they know peace, but in reality they are contending against David, God's chosen leader and warrior. It's always better to be underestimated.

Second Samuel 5:7 says, "Nevertheless, David captured the fortress of Zion, the City of David." How did he take that seemingly impregnable fortress? Verse 8 tells us, "Anyone who conquers the Jebusites will have to use the watershaft to reach those 'lame and blind' who are David's enemies" (v. 8). The verse continues, "That is why they say, the 'blind and lame' will not enter the place." In other words, David is challenging his warriors by saying that whoever leads the attack will be the commander of the army. First Chronicles 11:5–8 presents a parallel passage, which says that Joab took the lead. So Joab became the commander in chief of David's army. How did Joab do it? How did they capture this Jebusite city and make it into David's capital?

Archaeologists have discovered in Jerusalem that a watershaft was dropped inside the city. A tunnel was dug from that watershaft outside the city to the pool of Gihon. I've been to the pool of Gihon. It was the only source of water for the city of Jerusalem, which comes up later on in the days of Hezekiah. In fact, in the days of Hezekiah when Jerusalem was under attack, the pool of Gihon was hidden in that tunnel so the enemy wouldn't know there was an inside source of water for Jerusalem.

This is why Psalm 46:4 says, "There is a river whose streams make glad the city of God." The passage is talking about that pool of Gihon that brought in the water. Talk about hidden resources. When you give your heart to Jesus Christ, you receive a fountain on the inside. You have hidden resources. Christians have the same problems other people have, of course. The difference is that Christians can draw on resources and refreshment that God provides for them on the inside.

Joab went into the tunnel. He actually went up the watershaft and led an army through it. Before the Jebusites realize it, they are attacked and conquered from the inside. They underestimated David, and Jerusalem became David's capital.

David "became more and more powerful" (v. 10). Literally, it means that David has longer strides and a larger embrace. Figuratively, it means David's power is growing. He hits his peak. It's all working out for him. "The LORD God Almighty was with him." The secret of success is to have the Lord with you. If you don't, whatever you do is destined to fail. Philippians 4:13 says, "I can do everything through him who gives me strength." The Lord is with David. Is the Lord with you? Do you have Jesus leading in your life?

David understands why he is being blessed: "And David knew that the LORD had established him as king over Israel and had exalted his kingdom for the sake of his people Israel" (v. 12). David understood the source of his blessings. David saw why he was prosperous and victorious. The Lord was in his life, and the Lord had established him as king.

Verses 13–16 hit a negative note. "David took more concubines and wives in Jerusalem" (v. 13). David is living in specific disobedience to Deuteronomy 17:17. God had very clearly said that the king was not to multiply wives and concubines. This section of 2 Samuel also talks about the children who are born. These children cause problems down the road. The Bible is providing a foreshadowing of what's coming in David's life.

David's Conquest

It's not all peaches and cream for David, just like it isn't for Christians living for God today. "When the Philistines heard that David had been anointed king over Israel, they went up in full force to search for him, but David heard about it and went down to the stronghold" (v. 17). The stronghold is really the fortress. So his old enemies, Goliath's people, come on the scene to attack again. Why? It's always this way. The moment you crown Jesus the king of your life, get ready. The devil will attack you.

It is always after times of great spiritual commitment and victory that Satan comes with his strongest and most subtle temptations. Here come the Philistines. Don't forget, David is a man of war. He is trained in battle. He knows what to do. So he gets down into the fortress to prepare for battle.

"The Philistines had come and spread out in the Valley of Rephaim," also known as the "valley of the giants" (v. 18).

"David inquired of the LORD, 'Shall I go and attack the Philistines? Will you hand them over to me?'" (v. 19). Then David goes to God in prayer. By the way, David has learned his lesson. Back in the earlier chapters of David's story, there were times when he chose not to pray and seek the Lord. It caused him great sorrow and defeat. David has learned the importance of prayer. Please don't minimize the importance of prayer. It is absolutely vital. It is the powerhouse of the church.

It is essential to the victorious Christian life. Prayer is where spiritual energy is generated, and David knows it.

David inquires of the Lord, and he gets an answer. Verse 19 says, "The LORD answered him, 'Go, for I will surely hand the Philistines over to you.'" Good answer, as Richard Dawson used to say on *Family Feud*. It's comforting to get such a definite answer, especially right before a battle.

"David went to Baal Perazim, and there he defeated them. He said, 'As waters break out, the Lord has broken out against my enemies before me'" (v. 20). Baal Perazim literally means "the breach of waters." In other words, David says it is like the Lord flooded a stream. David is acknowledging that the Lord flooded his enemies and gave him the victory. This is the first battle.

"It ain't over 'til it's over." "Once more the Philistines came up and spread out in the Valley of Rephaim" (v. 22). They came again. This reminds me of those toys we used to buy for the children called Weebles. The advertising slogan went something like, "Weebles wobble, but they don't fall down." Maybe the Philistines were just wobbling the first time.

If you have a spiritual battle and the devil attacks you, pray and claim God's direction and God's blessings. When it is over, rejoice. Often, there's another attack. The battle won't be over until we are no longer on earth. As long as we are here in this world, we will fight battles. The battle is not over yet, but it will be one day. The devil is persistent. He keeps at you all the time. Just because you've won a spiritual victory doesn't mean it's all over. In fact, the most dangerous time is often right after you have won a spiritual victory. Stay alert for enemy attacks.

So the Philistines are back in the Valley of Rephaim. But look at David. What an example he is. "David inquired of the LORD, and he answered, 'Do not go straight up.'" Previously, when David asked the Lord, he was told to go. Now the Lord says to David, "Do not go straight up, but circle around behind them and attack them in front of the balsam trees." This time

God's plan is different. The first time it was frontal attack. This time it is ambush from behind.

What's the lesson for us? There are two very important lessons.

First, for each new battle in life, we need new directions from the Lord. David "inquired of the LORD" again and again. There are no carbon copies of God's will. Past directions for past victories may not work in a new situation. It is vital to always seek fresh direction from the Lord in every situation.

Second, God is not captive to any one method. David won the first battle by direct frontal assault. The second battle is an ambush. The approach is completely different. God is not confined to any one method. The goal in both battles was the same, and it was victory over the Philistines.

In every generation, the church has to learn how to find God's plan and God's direction. Methods that worked twenty-five years ago may not work today. Sometimes this concept is a difficult one for people to accept, especially if past methods were very successful.

There was a company many years ago that made buggies. It was quite a successful business. They made the best buggies around. Then Henry Ford invented the automobile. The buggy company tried to compete by building a bigger and better buggy. Unfortunately, the buggy people went out of business because they made a fundamental mistake. They thought they were in the buggy business when they were actually in the transportation business.

As Christians, we are in the business of getting the message of the gospel out to a lost world. That's our ultimate goal. The message never changes. But the medium through which the message is transmitted may change. It was Marshall McCluhan who first said, "The medium is the message." That may be true in some cases. But with the gospel, the message never changes. The medium might change, but not the message.

Five years ago I would never have imagined that church services could be broadcast in real time over the Internet. Now they can. That means the gospel message may reach an audience not available before. The message of the Bible is the same. But we have to be aware that though God may have used one method successfully in the past, He may have an altogether different method for us to use in the present. Jesus said in Luke 16:8, "The people of this world are more shrewd in dealing with their own kind than are the people of the light." We can learn quite a bit from the lost world that will help us spread the gospel.

Look at what God said in 2 Samuel 5:24, "As soon as you hear the sound of marching in the tops of the balsam trees, move quickly, because that will mean the LORD has gone out in front of you to strike the Philistine army." In other words, God told them to wait for the blowing in the balsam leaves.

What a picture these verses paint. It reminds me of Acts 2:2, "Suddenly a sound like the blowing of a violent wind came from heaven." Today, we need to pray and wait for the moving of the Spirit of God. When God's Spirit begins to move, let's go with it. Let's go with God. When we do, God will give us the victory.

Perhaps you sense a blowing of the balsam leaves as David did. God may be stirring some of His people. Somebody in a fellowship gets excited and on fire for the Lord and then a few other people catch it. Then there is a great move of God in the fellowship. Who knows what God may do if we will pray and wait on Him and when the wind of God blows, catch the wind and go with God?

Dickens's novel *A Tale of Two Cities* is a good read. It has interesting characters, a deep plot, and historical descriptions of two world cities, London and Paris. What is even more interesting to me is the constantly unfolding story involving two other world cities, Washington, D.C., and Jerusalem. Since September 11, 2001, the conflict between Arabs and Jews in the

Middle East has intensified. The role Washington plays may be diminishing. Nevertheless, Jerusalem, the City of David, remains on center stage in this drama that we call our lives. This other tale of two cities, unlike Dickens's novel, remains unresolved.

CHAPTER 12

Worship Matters, or Symbols and Cymbals of Worship

"Shout for joy to the LORD, all the earth. Worship the LORD with gladness; come before him with joyful songs."
PSALM 100:1–2

2 SAMUEL 6   What do you think worship means? Is it simply prayer? Is it praising God? Is it a mind-set or a feeling? Is it an individual or group experience? It seems that today the definition of worship is in flux.

One definition from the *American Heritage Dictionary* states that worship is "the reverent love and allegiance accorded a deity, idol, or sacred object." So that would mean worshiping God. Others might say the definition means adoring a teen idol such as a rock star. Another definition says to worship is "to participate in religious rites of worship." Churches often call their Sunday meetings "worship" services.

A telling article was printed in *USA Today* on March 7, 2002. It presents one of our modern culture's ideas of going to church for worship. The article, entitled "'Amen' to a Church-free Life," says that the state of Washington has the highest percentage of residents who say they have no religion. It goes on to profile several people who spend time on Sundays doing activities other than church. For example, thirty-two-year-old Jason

165

Wilson "is likely to be sleeping in—at least until the weather tells him which gear to pull out of the garage of his suburban Seattle home. Skis, snowboard, bikes, skates or golf clubs . . . No church for him. 'I don't spend a lot of time fretting about the meaning of the universe,' he says."

The article uses information found in a recent survey called the American Religious Identification Survey 2001. According to the survey, "25% of people in Washington say they have no religion at all, or call themselves atheist, agnostic or secular. Only 42% say someone in their household is affiliated with a church, synagogue or mosque."

The article may indicate some startling trends in America today. It says, "Washington reflects many of the religious and social values seen world wide today—'an emphasis on individuality, freedom of choice and an embrace of diversity,' says sociologist Ronald Inglehart of the University of Michigan."

Is the face of worship changing? Has church lost its relevance today? Is going to church a generational thing? Does our culture need less of God today? Worship is a difficult concept to grasp, but perhaps it could best be defined as a sincere and sacrificial expression of devotion to God. The focus of worship is on God, not on the human worshiper. Perhaps this is what doesn't sit well with people today. Nevertheless, this chapter in David's life presents worship as an expression of devotion to God, and he was a man after God's own heart.

What does the Old Testament say about worship? Second Samuel 6 addresses the subject. Ironically, it is one of the strangest but most helpful chapters in the entire Bible.

When the chapter opens, David is fully established as king over all Israel with Jerusalem as the capital. David analyzes his kingdom and realizes something is missing. He also knows that God has made him Israel's shepherd king. Of course, David has civic responsibilities as king, but he also has religious responsibilities as the shepherd king. As a political and religious leader, David knows his new nation needs to put worship in its proper place. Why? Psalm 144:15 says, "Blessed are the people whose God is the LORD." The Scripture makes it clear that a nation will never reach its full potential unless that nation puts God in His proper place. This is why it is so important for a nation's leaders to be of high moral character and to have spiritual insight. A nation cannot be ruled correctly without the presence and blessings of God.

In order for David to establish worship in its proper place in the new nation of Israel, he must bring the ark of the Lord to Jerusalem and establish it in the center of life. Why? Because the ark is a symbol of worship and of God's presence. The ark is also the Old Testament picture of Jesus.

There was a popular movie in the 1980s entitled *Raiders of the Lost Ark.* Maybe you saw it. The movie is about a quiet college professor named Indiana Jones who becomes involved in a worldwide search for the lost ark of the covenant. In the movie, Indiana Jones must outthink a group of Nazis who are also seeking to find the ark for Hitler, who believes that if a fighting army can carry the ark, the army will be invincible. The movie, while certainly not biblically accurate, was a blockbuster hit and helped to make director Steven Spielberg as famous as he is today.

But the movie also brought many questions about the ark into our contemporary culture. Where is the ark? Who took the ark? Is it hidden in Jerusalem under the temple mount? Is it hidden on Mount Nebo on the Jordan River's east bank? Is it in Ethiopia? Did the Nazis take it?

According to the web site *christiananswers.net,* a new view of the ark's location has become popular. A British journalist named Graham Hancock has written a book entitled *The Sign and the Seal: The Quest for the Lost Ark of the Covenant.* The book claims the ark was taken from ancient Jerusalem in the days of King Solomon. Some say that one of Solomon's sons, Menelik, took the ark to Ethiopia for safekeeping.

But let's remember that David, the new king of Israel, is trying to give worship its proper place in his kingdom. How does David obtain the ark? He puts together a group of thirty thousand people to get the ark and to bring it to Jerusalem.

English professors and teachers of literature love to emphasize the importance of symbols and what they mean. For example, the white-washed fence is a symbol of Tom Sawyer's influence over his friends. Fangs are a symbol of Count Dracula. Likewise, the ark of the covenant is a meaningful symbol of worship.

Just what was this ark? The ark was a wooden box overlaid on the outside and inside with gold. The inside of the ark contained three items. First, there were the two tablets of stone Moses brought down from Mount Sinai with the Ten Commandments written on them. Second, Aaron's rod that budded was inside. Third, a pot of manna from the wilderness experience was inside the ark. On the top of the ark was laid a solid slab of gold that was known as the mercy seat.

Each corner of the ark had golden rings, and there were wooden staves overlaid with gold inside the rings. On each side of this ark of the covenant there were gold cherubim. These cherubim faced one another, looking into the middle of the ark. On the day of atonement, blood was sprinkled on the altar, and the Bible says that the glory of God would come and dwell on the ark. So the ark was a visible symbol in the Old Testament of the presence of God. It is also an Old Testament picture of our Lord Jesus Christ.

Today, we know that Jesus is our ark. Jesus Christ is the one in whom the glory of God dwells, and He is the one who shed His blood in order that we might be reconciled to a holy God.

When the wilderness wandering was over, the priests bore the ark on their shoulders. When they came to the Jordan River, the waters parted and the ark of God led the children of Israel into the promised land of Canaan. During the period of the judges, the ark was used by the Israelites in battle. When they went out to battle, they knew that without the presence of God there could be no victory. To them, the ark in battle was a symbol of worship to God.

Unfortunately, the people of Israel made a fatal mistake. They thought just because they took the ark with them, it was a guarantee of God's presence. In other words, they started using the ark of the Lord for their own purposes. We know we can't use God. God will not be used by anybody. God will use us, but He will not let us manipulate Him. Their dependence shifted from God to a symbol of God. This is why the people of Israel took the ark into battle, and probably why in Spielberg's movie *Raiders of the Lost Ark*, Hitler tried to find the ark so his armies could take it into battle.

According to 2 Samuel 6:3, the ark of God had been kept in the house of a man named Abinadab. He lived about eleven miles southwest of Jerusalem. So David goes to get the ark of the Lord to bring it to Jerusalem. He will then establish it as the center of the life of the nation of Israel. With thirty thousand people, it sounds like David is getting ready for war. But he is not. David is getting ready for worship.

Worship Desecrated

In this chapter of 2 Samuel, worship is misused. But we won't find that out until later because it all starts off so wonderfully. Remember the large crowd of thirty thousand people that David takes to the house of Abinadab. They take the ark of God and put it on a new cart. The sons of Abinadab—Uzzah and Ahio—go along with the ark on its new cart. So far, so good. Or, is it?

David, the shepherd king, leads a worship service (v. 5). He plays music before the Lord. David is a musician and a composer of songs, and he's the one who organizes all of the choirs and orchestras of the people of Israel. So all kinds of instruments are being played in praise, adoration, and worship of the Lord. It must have been a magnificent sound. Was this true worship? Does this fit our definition of worship? Yes and yes. There is praise, excitement, and glorious music adoring God. In my opinion, this is the way worship ought to be. I believe it should be exciting to worship the Lord. David also participated in the worship, and he led his people to do the same. Too much worship today is dull, passive, and predictable.

Of course, there is the other extreme if emotions drive the worship instead of the Spirit. A few weeks ago I talked to a young man who told me that the phrase for life in his generation is "assume nothing." I can certainly see validity in his statement. Our world today is full of unknowns. Assumptions can lead to dashed expectations about job security or medical care or even committed marriages. This applies to worship as well. It is dangerous to assume that you're participating in worship by looking at external signs.

Just because there is a big crowd in a big building with loud music and religious activity doesn't mean you're experiencing true worship.

So David is leading worship and then it all changes. The group is moving along with the ark of God on the new cart. Then, the oxen stumble and the ark of the Lord is shaken (v. 6). Uzzah, one of Abinadab's sons, puts out his hand to steady the ark. His act is both physical and symbolic. It is physical because he actually puts out his hand to steady the ark. It is symbolic because many times we, as humans, try to bring about change in the things of God by using our human strength and wisdom.

Uzzah's action is probably second nature because he is comfortable around the ark. It had been in his house for about fifty years. He had been around the ark since his birth. But what Uzzah does is very human. Many people make the same mistake today. It may be that he became so familiar and so accustomed to the ark that he failed to understand how sacred and holy it was. People who are brought up going to church have to be cautious of this as well. Familiarity with spiritual and holy things can cause irreverence and misunderstandings in relationships with fellow Christians and with God. Complacency can be very dangerous.

So Uzzah makes a mistake. It turns out to be a fatal mistake. Uzzah and his family are not Levites. That's very important to remember because they were not priests. When the oxen stumble and the ark of the Lord moves, Uzzah immediately puts his hand on the ark to steady it. It's as if he touches a live wire. The Bible says that when he touched the ark, the anger of the Lord was kindled and Uzzah died on the spot (v. 7). Suddenly the worship ceases. The music stops. There is silence because here is a man who has touched the ark of the Lord, and he is dead. It's actually a reality check for David as he seeks to put worship in its proper place in his kingdom. It's also a reality check for us today.

When you first read this account, you may find Uzzah's death harsh. You may think his act was innocent and helpful. He was just preventing the ark from falling, right? Wrong. The worship going on in these verses is wrong. David is leading man-centered worship, not God-centered worship. It is a desecration of the things of God. Why? We desecrate worship when we go by the world instead of the Word. In other words, if worship does not follow the Lord's guidelines, it is not worship. It becomes simply another human endeavor. Remember, worship is an expression of devotion to God, not some entertainment for us.

David is actually conducting this worship service in disobedience to the word of God because the Bible is very clear about how and by whom the ark is to be transported.

Exodus 25 contains a description of how the ark is to be constructed and put together. Exodus 25:12–14 says, "Cast four gold rings for it and fasten them to its four feet, with two rings on one side and two rings on the other. Then make poles of acacia wood and overlay them with gold. Insert the poles into the rings on the sides of the chest to carry it." The ark is supposed to be carried on the shoulders of the Levites, the priests.

The worship of God is not a casual matter. I know that much in our culture has become more casual. For example, many businesses now support "dress-down" Fridays or allow the lack of standard English in E-mail communication. But worshiping God cannot be anything but formal. When you come to God's house to worship Him, you are coming into the presence of a holy God. God clearly directs us how we are to go about that matter. Jesus said in John 4:24, "God is spirit, and his worshipers must worship in spirit and in truth."

God gave us directions for worship in the Scriptures, and we should follow them. David does not follow these directions. David is conducting worship according to the ways of the world. Where did they get the idea to put this ark on a cart? Perhaps it was convenience. Perhaps it was the easy way out. Second Samuel 6:3 says, "They set the ark of God on a new cart." This is direct disobedience to the Scriptures. Remember, God had given instructions that the ark should be carried on the shoulders of the Levites. The ark could not be touched. David led his people not only in violating Scriptures, but also in worshiping God according to the ways of the world. We humans sometimes think our own logic is better than God's.

Where did this cart idea come from? In 1 Samuel 6, the Philistines decide to get rid of the ark, and the Bible says they put it on a cart. So David is actually following a pattern established by the world. The Philistines represent the ungodly, or the world. David allows worldliness to enter into the worship of God. Maybe he thought it wouldn't matter that much. He was wrong.

Churches today must deal with this issue. Those who lead worship should be especially mindful of how easily worldliness can creep in. The ways of the world should never dictate how God is worshiped.

In reality, the cart itself can be considered another symbol. It is a symbol of worshiping man's way, not God's way. There are several examples of carts being used in church worship today. One cart is rock music. Rock music is used in some churches today to worship God. I am aware that the term *rock* is a catch-all term today. Some music today called rock doesn't truly fit into the rock genre—true rock hard-core music has rebellious lyrics directed against a holy God. In other words, it is music that encourages immorality and violence.

Sometimes people are guilty of generalizing. In other words, some people might label any music they don't like as rock music. I'm not talking about that. I'm talking about music that is clearly satanic in its lyrics and in the dissonant sounds instead of harmony and melody. I'm talking about music designed to bombard and influence the subconscious mind. There are churches that currently use this kind of music to draw people to church. In this case, the rock music would be an example of a cart.

I recently read an article in a church growth magazine. There is a pastor of a church in Florida who basically says that rock music is what people listen to all week long. Therefore, on Sunday, the church should give them the same kind of music. In my opinion, this pastor is using a cart in the worship of God. God doesn't want us to worship with new carts. There is music that exalts the Lord Jesus Christ and talks about the blood of Christ and salvation. There is music that can exalt the Lord and enhance our worship of Him, but it is not the new cart of rock music.

I've been preaching about rock music since it first started. I actually played in a band when I was a backslidden teenager. I didn't enjoy it, though. God grabbed my heart, and I knew I had to get out of the band if I was going to be sold out to the Lord. Today, many would tell me to keep on doing my thing. It would not be a problem. I disagree. I think it would be a problem. I have always believed Christians should be different. There ought to be an evident separation from the world if you are God's child. As much as our modern human psyches don't like to admit it, to strive to be holy means to live a life separated from the things of the world.

Perhaps you feel you should read certain books or see certain movies to be culturally aware. Instead, you find yourself becoming more and more accepting of a man-centered worldview. It seems the line between holy and carnal becomes more and more blurred as we progress through time. Yet I believe that is only an illusion. The line is still there. It's not the line that becomes blurred. It's us humans.

Another new cart used in modern worship is marketing. We market trends in every other area of life. Why not market God, too? Since when did a lost world dictate how the people of God should worship God? Marketing strategies and surveys shouldn't guide our worship of God. The Scriptures should. This may not be the most popular view. But it is God's view. Remember, worship shows devotion to God. Making it convenient or entertaining to today's culture is not relevant at all.

A course was recently offered at a small liberal arts college in the American South. It caught my attention because the course description asserted that many people in modern society were substituting a trip to the movies for a trip to church. In other words, the idea of worship has morphed into shared movie-going experiences. It was a religion course entitled "Myths, Movies and Secularization." In the summary for the class, a scholar named Mircea Eliade is referred to for his work studying movies.

The summary states, "Eliade argues that human beings in non-religious cultures instinctively seek alternative ways in which to experience transcendence. He specifically asserts that cinema becomes a substitute for religion. This course will test the theory that cinema functions as sacred time and sacred space. . . . Students will . . . decide whether or not the cinema is indeed where the secular culture goes to church." I believe many Americans may use movies and entertainment as a substitute for true worship.

David makes a mistake. He introduces new carts in the worship of the Lord, and of course God's judgment comes. It always does. Think of Ananias and Sapphira when they pretended to give the church all they received from the sale of some property. Ananias lied to the Holy Spirit and was struck dead as a judgment (Acts 5:1–11).

Judgment will also fall on some churches today that are willing to compromise their convictions and to sell out the blood of the Lord Jesus. Some ask members not to mention the blood of Jesus because it might be considered offensive. The blood of Jesus is precious blood because it was shed on the cross to provide forgiveness for us. God's judgment always comes. Any church that sacrifices and compromises the truth by using the world's techniques to achieve spiritual result, gives death, not life, to the people who come.

David, the new king of Israel, has desecrated the worship of God.

Worship Described

After the upsetting events with Uzzah and the ark, David decides to park the ark for a little while. So David takes the ark to the house of Obed-Edom where it stays for three months. Then, 2 Samuel 6:12 says, "Now King David was told, 'The LORD has blessed the household of Obed-Edom and everything he has, because of the ark of God.' So David went down and brought up the ark of God from the house of Obed-Edom to the City of David with rejoicing."

During the three months when the ark was with Obed-Edom, it appears that David went through a time of real heart-searching. Remember David is a man after God's own heart, and his life can teach us many lessons today. One is that when David makes a mistake, he has enough of the heart of God in him to confess and acknowledge the mistake and get right with God. Evidently David is searching the Scriptures to find out how God wants His worship carried out.

In 1 Chronicles 15 there is a parallel account of this time in David's life, and there is additional information that indicates that David searched the Scriptures. He finds out what God's Word has to say about worship, and how the ark of God is to be correctly transported. First Chronicles 15:2 says, "Then David said, 'No one but the Levites may carry the ark of God.'"

Where did he find that out? In the Bible. "Because the LORD chose them to carry the ark of the LORD" (v. 2). "The priests and Levites consecrated themselves in order to bring up the ark of the LORD, the God of Israel. And the Levites carried the ark of God with the poles on their shoulders, as Moses had commanded in accordance with the word of the LORD" (vv. 14–15). David finally gets it. He decides to do it God's way. He decides to do it the right way.

Back in 2 Samuel 6 we see that David does it God's way. He obeys the Scriptures. He lets Levites put the staves of the ark on their shoulders just exactly as God says to do it. The worship starts again. "When those who were carrying the ark [no carts now] of the LORD had taken six steps, he sacrificed a bull and a fattened calf" (v. 13).

From his Scripture study, David now understands that the worship of God is based on sacrifice. For you and me in our New Testament day, this means that all genuine worship focuses on what Jesus did for us on the cross of Calvary. The sacrifice that Jesus made in shedding His blood is the focal point of all worship. True worship of God centers on the Lord Jesus Christ. It exalts Christ. It acknowledges what Jesus did for us on the cross.

David finally gets it right. Second Samuel 6:14 says, "David wearing a linen ephod, danced before the LORD with all his might." An ephod was a fine, linen garment worn by the priests. By doing this, David simply takes his place with the people of God. He lays aside his royal robes and dances before the Lord with all his might because he is happy in the Lord. For a little while, he lays aside his role as king and takes the humble garment of a Levite.

WORSHIP MATTERS — 177

Second Samuel 6:15 says that David "and the entire house of Israel brought up the ark of the LORD with shouts and the sound of trumpets." The cymbals are crashing and the trumpets are blowing and the harps are playing and the people are shouting. It's a happy affair when God's people get together for genuine worship.

"They brought the ark of the LORD and set it in its place inside the tent that David had pitched for it, and David sacrificed burnt offerings and fellowship offerings before the LORD" (v. 17). Again, true worship has at its heart the spirit of sacrifice.

David blesses the people (v. 18). People ought to get a blessing when they worship. Then David gives the people some bread and flesh and wine. In other words, he gives them nourishment (v. 19). Then the people depart to their houses. Today, people ought to be fed when they worship. They ought to hear something that will feed their hearts and souls through the days of the week. This is the reasoning behind Wednesday night services in some churches. I know they are not as popular as they used to be, but these services give spiritual food to help people make it until Sunday.

People ought to get fed when they worship at church. I think of what Jesus said when the hungry multitudes were brought to Him. Jesus looked at the disciples and said, "You give them something to eat" (Matt. 14:16). Honestly, I think about that every time I preach. God tells me to give the people something to eat. Worship involves the preaching of the Word, which is the breaking of the bread that feeds the hearts of God's people.

Because David was willing to correct his ways after leading his people down the wrong path, we are able to understand the description of true worship today.

Worship Despised

David has successfully brought the ark to Jerusalem, which was his goal. As Israel's shepherd king, he wants to put worship of God in the center of Israelite life. And all goes according to plan. Right? Well, not exactly. We learn that not everyone shares David's joy back in 2 Samuel 6:16. It says, "As the ark of the LORD was entering the City of David, Michal daughter of Saul watched from a window. And when she saw King David leaping and dancing before the LORD, she despised him in her heart."

Michal is not only the daughter of one king, but she's the wife of another king. She is the daughter of King Saul. She is the wife of King David, and sadly, their marriage is a disaster from the outset because she is an idol worshiper. Michal is also a symbol. She represents those people who despise the things of God and who show no appreciation for spiritual things. They resent anything spiritual that they see in anybody else. When they see a person exhibiting joy in the Lord, they become upset. Michal is a self-righteous, religious bigot. She represents those people who think their way is the only way. Michal is the Old Testament sister to the New Testament elder brother in the story of the prodigal son.

When the elder brother comes in from the field on the day his younger brother, the prodigal, returns, he hears music and sees dancing. He witnesses the family rejoicing because a son who was lost comes home. The elder brother is upset. Michal is also upset when she sees people rejoicing in the Lord.

"When David returned home to bless his household, Michal daughter of Saul came out to meet him" (v. 20). David has just come from a worship service. He's grateful to God that he was able to bring the ark to Jerusalem. The amens and hallelujahs of his people are ringing in his ears. The joy of the Lord is bubbling up in his heart. He certainly wants his own family to share in the worship. Just as sure as the Lord is around to bless you, the devil will be around to blast you. There will always be one of these Michals around with a bucket of cold water to pour on you to kill your joy in the Lord.

With sarcasm in her voice, she says, "How the king of Israel has distinguished himself today, disrobing in the sight of the slave girls of his servants as any vulgar fellow would!" (v. 20). She's chiding him for taking off his royal robes and for dressing like a common person in the kingdom. Actually, to me she seems jealous. She knows her husband, King David, has a special relationship with God, and she doesn't. She may even resent sharing him with God.

Michal represents those people who may be church members today who look down their noses at others who are happy in the Lord. David basically wants his wife to know that he's sharing his worship with the common people. Yet she scoffs at him and his actions. God help a church when it gets to the point that the common people can't come to the services to receive a blessing.

Michal "had no child unto the day of her death" (v. 23). Figuratively speaking, the Michals among us never win souls to Jesus Christ. The Michals never have spiritual children. They complain about and criticize the church experience. Unfortunately, they live joyless lives.

In researching the word *worship*, I learned that the English origin of the word means "worthship." To me, this implies that what we worship should be worth the homage paid to it. I wonder if in America today, most people could say that what they worship is worthy of the time, the expense, and the attention they pay to it. I think of sports events, famous actors, musicians, television shows, even academics. We are created by God to serve Him and to worship Him. He is the only one worthy of our worship. Yet in today's society, many objects and people are worshiped instead of God.

David's story of the cart and the ark is relevant for us in the twenty-first century. He attempted to bring worship to his people in his own human way. By doing so, he precluded God from receiving the worship due Him. Even though it seems that most aspects of our modern society have become less formal, let's remember that worshiping God is a serious matter with serious consequences. It is not a casual occurrence. As our society progresses more and more to a more man-centered way of life, the true worship of God takes on an increasingly important role. Thankfully, through David's experience in 2 Samuel 6, we can be reminded that only the one true God is worthy of our worship.

CHAPTER 13

Dream Matters, or a Dream Deferred

"What happens to a dream deferred?
Does it dry up like raising in the sun?"
LANGSTON HUGHES

2 SAMUEL 7   This poem, entitled "Montage of a Dream Deferred," was written by Langston Hughes. He was a famous African-American poet and writer during the Harlem Renaissance. He also worked as a journalist, dramatist, and children's author. Sometimes I like to read poetry because I feel that I get a lot of "bang for my buck," so to speak. Poetry is a compressed type of writing often with profound or universal meanings. Hughes asks, "What happens to a dream deferred?" Then he mentions several possibilities. The dream could "dry up like a raisin in the sun," or it could "fester like a sore" or "sag like a heavy load."

To me, Hughes's poem is universal because virtually ever human being has some dream in life that somehow is deferred.

For the Christian, God may be the one who delays the realization of the dream. Perhaps at some point, you had great dreams for God. Maybe you felt there were tasks you wanted to accomplish for Him. You set out to achieve those goals. Somewhere along the way, however, those dreams were deferred and never fulfilled.

Maybe when you were younger you felt like God wanted you to be a preacher. You may have had a great desire in your heart to preach the gospel. But those plans were not realized. Perhaps when you were younger you wanted to be a lawyer and then run for political office. You dreamed of being one of two United States senators from your state. Perhaps you wanted to become a missionary, an airline pilot, or a Christian businessperson giving large sums of money to the work of the Lord. Yet none of these plans was fulfilled. Instead, your dreams evaporated. Through various circumstances in your life, the Lord may have said those dreams weren't for you at all.

King David, our Braveheart, also dreams a dream. Yet it becomes apparent that his dream is not in God's plan for his life. In many ways, he's living good days at this point. In fact, these are the best of times for this man who is now the king of Israel. Jerusalem has been established as his capital. The ark of the Lord has been brought into Jerusalem, and David has prepared a special tent of worship where the ark is placed. In addition, the Lord has given him rest from all of his enemies. It is a time of peace. If there had been pollsters in David's day, the news networks would report David's approval ratings at an all-time high.

So David is living great days with a dream in his heart. But as we shall see, his will be a dream deferred. It will not be fulfilled. Let's first consider the proposal of David.

David's Proposal

David is enjoying a time of rest in his life. Our dreams often rise up from our subconscious when we have time to rest. Second Samuel 7:1 says, "The king was settled in his palace." In other words, the king is in his palace, resting on his throne. Then we find out he has a visitor. The second verse tells us it was none other than Nathan the prophet, who was actually a frequent visitor. Nathan plays a crucial role in David's life. He was a spiritual advisor for King David. They were undoubtedly good friends, but Nathan also acted as spiritual mentor for David.

Leaders sometimes have spiritual advisors. Think of Billy Graham. Many times, he was a counselor and confidant to presidents. In Dr. Graham's book, *Just As I Am*, he centers his biography on the different presidents of our nation with whom he had contact. Unfortunately, some times brought embarrassment to Dr. Graham. But some wonderful things also took place. For example, he had a relationship with President Eisenhower. God was able to use Billy Graham to bring Eisenhower to an understanding and acceptance of the gospel. In fact, the Lord used Graham to give Eisenhower assurance about heaven shortly before his death.

Sometimes there is an unusual relationship between leaders and men of God, between those in the realm of government and those in the realm of the things of the Spirit.

Spiritual advisors aren't just for national leaders, though. A recent newspaper article from *The Greenville News* entitled "They're Listening for the Voice of God" chronicles the rise of spiritual advisors or spiritual directors in modern life. These spiritual directors are defined as "people who help today's pilgrims listen for the voice of God." In fact, there's even an eleven-year-old organization called Spiritual Directors International or SDI.

According to Thomas Hart, who wrote *The Art of Christian Listening* in 1980, spiritual directors provide "heightened sensitivity to God's movement in one's life and a fuller response to it." The idea of spiritual directors is not new, and it is not tied to one specific denomination. Yet maybe the idea of taking time out to seek God's direction is foreign to people living in our busy modern world. As the article points out, "Integral to spiritual direction is the concept of retreats, quiet time-outs for reflection and listening for God's presence." Since David has time off from battle, and he has time to think, he has a perfect time to meet with his spiritual advisor, Nathan.

Picture Nathan and David enjoying some fellowship together as they talk of the Lord. David lays bare his heart to Nathan about his dream. Perhaps David's time of rest made him more reflective. Maybe he begins to examine his life, and he sees that he has a beautiful cedar palace for himself. He even says to Nathan the prophet in 2 Samuel 7:2, "Here I am, living in a palace of cedar, while the ark of God remains in a tent." David has a desire in his heart to do something important and symbolic for the Lord. David has a dream of building a magnificent temple for the worship of the living God.

Of course, Nathan loves this idea. It makes me believe that Nathan was a Baptist preacher! What Baptist preacher doesn't want to hear a church member say he or she wants to give some money to start a building fund? David wants to be a giver instead of a receiver, and this must have thrilled Nathan. It's wonderful when God's people get to the point where they want to give back to the Lord.

Nathan encourages David in what he wants to do. Nathan says, "Whatever you have in mind, go ahead and do it, for the LORD is with you" (v. 3).

It will become apparent later that Nathan has not prayed about this matter before he responds to David, but this is not Nathan's fault. The spiritual advisor was expected to encourage the leader in worthwhile endeavors. Really, this is a beautiful picture of encouragement. Nathan is encouraging David in the things of the Lord. We should all encourage others.

Hebrews 10:24–25 address the concept of encouragement: "And let us consider how we may spur one another on toward love and good deeds. Let us not give up meeting together, as some are in the habit of doing, but let us encourage one another—and all the more as you see the Day approaching." In other words, one thing all believers can do is encourage each other. This applies to our lives today. We can use our church meetings as an opportunity to encourage each other in the things of the Lord.

So we hear David's proposal. His dream is to house the ark in something other than tent curtains. Now let's consider David's promise.

David's Promise

That night, Nathan evidently receives a clear message from the Lord. He has encouraged David to build a house for God, but then the word of the Lord comes to Nathan the prophet. You could say he basically has a denial of the building permit from the Lord. The Lord refuses to grant David's dream. The Lord tells Nathan that David will not be allowed to build Him a house. It is a firm refusal. The Lord gives no reasons why. Later David will understand why, but at this point he does not. There is no account in this chapter that God explains it to him. God doesn't have to explain it.

Have you ever found yourself in a mystery of God's purpose and providence? Sometimes God has a "no" for us. We don't understand why. In our reasoning, we see our heart's desire as something that will bring honor and glory to the Lord.

The Lord makes it very clear to Nathan that David is not to build a house for Him. In fact, God says, "I have not dwelt in a house from the day I brought the Israelites up out of Egypt to this day" (v. 6). And, "I have been moving from place to place with a tent as my dwelling." This is a beautiful foreshadowing of what happens when Jesus comes into the world. John 1:14 says that "the Word became flesh and made his dwelling among us." In other words, God says He walked among us in a tent. He never requested a house. Then, in these verses, He begins to go over what He has done for David, what He is doing for David, and what He will do for David.

"I took you from the pasture and from following the flock" (v. 8). "I have been with you wherever you have gone . . . Now I will make your name great" (v. 9). He moves into the future: "And I will provide a place for my people Israel and will plant them" (v. 10). We now learn God's plans for the future.

The last sentence of verse 11 is particularly beautiful. "The LORD declares to you [David] that the LORD himself will establish a house." Do you get what God is saying? It's very exciting. David has the dream and desire to build the Lord a house. But the Lord stops him and says that instead He will build David a house! Notice how gentle the Lord is with David. Inside the Lord's refusal is a beautiful promise. This is exactly how God deals with His children. Sometimes God tells us "no." There are some things we desire to do for the Lord that are not part of God's plan for our lives. Remember David's dream every time you receive a refusal from God.

Incidentally, the use of the word *house* here is different from its use in the opening verses. "Are you the one to build me a house?" (v. 5). God is talking about a material house or a temple. God uses the same word, but He doesn't mean a material house. David already has a material house (v. 11). He means that He is going to create a dynasty of David's family.

On Easter Sunday, 2002, newspapers reported that England's "Queen Mum," or Queen Elizabeth's mother had died in her sleep on Saturday afternoon. Both Elizabeth and her mother come from the house or the dynasty of Windsor. That is their family name. Likewise, God promises David a house or a dynasty, which is actually one of the greatest promises in the entire Bible. In fact, this chapter of 2 Samuel is one of the most important chapters in the Bible because God's promise to David is at the heart of all Old Testament prophecy. Everything the Old Testament prophesies, hopes for, and announces is wrapped up in the promise God makes to King David. This promise helps us understand the New Testament more completely.

God promises David, "When your days are over and you rest with your fathers, I will raise up your offspring to succeed you" (v. 12). In other words, when David's reign is over and David dies, God will set up seed after him "who will come from your own body, and I will establish his kingdom. He is the one who will build a house for my Name, and I will establish the throne of his kingdom forever" (vv. 12–13).

The immediate reference here is to David's son Solomon, who will follow his father to the throne to become the third king of Israel. God says to David that it will be his seed or his son Solomon, who will build a house for God. David's dream becomes a dream deferred.

God says, "I will be his father, and he will be my son. When he does wrong, I will punish him" (v. 14). "But my love will never be taken away from him, as I took it away from Saul, whom I removed from before you. Your house and your kingdom will endure forever before me; your throne will be established forever" (v. 15).

What is so remarkable about that? This promise had an immediate fulfillment in Solomon. But it could not be completely fulfilled in Solomon. The promise extends far beyond Solomon. David catches the meaning immediately. It takes us a little longer to get a grip on what God is saying. Sometimes the promises of God in the Old Testament had immediate fulfillment. But they also had ultimate or complete fulfillment in the future. God promises to establish his kingdom forever. The promise must go beyond Solomon and his successors because they were all mortal kings. They all lived a period of time, but they died. If someone's kingdom is going to be established forever, there has to be a king somewhere down the road who will be immortal. Do you know a king who will live forever? It's Jesus, of course.

First Timothy 1:17 says about Jesus, "Now to the King eternal, immortal, invisible." Jesus is the king who lives forever and whose kingdom will last forever. Jesus Christ is none other than the son of David in ultimate prophecy.

Luke 1:28–33 gives the fulfillment of this prophecy that goes all the way back to 2 Samuel 7. The angel is telling Mary that she has been chosen to be the virgin through whom the son of God, the Lord Jesus Christ, will come. Luke 1:31–33 says, "You will be with child and give birth to a son, and you are to give him the name Jesus. He will be great and will be called the Son of the Most High. The Lord God will give him the throne of his father David, and he will reign over the house of Jacob forever; his kingdom will never end." What God predicted for David way back in the Old Testament is fulfilled in the person of the Lord Jesus Christ.

Jesus Christ is coming back one day. He will establish His kingdom on this earth, and He will reign forever. That's a wonderful promise. And yes, to David his dream was deferred, but God definitely had a plan in the delay.

Here is David with a dream in his heart. He comes up with a proposal to build God a house, and God turns around and makes a promise to David to build him a house that will last forever. If God says no to you, keep in mind that He has a bigger promise He is going to fulfill that will link you into His eternal plan for the universe. Yes, that's a dream deferred, but it's also a bigger dream. Second Samuel 7:17 says, "Nathan reported to David all the words of this entire revelation." Nathan has a job to do. He must go back to King David as spiritual advisor and tell him that he will not be able to carry out his dream. Sometimes it takes courage for the man of God to tell the truth, especially to those in power.

Nathan does his job. He goes to David and tells him that he cannot complete his proposal. Nathan tells David that his dream is not part of God's perfect plan. Nathan then tells David that his son Solomon will carry out his father's dream. Then Nathan tells David that God has made him a promise that will link David to His eternal plans forever.

Now let's consider David's prayer.

David's Prayer

How does David respond when God delays his dream? "Then King David went in and sat before the LORD, and he said: 'Who am I, O Sovereign LORD, and what is my family, that you have brought me this far?'" (v. 18).

This prayer of David continues from this verse to the end of the chapter. If you read it, you will not find one note of bitterness in David. David's heart harbors no resentment, and he doesn't whine to God or pry for information. What about you? Can you take it when God delays your dream? Can you accept a refusal from God without letting bitterness build in your heart?

Picture King David, a mighty and great king. In the first verse of this chapter, David sits in his house. Now, in verse 18, King David steps off his throne and sits before the Lord on His throne, like a little child. David prays one of the most beautiful prayers in the entire Bible. It starts off with praise. That's a good way to start your praying. Then he acknowledges his smallness before the Lord by asking, "Who am I?"

David says, "What more can David say to you? For you know your servant, O Sovereign LORD" (v. 20). David is admitting that he doesn't know anything else to say. Have you ever reached the point in prayer where you don't know anything else to say?

David goes on and says, "For the sake of your word and according to your will, you have done this great thing and made it known to your servant" (v. 21). He's praising God for His greatness and His wonderful works.

"How great you are, O Sovereign LORD" (v. 22). He could have burst into a chorus of the hymn, "How Great Thou Art." That's the way to pray. "There is no one like you, and there is no God but you." When you can praise God for His greatness and say there is none other like Him, that's sincere prayer.

David moves from praise to petition. He makes requests of God. "And now, LORD God, keep forever the promise you have made concerning your servant and his house. Do as you promised, so that your name will be great forever" (v. 25). He is asking the Lord to do what He said He would do. David is now asking God to fulfill the promises made to him.

Romans 4:21 says about Abraham, "Being fully persuaded that God had power to do what he had promised." Abraham had confidence in the promises of God and in the ability of God to do what He had promised to do. Likewise, David is praying God's promise back to Him in prayer. The promises of God fall upon our hearts from heaven. Then in prayer we can return those promises to God. When you receive a promise from God's Word, you can claim it in prayer. Then if you pray the promise back to God, you can count on the answer to that prayer.

Matthew Henry, the great commentator, said that it is by turning God's promises into petitions that they are turned into performances. That's something to think about.

That's exactly what David does. In verses 27–28, David is talking to God reminding him of his promises. "'I will build a house for you.' So your servant has found courage to offer you this prayer. O Sovereign LORD, you are God! Your words are trustworthy, and you have promised these good things to your servant." David is praying the promises back to God.

"Now be pleased to bless the house of your servant, that it may continue forever in your sight; for you, O Sovereign LORD, have spoken, and with your blessing the house of your servant will be blessed forever" (v. 29).

When God says no to you, keep in mind that He does so because He has a better plan in mind. Although God did not allow David to build His house, he allowed the house to be built by his son Solomon.

In 1 Chronicles 22:6–10, God explains the dream deferred to David. "Then [David] called for his son Solomon and charged him to build a house for the LORD, the God of Israel. David tells Solomon: "My son, I had it in my heart to build a house for the Name of the LORD my God. But this word of the LORD came to me: 'You have shed much blood and have fought many wars.' You are not to build a house for my Name, because you have shed much blood on the earth in my sight. But you will have a son who will be a man of peace and rest, and I will give him rest from all his enemies on every side. His name will be Solomon, and I will grant Israel peace and quiet during his reign. He is the one who will build a house for my Name. He will be my son, and I will be his father. And I will establish the throne of his kingdom over Israel forever.'"

So at some point, God shows David why He would not let him build the temple. It is because David was a man of war. David's son Solomon will be allowed to build the temple because he is a man of peace.

I don't know why God says no to some of our dreams. But I can make you a promise. Though He may not let you know the reasons why now, He will let you know later. You may not find out in this life, but you will know in the next life, and you will understand and agree that God did everything exactly the way He should have. When we get to heaven and look back on all of the things we didn't understand, and we see the full plan and purpose of God for eternity, every one of us will agree with God's timing. God doesn't make any mistakes in our lives.

David didn't sit in a corner and pout when his dream was deferred. He decided that if he couldn't build the house, he would help his son Solomon by getting things ready. In fact, the Lord gave David credit for building the temple. Second Chronicles 6:8 says, "The LORD said to my father David, 'Because it was in your heart to build a temple for my Name, you did well to have this in your heart.'" God acknowledged the dream inside his heart. You may not be the one God chooses to construct the building, but God will give you credit if the dream is in your heart. He will give you credit for what you would do for Him, if you could do for Him.

I met a man named Leonard Wright when I was a teenage boy. He was a true Christian man. He was the building super-intendent of our home church. He used to go with us to youth camp. I remember the campfires and the time of testimony. Mr. Wright would often give his testimony. He would reminisce about how as a young man he wanted to be a missionary for the

Lord. His family was poor. They were sharecroppers, and he was not able to get an education. He told us that he was disappointed that he never was able to become a missionary. He used to say to us, "But you know, God is letting me be the building superintendent of our church, and God lets me have the opportunity to teach you and lead you. I'm just trying to help get you ready to do for God what I wanted to do for God, but was not able to do." Mr. Wright's dream was deferred.

Did you also wish to be a missionary, but something prevented you? Then give some money so that somebody else can be a missionary. Did you dream about becoming a preacher, but it didn't work out? Then encourage some young man God has called by helping him go to school to prepare himself to preach God's Word. David knew he could not build the temple, but he gathered all the materials together to make it possible for his son to do it.

All of our dreams may not come true, but God knows our hearts. If you are sincere in serving Him as best you know how, even when God says no, He will acknowledge what you want to do in your heart and give you credit down the road.

One of your dreams in life may become a "dream deferred" as Langston Hughes says. That dream doesn't have to dry up "like a raisin in the sun" or sag "like a heavy load." God sometimes intentionally delays our dreams because it suits His purposes. To me, Langston Hughes's poem creates a sad mood in the reader and reflects a disappointed tone from the author. Perhaps Mr. Hughes never realized that King David also had dreams that were deferred. But they still came true.

CHAPTER 14

Grace Matters,
or Grace Expectations

Amazing grace, how sweet the sound
That saved a wretch like me!
JOHN NEWTON

2 SAMUEL 9   The spiritual concept of grace can be defined several ways. To some, it is "that which affords joy, pleasure, delight, charm, sweetness and loveliness."[10] To others, it can be considered "good will, lovingkindness, mercy, etc." The most common definition from the Bible, however, is probably that grace is "the kindness of a master toward a slave. Thus, by analogy, grace has come to signify the kindness of God to man."[11]

When I was in high school, a novel entitled *Great Expectations* by Charles Dickens was required reading. I did not enjoy the reading assignment much until I waded through about half the book. Then I became quite interested in the fates of the characters I met. I now view this book as one of the best English novels ever written because of its excellent plot and its universal themes.

One of the themes of the novel is the biblical concept of unmerited grace. In other words, one of the book's themes is grace as "the concept of kindness given to someone who doesn't deserve it."[12]

The protagonist of the book is an orphan boy nicknamed Pip. His mean sister and her good-natured husband named Joe Gargery bring him up. One evening, as Pip sits in a cemetery looking at the tombstones of his parents, he meets an escaped convict. He helps the convict by bringing him food and a file to loosen his leg irons. The convict is captured anyway. Pip is then sent to live with a spinster named Miss Havisham in whose home he meets and falls for a beautiful girl named Estella. Since Pip is poor, he has no expectation of becoming an educated gentleman. To his surprise, however, an anonymous benefactor makes it possible for Pip to study in London and receive an education. His expectations change. In the end, Pip finds out that his benefactor was not Miss Havisham as he suspected, but instead Abel Magwitch, the convict he once aided.

To me, Pip's story is an illustration of grace. He doesn't expect to become an educated gentleman. But because of the grace Abel Magwitch shows him, Pip's expectations change, and he is given tools that enable him to succeed.

This same kind of grace is illustrated many times in the Bible. In fact, King David, our Braveheart, receives the same kind of grace from the Lord, but he also bestows this kind of grace on his subjects. The grace he bestows on one of those subjects, Saul's grandson Mephibosheth, is the subject of 2 Samuel 9.

At this point in the story, David has come to the pinnacle of his royal career. He has enjoyed victory after victory. Now he can rest. These are indeed good years for David. What does David do? Does he rest on his laurels? Does he become introspective? Or does David remember the promises he has made to his friends in years past? Success is a test of true character.

This chapter may actually present the greatest episode in David's life. To me, the account of David and Mephibosheth illustrates one of the greatest truths in the Bible.

The Old Testament is a beautiful illustration book of New Testament truths. This is precisely why the Old Testament is valid today. One of the greatest truths in the New Testament is the grace of God. Ephesians 2:8–9 says, "For it is by grace you have been saved, through faith—and this not from yourselves, it is the gift of God—not by works, so that no one can boast." The grace of God, undeserved by humankind, is one of the great themes of the Bible and also of classic literature like *Great Expectations*.

God's Grace Seeks Us

Like the grace that Abel Magwitch shows to the orphan Pip, the grace of God reaches out to us. It seeks us, and it finds us.

It is the same way with David as he enjoys a time of peace and rest after his many victories. In 2 Samuel 9:1 he asks, "Is there anyone still left of the house of Saul to whom I can show kindness for Jonathan's sake?" He is definitely not your average king. Here is a king looking for an enemy so he can do something kind for him. And David wants to show this kindness for Jonathan's sake.

The word *kindness* occurs three times in this chapter. It occurs here. It occurs in verse 3, "God's kindness." It occurs again in verse 7, "I will surely show you kindness." The root of this word originally meant the milk of a mother for her child. It is an expression of kindness and affection. Raised to its highest level, it is a word that depicts the loving-kindness of God that flows toward us.

Remember, David is a man after God's own heart. I don't think there is ever a time in his life when he is more Godlike than he is here. He seeks to find someone in the house of Saul so he can show kindness to them.

It is David's nature as king that motivates him to show kindness to his subjects. In the same way, God is motivated by His kindness toward you and me. The Bible makes it very clear that the wonderful grace of God is an expression of the kindness of God.

For example, Ephesians 2:7 says, "In order that in the coming ages he might show the incomparable riches of his grace, expressed in his kindness to us in Christ Jesus." The kindness of God is expressed in the grace of God. You and I are not saved because we deserve to be saved. We are saved because of the love, mercy, grace, and kindness of God.

David wants to show kindness, the kindness of God, to a member of the house of Saul. There is another motivation here, too. Back in verse 1, David asks, "Is there anyone still left . . . to whom I can show kindness for Jonathan's sake?" Remember Jonathan? He was David's truest friend. David and Jonathan loved each other like brothers. You may remember that Jonathan and David entered into a covenant with each other, and Jonathan asked David to make him a promise. Back in chapter 20 of 1 Samuel, David makes a promise to Jonathan.

Basically, David commits himself to be kind to Jonathan's offspring. He promises to show kindness to Jonathan's family.

First Samuel 20:15 says, "Do not ever cut off your kindness from my family—not even when the LORD has cut off every one of David's enemies from the face of the earth." So, Jonathan makes a covenant with David and asks him to promise to be kind to his family in the future.

As David sits on his throne enjoying his time of peace, he looks for someone to whom he can keep this promise. He remembers making a promise to his best friend Jonathan. For Jonathan's sake, he wants to show the kindness of God to some member of Jonathan's family. David personifies grace here. This is what it is all about. It's the reason why we're saved. Jesus Christ made it possible for God to extend grace to us. Salvation is available to us because of the work of Jesus Christ on the cross of Calvary.

David begins his search. He finds Ziba, who is a servant of the house of Saul. Ziba is called before King David and asked if there's anyone left in the house of Saul. Ziba knows that Jonathan's son Mephibosheth is out there.

According to 2 Samuel 9:3, "Ziba answered the king, 'There is still a son of Jonathan; he is crippled in both feet.'" In other words, Jonathan's son is crippled. Back in 2 Samuel 4 we are told how Mephibosheth was crippled. It happened on the day when Mephibosheth lost both his father Jonathan and his grandfather Saul on Mount Gilboa in battle. It was a terrible disaster.

With the deaths of Saul and Jonathan, the house of Saul crumbled. When the news of their deaths reached the home where a nurse was keeping little Mephibosheth, she panicked and fled with him: "As she hurried to leave, he fell and became crippled. His name was Mephibosheth" (2 Sam. 4:4).

The boy was crippled by a fall. His feet didn't heal properly, and he was never able to walk correctly. Though the Bible does not say it, I believe David shared part of the blame for Mephibosheth's handicap because David was an enemy of the house of Saul. There were probably some people who whispered constantly in Mephibosheth's ear that it was all David's fault.

Symbolically, Mephibosheth represents people who are spiritually crippled and some who are spiritual invalids. Perhaps they blame God for making them a certain way or for allowing circumstances to happen to them. Mephibosheth is the symbol of a lost sinner in need of a Savior. Romans 5:12 says, "Sin entered the world through one man [Adam]." That's our human family. We are born in our sinful condition, crippled by a fall. When Adam fell, the whole human race fell.

When I'm in a person's home talking about Jesus, I try to explain what the Bible means by saying we have all sinned. I use the illustration of a bowl of oranges. I ask the person to imagine a bowl of oranges on the table. The bowl is then pushed off the table. When the bowl falls, the oranges fall. The fall is what happened when Adam sinned in the garden. When Adam fell, the whole human race fell. As humans, we are born into the wrong family, and we are crippled by a fall just as Mephibosheth was. Adam's fall made us sinners by nature.

The name *Mephibosheth* means "one who scatters" or "seething dishonor." Here is a boy born into royalty. He would have been next in line after Saul and Jonathan. Instead of becoming a ruler, he becomes a cast-off, a nobody. His self-esteem must have been very low. In fact, he calls himself a "dead dog" (2 Sam. 9:8). After sin causes us to fall, it hits our self-esteem. Sin will make a nobody out of anybody. God doesn't destroy self-esteem; our sin does. Our sin is the problem.

In verse 4, King David asks where Mephibosheth is. He's interested in his location. Ziba, the servant, happens to know where he is. Ziba tells David that Mephibosheth is in the house of Machir in Lo Debar. Lo Debar was a little village right across the Jordan River. The name *Machir* means "sold." That's a picture of what sin does to us. It sells us out. Lo Debar means "no pasture" or "no ability to get nourishment." So here is a person, crippled by a fall, and he winds up in a place sold out with no pasture. The truth is that Mephibosheth is barely surviving. The same thing happens with every human attempt to find satisfaction, peace, and fulfillment outside of God. It's all Lo Debar or no pasture at all.

Are you trying to find satisfaction for your soul in finances? It's another Lo Debar, no pasture. Do you think sports will satisfy your soul? It's another Lo Debar, no pasture. Do you think your pleasures are going to bring satisfaction to your heart? It's another Lo Debar, no pasture. Do you think material possessions will satisfy you? They're another Lo Debar, no pasture.

"King David had him brought from Lo Debar" (v. 5). David takes the initiative. He makes the move. The grace of God always makes the first move toward the soul. People talk about sinners seeking the Lord. In fact, some church growth experts talk about seeker services. But that term is a misnomer. The lost world is not seeking God. Lost people are not knocking down church doors because they are seeking soul satisfaction inside. Romans 3:11 says, "There is no one who understands, no one who seeks God." The seeker is not the sinner; the seeker is the heavenly Father. He is the one who reaches out and seeks the lost and crippled soul. Jesus put it this way: "For the Son of Man came to seek and to save what was lost" (Luke 19:10).

David sends his men to get Mephibosheth. Work with me for a moment and use your imagination. Mephibosheth is over there in a little hut in Lo Debar, the place of no pasture. One day there is a knock on his door. He becomes frightened when he realizes that King David's men have found him and are standing outside his door. Terror fills his heart. His family's enemy is right outside the door. In the Middle East in those days, when a new king began his reign, he would destroy all members of the previous ruling family. Mephibosheth wants to run, but he can't because he is crippled.

The knocking continues on his door. Mephibosheth's heart is a trembling leaf. He could appear on the new reality show *Fear Factor* because his fear is happening in living color.

Figuratively speaking, this is a picture of what happens when the Holy Spirit convicts a sinner. Jesus said in John 16:8, "When he [Holy Spirit] comes, he will convict the world." It is not a pleasant experience to hear the Holy Spirit knocking on your soul's door knowing that He is going to convict you of your sins. The Holy Spirit is the great sheriff who arrests us and brings us into the presence of the King of the universe.

King David's men put Mephibosheth into a wagon for a trip of approximately fifty miles. As they cover each mile, Mephibosheth's blood pressure rises. He is headed to his own death. Mephibosheth thinks David is on a search-and-destroy mission. Nevertheless, Mephibosheth knows that no matter what, David has sought him and found him. This is the first trait of God's grace. It seeks us.

God's Grace Saves Us

They finally arrive at the palace. In verse 6, Mephibosheth is brought into the throne room of King David. Mephibosheth falls on his face to show reverence. Of course, he is scared to death. He doesn't know his fate. "David said 'Mephibosheth!'" Instead of sounding vengeful, David's voice sounds kind (v. 6). There was all of the love, all of the kindness, and all of the forgiveness you can imagine when the king calls Mephibosheth by name.

God knows you by name, too. He knows your identity. Jesus said about the Shepherd who seeks the sheep in John 10:3, "He calls his own sheep by name." You are not a nameless individual. You may feel like one after walking through a large airport or waiting in a long line to pay your taxes. But you are not a nothing. I often hear people refer to the homeless population as numbers or statistics, as if they are not people. Homeless people have names. Each one is somebody who is an object of God's love, and He knows him or her by name. Jesus always calls people by name when He is seeking them.

Remember Zacchaeus? Jesus was walking through Jericho one day and saw him up in a sycamore tree. Jesus called him by name, and it made a difference. Think of Saul of Tarsus. He was in a rage persecuting Christians. On the Damascus road, a light from heaven knocked him into the dust of conviction. From heaven, a voice called, "Saul, Saul" (Acts 9:4). God knows our names.

Mephibosheth still doesn't know what to expect. He is scared to death. David says, "Don't be afraid" (2 Sam. 9:7). In other words, he tells him to relax because everything will be all right. That phrase, "don't be afraid," is a gospel phrase. It's a Jesus phrase.

David then says, "I will surely show you kindness for the sake of your father Jonathan." This is what grace does when it saves us. Mephibosheth, because of his birth, deserves judgment and death. Yet he receives forgiveness and kindness. Then David says, "I will restore to you all the land that belonged to your grandfather Saul." When God saves us, He also restores to us everything Adam lost for us and even more.

Mephibosheth is overwhelmed. He thought he was going to be dead. Instead of execution, he experiences grace. He is saved. Yes, conviction is an unpleasant experience. But after conviction, if you receive Jesus as your Savior, conversion comes, and that is a glorious experience.

Mephibosheth is moved. He bows and says, "What is your servant, that you should notice a dead dog like me?" (v. 8). When I read this verse, I think back to the Book of Ruth. When Boaz sees Ruth, he starts leaving some extra handfuls of grain along the path so she can find them. It dawns on Ruth what he is doing, and she says in Ruth 2:10, "Why have I found such favor in your eyes that you notice me—a foreigner?" She doesn't get it. I can understand it perfectly. She finds grace in Boaz's sight because she is beautiful! What I can never understand, however, is why God would look down on an unworthy, hell-deserving sinner like me and choose to save me by His wonderful grace. It's incomprehensible.

God's grace seeks us. God's grace saves us. And it even goes beyond that.

God's Grace Satisfies Us

Many people today are living frustrated, unfilled lives. They feel they are not living the satisfied life. The secret to a satisfied life is God's grace. It meets every need of your life. It lifts every burden of your heart.

In 2 Samuel 9:9, the king calls Ziba in and says, "I have given your master's grandson everything that belonged to Saul and his family." Likewise, when you come to the Lord, you receive the riches of His grace. David says, "You [Ziba] and your sons and your servants [that's thirty-six people] are to farm the land for him and bring in the crops, so that your master's grandson may be provided for" (v. 10) Picture thirty-six people working full-time to provide for one crippled boy. That's grace. That's sufficiency. God said to Paul one time, "My grace is sufficient for you" (2 Cor.12:19). It applies to us as well. Whatever your need is, day by day, God has grace to provide for that need.

There is a sweet and encouraging example of God's grace in 1 Peter 1:6: "Wherein ye greatly rejoice, though now for a season if need be, ye are in heaviness through manifold temptations" (KJV). The word *manifold* literally means many-colored or kaleidoscopic. So the verse refers to many-colored temptations. In other words, life's trials and difficulties come in all colors and shades. Sometimes they come in the black of death and disaster. Sometimes they come in the blues of depression and despair. What should we do?

First Peter 4:10 says, "As every man hath received the gift, even so minister the same one to another, as good stewards of the manifold grace of God" (KJV). The same word is used here referring to the many-colored grace of God. Do you get the connection? The many-colored trials and the many-colored grace. It doesn't matter what color the trial is because God has a matching grace to take care of every need. God's grace satisfies us. It gives us provision. It meets our daily needs.

In fact, God's grace not only satisfies by provision, but also by position. The grace of God gives us a satisfying position. Second Samuel 9:7 says, "You will always eat at my table." That statement occurs four times in the rest of that chapter: "Mephibosheth . . . will always eat at my table" (v. 10). "Mephibosheth ate at David's table like one of the king's sons" (v. 11). "He always ate at the king's table, and he was crippled in both feet" (v. 13). What does it all mean?

David is saying that he is going to treat Mephibosheth just like one of his own sons. When mealtime comes, Mephibosheth sits at the dinner table just like he is one of David's sons. Imagine hearing the clang of the dinner bell. Supper is served. In comes King David and all of his children. Then the servants enter. Finally, hobbling on crippled feet comes Mephibosheth. He knows he is lame, and he knows his condition. Think of Mephibosheth with his lame feet under the king's table. He knows he doesn't deserve to be there, but he is there because of grace. David has bestowed grace upon him for his father's sake.

You may wonder why Mephibosheth was the recipient of David's grace. He came just as he was. King David didn't put any conditions on him. Mephibosheth did not have to walk first in order to be fed. King David did not require Mephibosheth to become his friend first. No, Mephibosheth came just as he was and fell at the feet of King David and said, "Your servant." It was total surrender on Mephibosheth's part.

The character Pip in the novel *Great Expectations* was the recipient of grace in his life much the way Mephibosheth was. Both Mephibosheth and Pip did not expect to have grace bestowed upon them. Yet they did. Pip was able to realize some great expectations in his life and become an educated gentleman. Mephibosheth was able to become a part of the king's family.

As Christians, we can have "grace" expectations knowing that God's grace seeks us, saves us, and satisfies us. God's grace doesn't guarantee an easy life for believers. But it does mean we can have great expectations for God's grace to meet our needs in our daily walk with God.

CHAPTER 15

Scandal Matters,
or "You're the Man"

"Man is the only animal that blushes, or needs to."
MARK TWAIN

2 SAMUEL 11–13   Picture this. Three teenaged boys talking to each other in line at a restaurant the other day. As each decides whether to put red or blue jello on his tray, they talk about a baseball team on which two of the boys play. One kid, who has on a red shirt, is talking about Jeff's fabulous home-run hit.

"You're the man, Jeff! You're the man!" the kid wearing red says to Jeff as he reaches for his lemonade from the attendant. It catches the ear because none of the boys is a man yet.

Jeff beams, full of pride of course, but that phrase causes me to flash back and think of a conversation between King David and his trusted spiritual advisor, Nathan. God's prophet Nathan uses the same phrase in a conversation with David, but Nathan does not say it because David hits a home run. Nathan says it in a tragic conversation with David.

There are two definitive personalities in the life and reign of King David. Most people think of these people when they think of him. The first person is Goliath. His name reminds us of David's greatest victory. The second person is Bathsheba, who reminds us of the greatest defeat in David's life.

The affair of David and Bathsheba is a watershed event in the life of King David. David is at the zenith of his reign. He has been king for approximately twenty years. He is about fifty years old. He is financially secure. His subjects praise him, and he has been extremely successful as king. In some ways, David has arrived. He's "the man." But it is dangerous for any of us, especially Christians, to become complacent.

This is one reason the story of David and Bathsheba is so compelling. Another is that humans are fascinated with any hint of a sexual affair. The story has universal themes, and there are always consequences. It's also part of human nature to desire to watch the downfall of someone in power.

"The Man's" Sin

The opening verses of 2 Samuel 11 set the stage. It is springtime. Normally, armies go to battle at this time. But David decides to wait in Jerusalem. Maybe deep inside he thinks he has fought all his battles and won all his wars.

One night David is restless. He can't sleep. If he had gone to battle, he would probably be sleeping like a baby. The Bible says he arose from his bed and went to the roof of his house in Jerusalem. He sees a stunningly beautiful woman bathing on a neighboring housetop. Her name is Bathsheba. David is smitten with her, and he sends for her to come to him. They have an affair.

Bathsheba is already married. She is the wife of Uriah, one of David's most faithful and capable soldiers. She is also the daughter and granddaughter of two of David's most trusted warriors. He violates his honor, her honor, and her family's honor with this indiscretion.

There was a famous emperor in ancient Rome named Julius Caesar. His fame has been heightened by the tragedy Shakespeare wrote about him. One of the most famous phrases attributed to Julius Caesar is "veni, vidi, vici." He utters this after he goes to Asia Minor and defeats Pharnaces in just five days. The phrase means, "I came, I saw, I conquered." Notice the verbs in David's story. They are similar. Verses 2–4 show that David saw Bathsheba, he sent for her, and then he took her.

Those three words wrap up the whole sin package. Seeing the temptation, sending for the temptation, and taking the temptation. Think about Eve in the Garden of Eden when sin was established in the human race. She saw, she took, and she ate. The devil's methods have not changed, and sin has not changed. The way humans sin is simple and as old as the Garden of Eden itself. David's sin is also simple. He sees, he sends, and he takes. End of story. Or is it?

Perhaps David temporarily forgets he is a man after God's own heart. Maybe he forgets that he had God's anointing upon him. The Spirit of the Lord was working in his life. It is usually true that when a person has great influence and prominence in the public eye, his or her sin has more impact on the lives of others. You could say that those in the public eye are role models. I know that many entertainers and TV personalities disregard this aspect of their fame. Nevertheless, people in the public eye are usually held to a higher standard of conduct. This has not changed in all the generations since David's. In a moment of sexual arousal, he forgets who he is and what the consequences of his actions will be.

It's just a one-night stand, and then it's over. He sends Bathsheba back home, thinking nobody knows anything. Proverbs 9:17 says, "Stolen water is sweet; food eaten in secret is delicious!" Secret sin is exciting. There is something exhilarating about the chase. David probably felt more like a lover than a sinner when he committed sin with Bathsheba. I'm told the part of the brain that governs sexual desire also governs our spiritual motivations. Perhaps David felt somewhat righteous and religious during the moment of passion he enjoyed with Bathsheba. Sin often subtly and surreptitiously confuses a person into thinking he is doing the right thing when in reality he is doing the wrong thing.

So David sends Bathsheba back to her home, and all is well. David is unscathed. Not exactly. According to verse 5, word from Bathsheba arrives at the palace for David. Her message consists of three short words. Yet these words probably brought David to his knees. His life changes forever. Bathsheba's message was, "I am pregnant."

Today's tabloid newspapers and television shows could have had fun with this scandal in the palace. Imagine the headlines. "King and soldier's wife create love child." Or "King's spring fling."

David has a choice at this point. He can either confess his sin, or he can attempt to cover his sin. Sadly, he chooses the latter. From verse 6 to the end of this chapter, King David, the man after God's own heart, tries to hide his sin.

His mind begins searching for a plan. He decides to bring Bathsheba's husband Uriah home from the field of battle. "David sent this word to Joab [his general]: 'Send me Uriah the Hittite.' And Joab sent him to David" (v. 6).

Uriah comes home. He and David make small talk. David finds out what's happening on the battlefield. Of course, this is all a ploy on David's part. He says to Uriah, "'Go down to your house and wash your feet.' So Uriah left the palace, and a gift from the king was sent after him" (v. 8). You're the man, David.

You know what David is thinking. He will send Uriah home, and he will spend the night with his wife. Then she will announce her pregnancy. Everyone will assume that it is Uriah's child. Sounds like a good plan to David. He had his fun, and now he will wipe away the consequences.

Uriah is a good man and a good soldier. He shows true character. His valiant behavior throws a kink in David's plan. "But Uriah slept at the entrance to the palace with all his master's servants and did not go down to his house" (v. 9). David is told the next day that Uriah never went home. Uriah slept right outside the palace door.

David calls for a meeting with Uriah. He inquires why he stayed away from his home. Uriah delivers one of the most magnificent statements of commitment and loyalty to his king you'll ever read anywhere in literature. Uriah says, "The ark and Israel and Judah are staying in tents, and my master Joab and my lord's men are camped in the open fields. How could I go to my house to eat and drink and lie with my wife? As surely as you live, I will not do such a thing!" (v. 11). Where did Uriah learn to be a man of loyalty and commitment to that degree? From David! He learned it by following his king's example.

David realizes his cover-up is going to be more difficult than he thought. So the plot thickens. David tries another approach. David calls Uriah in again. He has a meal prepared for him. But that's not all. He also says that Uriah "ate and drank with him, and David made him drunk" (v. 13).

King David, the political and spiritual leader of the land, thinks he has it all figured out. He knows alcohol and sex go together. He is hoping Uriah will go home drunk and spend the night. But Uriah is a better man drunk than David is sober. Uriah doesn't bite the bait. David's problem is now growing into a crisis. He becomes desperate to hide his palace scandal.

Adolph Hitler called his plan to exterminate the Jews in Nazi Germany "the final solution." In his desperation, David formulates his own final solution for his sin problem. He knows Uriah is headed back to battle. So David scribbles a note and closes it with the king's seal. The note is addressed to General Joab. It instructs Joab to place Uriah in the hottest part of the battle. David wants Uriah to be killed in battle. Ironically, David tells Uriah to deliver the message, Uriah's death sentence, to Joab. Uriah faithfully complies.

Joab receives the note from the king, and he probably figures out the whole story. He crumbles the note into his pocket. It's his ace in the hole. Perhaps Joab could have used the information to blackmail the king. Nevertheless, Joab follows his instructions.

As Paul Harvey would say, here is "the rest of the story." David's plan works, for verse 21 says, "Your servant Uriah the Hittite is dead." David's sin has progressed. His lust has now become murder. Sin is like that. It works in bunches. Sins produce other sins. David, what have you done? You have murdered one of your own finest soldiers.

David then takes further action. After Uriah's murder, he sends for Bathsheba. She becomes his wife. Finally, David thinks he has settled the matter and that the consequences of his sin are gone. But David is wrong. "But the thing David had done displeased the LORD" (v. 27). God saw it all, and He was displeased.

God is omniscient. He sees and knows all. It is not possible to hide from God. The Bible says, "Be sure your sin will find you out" (Num. 32:23). It is probably harder to doubt this truth today than it has ever been before. In our world, we constantly learn of the capacity of computers to record and retrieve personal details of people's lives. Think of the increasing presence of video cameras when we check into motels or buy fuel at gas stations. Scientists now have the ability to identify human or animal remains from the tiniest particles of DNA. There are even sophisticated cameras on space shuttles and satellites that photograph earth with such precision that they actually show the hairs on our heads. Infrared cameras even photograph beneath the surface of the earth. How can we doubt God's presence, order, and plan for the universe? We may see chaos, but God's order and knowledge are inherent in all.

And David, our Braveheart, has displeased the Lord.

"The Man's" Sorrow

Approximately nine months pass between chapters 11 and 12. David plays the hypocrite. He lives a fiction. He pretends all is right with his world, but it is not. The psalms David writes during this nine-month period indicate that he is an unhappy man.

For example, Psalm 32:14 says, "For day and night your hand was heavy upon me; my strength [life juices] was sapped as in the heat of summer." He has literally and figuratively dried up. He is a physical and emotional wreck. He is devastated spiritually. His relationship with God is shattered: "He who conceals his sins does not prosper" (Prov. 28:13). David is not prospering.

Then Nathan reenters the scene. Second Samuel 12:1 says, "The LORD sent Nathan to David." Nathan is the prophet. He is David's good friend. Yet during this nine-month period, David has even turned away from his friends.

Nathan comes back into David's life at this point because God sends him to David. David had been doing quite a bit of sending himself. He sent for Bathsheba. He sent for Uriah. He sent a message to Joab. But it is the Lord who sends Nathan to David.

Nathan doesn't come over to make small talk. The Lord sends Nathan to tell David a story. Stories are one of the most powerful ways to communicate truth. Humans respond to narratives. So Nathan tells David a story about two men. One is rich, and one is poor. The rich man has plenty of land and livestock. The poor man possesses only one little pet lamb. In fact, the poor man's lamb "was like a daughter to him" (v. 3).

Nathan says, "Now a traveler came to the rich man, but the rich man refrained from taking one of his own sheep or cattle. . . Instead, he took the ewe lamb that belonged to the poor man and prepared it for the one who had come to him" (v. 4). There is symbolism working in this story. David is the rich man. Uriah is the poor man. Bathsheba, of course, is the pet lamb. And the traveler just passing by is a metaphor for sin itself. Instead of taking one of his many lambs to feed the traveler, the rich man takes the pet lamb of the poor man. "David burned with anger against the man" (v. 5). A story can rouse powerful emotions in the human heart. Nathan's story riles David's sense of justice.

David says, "As surely as the LORD lives, the man who did this deserves to die! He must pay for that lamb four times over, because he did such a thing and had no pity" (vv. 5–6). David hasn't figured out that he has just implicated himself. The sword is now at his throat. He hasn't made the connection between the rich man in the story and himself. Thankfully, Nathan, like some preachers of the gospel today, has the courage to tell it like it is.

Nathan then utters four heart-stopping words to David. He says, "You are the man!" (v. 7). In other words, it is you, David. You're the man. You haven't hidden anything.

Nathan then preaches what is really a moving sermon to David, and David realizes that every possession he owns and every position he has held has come from the Lord. Nathan has forced David's moment of truth to its crisis.

"Then David said to Nathan, 'I have sinned against the LORD'" (v. 13). The realization has hit home. David shows again why he is a man after God's own heart. David personally confesses his sin. He does not blame somebody else. He doesn't whine about a repressed childhood as the youngest of eight kids. He doesn't use the excuse of genetic make-up. David doesn't say he has a sexual addiction. No, David takes responsibility for his actions. In fact, it is around this time in David's life that he composes Psalm 51, one of the most moving passages in the Bible.

Proverbs 28:13 says, "He who conceals his sins does not prosper, but whoever confesses and renounces them finds mercy." David experiences the forgiveness and mercy of the Lord.

So what happens to David? Nathan tells him, "The LORD has taken away your sin. You are not going to die. But because by doing this you have made the enemies of the LORD show utter contempt, the son born to you will die" (v. 13–14). David will have to live with the consequences of his actions. Even God's forgiveness cannot remove them.

Bathsheba gives birth, but after a few days, the baby boy becomes ill. David knows why. He prostrates himself and pleads with the Lord. He fasts and prays, begging with God to spare the life of his child. But the baby dies. You're the man, David. Yes, you're the man.

"The Man's" Shame

The sins of the father are visited on the sons. This is true of David as we are told in 2 Samuel 13. This is a vulgar and filthy chapter. It's all about lust and rape and incest.

The opening verses of the chapter introduce us to Tamar, one of King David's daughters. She is a beautiful girl. Amnon is also a character in the chapter. He is the heir apparent to David's throne. He is also a sexual predator. He plots with a friend and acts like he is ill. He asks for Tamar to come into his room to make food for him. Instead, he takes advantage of his own sister and rapes her. She protests. She is unwilling. But the deed is done. But after Amnon rapes her, he immediately hates her. He actually feels more hatred toward her after the rape than the love he felt earlier (2 Sam. 13:15).

America today is swarming with Amnons who see women only as objects to be exploited. One can certainly understand why some women's groups have formed and become so popular in America. Their philosophies may be radical, but some of their reasoning is valid. Men use women and then leave them like dried-up, juiceless oranges tossed into a dumpster.

Amnon's act is diabolical not only because he rapes Tamar physically, but he also violates her emotionally. He destroys her spirit. Instead of being a beautiful young girl, she is now a bruised girl walking around in mourning clothes.

What does David do? "When King David heard all this, he was furious" (v. 21). He becomes very angry, but he does nothing about the situation. David doesn't say anything to Amnon, his son, for raping his daughter. How could he say anything to his boy for doing what he himself had done? Parents cannot live in sin and then expect their children to live on a higher level. Parents who do this will have absolutely no moral authority or leadership in their homes.

Don't forget about Absalom, David's other son. He is watching what his father is doing, too. When he sees his father do nothing about Amnon's crime, Absalom seethes. "He [Absalom] hated Amnon because he had disgraced his sister Tamar" (v. 22). For two years, Absalom waits and watches his father, perhaps hoping he will deal with the situation. David does nothing. Absalom has reached the boiling point. He plans a banquet, and he talks David into allowing all of his sons to attend. Absalom crafts a plan. He tells his servants to get Amnon drunk so they can kill him.

Absalom speaks to his servants. He says, "Listen! When Amnon is in high spirits from drinking wine and I say to you, 'Strike Amnon down,' then kill him" (v. 28). This is the second time, in this passage of Scripture, where liquor plays a vital role.

Somehow King David receives word that all of his sons are dead. They aren't. Just one is dead. "The report came to David: 'Absalom has struck down all the king's sons; not one of them is left.' The king stood up, tore his clothes and lay down on the ground" (v. 30). He grieves. Perhaps David remembers his night with Bathsheba while he mourns. Surely, he could have never predicted this outcome.

David then receives word that it is Amnon who is dead. But Absalom leaves. Verses 34 and 37–38 emphasize the fact that Absalom flees. He leaves his father. "The spirit of the king longed to go to Absalom, for he was consoled concerning Amnon's death" (v. 39).

Did you catch that? Here is a man whose family has disintegrated to such a degree that he is relieved that one of his own children is dead. Perhaps he is relieved because now he does not have to deal with Amnon and his sin.

The famous American author Mark Twain is known for saying, "Man is the only animal who blushes—or needs to." It's a thought-provoking statement. Man blushes in contrast to other animals because man sins. God gives us free will to decide our own actions. It's the choices we have to sin or not to sin that make us human.

Unfortunately, there's no magic age at which your temptations to sin are over. We never get too old or too far along to be above the potential and possibility of sin. David was fifty years old when he chose to have an affair with Bathsheba. His one sin tarnished his reputation for the rest of his life.

Remember those teenaged boys talking in the restaurant that day? I guess the phrase, "You're the man!" was meant as a compliment. After all, the one kid was saying it to the other kid who had hit a home run. But when Nathan is sent by God to tell David the lamb story, the phrase takes on a different meaning. It's a phrase that can change meanings according to context.

David is a man after God's own heart, even though he sinned and brought shame on his family. This is because of David's willingness to repent and to get right with God. David is God's man for God's time just as you and I are. Hopefully, God can say to us, "You're the man" or "You're the woman" the way the teenage boys used it because we are also striving to be people after God's own heart.

CHAPTER 16

Rebellion Matters,
or "Absalom, Absalom!"

"Do not be deceived: God cannot be mocked.
A man reaps what he sows."
GALATIANS 6:7

2 SAMUEL 14–18   There are many biblical allusions or references in literature. Maybe you have studied some examples. Authors often choose to use biblical allusions as explanations. These references are also deeply rooted in our culture. For example, if someone does a good deed for someone else, that person may be called a "good Samaritan." If a person shows great wisdom in making decisions, it may be said that he or she has the "wisdom of Solomon."

King David's story is full of universal truths. Many aspects of his interesting life are referred to in our culture's literature and conversation. David's tragic relationship with his son Absalom is no exception.

In 1936 the American Southern writer William Faulkner published a novel entitled *Absalom, Absalom!* Faulkner's title is an allusion to David's rebellious son. In 1681 the British poet John Dryden published a satiric poem entitled "Absalom and Ahitophel," based on the biblical account of Absalom and Ahithophel. The poem is really a debate between Catholics and Protestants. Finally, in Alan Paton's 1948 novel entitled *Cry, the Beloved Country,* the author creates a black South African character named Absalom Kumalo. He is a rebellious preacher's son who kills a white man and is sentenced to death. The novel explores Absalom's guilt and the guilt of his society at large.

All three of these literary works allude to Absalom. But it is the character of Absalom Kumalo in the third work that may be most like David's son. This is because Paton's Absalom tries to find his own way apart from his father, as David's son did.

David has a trial on his hands with his son Absalom. In fact, David reaps with Absalom the seeds of sin he had sown with Bathsheba. I heard an evangelist named Angel Martinez preach a memorable message years ago. His sermon had three main divisions. The first division was that we reap what we sow. The second was that we reap more than we sow. Finally, the third division was that we reap later than we sow. All three points are true for David, our Braveheart.

After David committed adultery with Bathsheba and greatly displeased the Lord, the Lord made it plain through the prophet Nathan that David would spend the rest of his days enduring the consequences. Indeed, David did reap what he sowed. And most of David's problems come from within his own house.

Second Samuel 12:11 says, "This is what the LORD says: 'Out of your own household I am going to bring calamity upon you.'" God says David will experience calamities as the direct result of his own sin—and David does.

At this point in David's story, some disasters have already befallen his family. For example, Amnon, David's heir apparent, rapes his own sister, Tamar. Then, in premeditated anger and vengeance Absalom, another son of David, kills his brother Amnon. David does nothing. He can't. He is rendered completely impotent because he has lost his moral authority, and his family knows it.

Absalom has an anger problem, and it causes rebellion to swell in his heart. He murders his brother and then runs to Geshur, the homeland of his mother's people. He stays there seething with anger toward his father for three years. King David longs to go to Absalom in Geshur, but he doesn't. He chooses not to take the initiative to make the situation better. David will pay a tremendous price for this decision later.

Reaping Absalom's Return

Remember Joab, David's army commander? Joab becomes aware of David's concern for Absalom (2 Sam. 14:1–2). He decides to manipulate the situation. Joab devises a dramatic plan using a wise widow and an imaginary case to convince the king to bring Absalom back home. Joab's plan works. David says to Joab, "Very well, I will do it. Go, bring back the young man Absalom" (v. 21). "Then Joab went to Geshur and brought Absalom back to Jerusalem" (v. 23). So Absalom is able to come back to Jerusalem unharmed.

For several years, Absalom has needed a father. He needs a father's forgiveness and love. He does not receive either of these upon his return to Jerusalem. "But the king said, 'He must go to his own house; he must not see my face.' So Absalom went to his own house and did not see the face of the king" (v. 24). Father and son remain estranged.

For about two years, Absalom lives under virtual house arrest. He stews about his situation, becoming more and more discontent. Think about it. He's just a kid. He needs a strong father who will take control of the situation and do what is right. But it doesn't happen.

Second Samuel 14:25 gives a visual description of Absalom: "In all Israel there was not a man so highly praised for his handsome appearance as Absalom. From the top of his head to the sole of his foot there was no blemish in him." Absalom was good-looking. Girls might call him a "hunk" today. He is strong and handsome. He probably reminds many Israelites of his handsome father when he was younger.

Absalom has long, flowing hair. In fact, when he cuts his hair annually, about five pounds come off. Absalom loves his hair. Ultimately, his hair will hasten his demise (v. 26).

"Absalom lived two years in Jerusalem without seeing the king's face" (v. 28). Absalom's resentment builds. But the king avoids his son, and this makes the situation worse. He needs his father's love. Instead, his father shirks his responsibility to his son.

Finally, Absalom sends for Joab to help him resolve the situation. Sometimes kids have to act like parents if their parents refuse to act like adults. Absalom says to Joab, "Come here so I can send you to the king to ask, 'Why have I come from Geshur? It would be better for me if I were still there!' Now then, I want to see the king's face, and if I am guilty of anything, let him put me to death" (v. 32).

Absalom knows two things for sure. He knows he is full of iniquity. This is the guy who killed his brother. He also knows his father won't kill him. Absalom considers his father to be completely ineffectual. Nevertheless, Absalom wants to see his father, so he arranges a meeting through Joab.

"Joab went to the king and told him this. Then the king summoned Absalom, and he came in and bowed down with his face to the ground before the king. And the king kissed Absalom" (v. 33). Think it's a reconciliation? Not exactly. Absalom prostrates himself on the ground outwardly before his father, but inwardly he is defiant toward his father. Absalom shows humility and submission on the outside. But it's a different story on the inside.

David makes hard choices in this situation with his son. He doesn't welcome Absalom back on the basis of forgiveness. Imagine what would have happened if David had acted like the prodigal son's father. Absalom's rage may have melted away.

But David doesn't greet his son with a kiss and a fine robe, and he doesn't prepare a fatted calf upon his return.

Reaping Absalom's Rebellion

You might think the story ends there as Absalom and David are reunited. But it doesn't. In fact, Absalom hatches a plot to overthrow his father. Inside the heart of Absalom there is still deep resentment against his father. That resentment becomes outright rebellion.

Absalom creates a plan and follows it for four years. Second Samuel 15:1 indicates that Absalom provides himself with chariots and horses. This is an indication of his rebellion, because the Lord specifically prohibited these items. Psalm 20:7 alludes to this: "Some trust in chariots and some in horses, but we trust in the name of the LORD our God." The Lord had made it very clear that His people were not to put their dependence in chariots and horses, which were actually a symbol of royalty.

But Absalom is prideful. He thinks he knows more than God. Absalom's rebelliousness becomes obvious as his plan to overthrow his father unfolds. He assigns fifty men to run before him. They could be called his "posse." He gets up early to wait each day at the gate near the palace. In reality, the city gate played the role that our courthouses do today. Matters were adjudicated here. This was "the people's court" for ancient Israel. Absalom would ask citizens about their problems. They would tell him. Absalom would listen and then pacify the people by telling them they had valid complaints. By doing so, Absalom makes life difficult for his father. He causes the people to think they have no representation with the king. He also creates dissatisfaction as he drives a wedge between the king and his subjects.

Absalom says, "If only I were appointed judge in the land!" (2 Sam. 15:4). Is this some subtle brainwashing? Perhaps it's not so subtle. Is Absalom's self-absorption becoming more obvious? His use of the word *I* indicates an affirmative answer.

In effect, Absalom is tearing David down in order to build himself up. He is showing false humility and making the people feel like he cares for them. His actions set the pattern for rebels of all generations. There are modern Absaloms, historical Absaloms, and literary Absaloms who have used his pattern.

Absalom does to his own father, a good man, what David never did to Saul, a bad man. He actually causes division among the people of God. "Absalom behaved in this way toward all the Israelites who came to the king asking for justice, and so he stole the hearts of the men of Israel" (v. 6).

Absalom has been a ticking time bomb. At this point, he is about to explode. His seething hatred causes his desire to assassinate his own father. There really is no more volatile hatred than that between family members.

In Second Samuel 15:7–9, Absalom's rebellion is disguised as religion. Absalom goes to his father and asks if he can go to Hebron to pay a vow to the Lord by conducting a religious retreat (v. 7). Looks like Absalom now wants to dedicate his life to the Lord. Yeah, right! He is a lying hypocrite, but David cannot see it. He's not planning a religious retreat at all. He is planning to organize a rebellion against David. David still won't deal with the problem. He tells Absalom he can go, probably hoping his son will now get right with God.

So Absalom goes to Hebron. "Then Absalom sent secret messengers throughout the tribes of Israel to say, 'As soon as you hear the sound of the trumpets, then say, "Absalom is king in Hebron."' Two hundred men from Jerusalem had accompanied Absalom. They had been invited as guests and went quite innocently, knowing nothing about the matter" (v. 10).

The last part of verse 12 says, "The conspiracy gained strength, and Absalom's following kept on increasing." His plan appears to be working. Absalom builds a following. As soon as he believes the majority of people support him instead of his father, he signals for the trumpet to be blown. Then he proclaims himself king in Hebron, following dear old dad's footsteps.

It's a full-fledged insurrection at this point. David is actually terrified because he is seeing Nathan's prophecy acted out in living color. He realizes his own son is ruthless.

The big question at this point is who will support whom. Some support the conspiracy of Absalom. Others are loyal to King David. Perhaps one of the most positive outcomes of troubling times is that they reveal people's true colors. Think of the incredible support and unity that occurred after the attacks on America on September 11, 2001. The storms of life separate true friends from false ones. Who were David's true friends? Who stayed loyal to Absalom? The verses in these chapters highlight several people and the differences between them.

First, there is Ahithophel (v. 12). He is one of David's special counselors and trusted confidants. He could have been a frequent guest on the Oprah Winfrey show had he been around today. David trusts his unusual wisdom and consults him on major decisions. He is also Bathsheba's grandfather. He knows information about David that nobody else knows. David confides his very heart to him. Surely David can count on Ahithophel's loyalty. Perhaps not. "While Absalom was offering sacrifices, he also sent for Ahithophel the Gilonite, David's counselor, to come from Giloh, his hometown." David's trusted counselor joins the rebellion against him. Perhaps Ahithophel is nothing more than a groveling opportunist who sees a brighter future with the young and vibrant Absalom.

Verse 31 of chapter 15 says, "Now David had been told, 'Ahithophel is among the conspirators with Absalom.'" David is stunned. His friend has betrayed him. David prays, "O LORD, turn Ahithophel's counsel into foolishness."

Verses 21–23 in chapter 16 say, "Ahithophel answered, 'Lie with your father's concubines whom he left to take care of the palace. Then all Israel will hear that you have made yourself a stench in your father's nostrils, and the hands of everyone with you will be strengthened.' So they pitched a tent for Absalom on the roof, and he lay with his father's concubines in the sight of all Israel. Now in those days the advice Ahithophel gave was like that of one who inquires of God. That was how both David and Absalom regarded all of Ahithophel's advice." Ahithophel uses his great influence to encourage Absalom to commit outright fornication in front of the whole kingdom to show the people how much he hates his father.

In Second Samuel 17, Ahithophel gives military counsel. The plot thickens because David has sent Hushai to Hebron to act as counterintelligence to Ahithophel. In other words, Hushai is there to give the opposite counsel. In a strange twist, Absalom declines the counsel of Ahithophel and takes Hushai's advice. Bad day for Ahithophel. "When Ahithophel saw that his advice had not been followed, he saddled his donkey and set out for his house in his hometown. He put his house in order and then hanged himself. So he died and was buried in his father's tomb" (v. 23). He committed suicide just like Judas. Ahithophel was David's Judas. He lived like Judas, and he died like Judas.

Betrayal hurts. Psalm 55 expresses just how much it hurt David: "If an enemy were insulting me, I could endure it; if a foe were raising himself against me, I could hide from him. But it is you, a man like myself, my companion, my close friend, with whom I once enjoyed sweet fellowship as we walked with the throng at the house of God" (vv. 12–14). In other words, David and Ahithophel were close. They worshiped together. Verse 15 says, "Let death take my enemies by surprise; let them go down alive to the grave, for evil finds lodging among them."

Another person who betrays David is Shimei. David hears that Absalom's rebellion is meeting with success, so he leaves Jerusalem. He knows his son is a bloodthirsty killer. As David is leaving Jerusalem, he meets Shimei. Second Samuel 16:5 says, "As King David approached Bahurim, a man from the same clan as Saul's family came out from there. His name was Shimei son of Gera, and he cursed as he came out." Verses 7–8 say, "As he cursed, Shimei said, 'Get out, get out, you man of blood, you scoundrel! The LORD has repaid you for all the blood you shed in the household of Saul, in whose place you have reigned. The LORD has handed the kingdom over to your son Absalom. You have come to ruin because you are a man of blood!'"

Shimei certainly doesn't mince words. He shows open hatred toward David. He sees David as he is leaving Jerusalem and basically tells him to get out of town. Unfortunately, there are plenty of people like Shimei in life.

"Then Abishai son of Zeruiah said to the king, 'Why should this dead dog curse my lord the king? Let me go over and cut off his head"(v. 9). At least Abishai is still loyal. He wants to decapitate Shimei.

What does David do? He says, "Leave him alone; let him curse, for the LORD has told him to" (v. 11). David is actually saying that God is sending him a message through this man.

Sometimes the Lord has to be blunt with us. It may be painful. But the Lord sends a Shimei to relay His message. If what the Shimei of life say is true, we can learn from what is said and be helped by it. That's what David does. He realizes that he deserves what Shimei says, and he forgives him.

Another individual involved in the story is Ittai. He is a Gentile mentioned in 2 Samuel 15:19–21. He is loyal to David. Other loyalists are Shobi, Mahir, and Barzillai. These men bring supplies to David in 2 Samuel 17:27–29. They symbolize people who give all they can to further the cause of Christ.

Even though David has supporters, his situation is bleak. Verse 23 of chapter 15 says, "The whole countryside wept aloud as all the people passed by. The king also crossed the Kidron Valley." Picture David now sixty years old. He and a small army cross Kidron, over Olivet. He has been rejected just like Jesus was when He went to Gethsemane.

"David continued up the Mount of Olives, weeping as he went; his head was covered and he was barefoot. All the people with him covered their heads too and were weeping as they went up" (v. 30). He is a fugitive again. This time his own son is chasing him.

"David arrived at the summit, where people used to worship God" (v. 32). What does David do? He worships God. Thoughts of his sin with Bathsheba and of the prophecies Nathan told him must have come to mind. "Do not be deceived: God cannot be mocked. A man reaps what he sows" (Gal. 6:7).

Reaping Absalom's Ruin

David is still the brilliant military strategist he has always been. He devises a strategy whereby he organizes his forces into three different groups. They prepare to fight. Absalom leads the battle himself. David tells his men, "Be gentle with the young man Absalom for my sake" (2 Sam. 18:5). He asks them not to kill Absalom. David has recovered his compassion.

David's men plan the battle for the Forest of Ephraim, because David knows he can offset Absalom's numerical advantage in the woods. Twenty thousand men are killed that day. According to verse 8, more men are killed by the woods than by the sword.

Remember that Absalom in his youth and pride is leading the battle for his side. "Now Absalom happened to meet David's men. He was riding his mule, and as the mule went under the thick branches of a large oak, Absalom's head got caught in the tree. He was left hanging in midair, while the mule he was riding kept on going" (v. 9). Absalom's beautiful hair is what stops him! His hair gets caught in a tree, and he cannot break free.

A soldier tells Joab about Absalom in the tree. Joab asks if he has been killed. He has no compassion. The soldier reminds Joab that the king requested gentle treatment for Absalom. Joab disagrees. He says, "I'm not going to wait like this for you!" (v. 14). So he takes three javelins and thrusts them through Absalom's heart.

Then the rest of the soldiers join in a vicious and savage assault on Absalom. Finally, they cut him down and throw him in a pit and pile it full of rocks. Absalom is treated savagely.

King David waits at the gate for word of his son's fate. He finds out the tragic news that Absalom is dead. According to 2 Samuel 18:33, "The king was shaken. He went up to the room over the gateway and wept." His heart is grief-stricken. His sorrow is worsened by thoughts that his sin may have caused his own child's death. He prays in the bed chamber. Perhaps his mind traveled back to another time in another bed chamber where he and Bathsheba sinned. Who knew he would lie on a bedroom floor crying, "O my son Absalom! My son, my son Absalom! If only I had died instead of you—O Absalom, my son, my son!"

There are many universal truths we can take away from Absalom's story. Parents often see their own sins arise in their children. Where did Absalom learn to murder? He learned it from David. Where did Amnon learn sexual immorality? He learned it from David. The private sins of parents may be public sins with their children, because children normally go further in sin than their parents do.

Absalom needed David's time. He also needed David's guidance and discipline. Loving parents discipline their children. If parents choose not to deal with rebellion in their children, more Absaloms will become adults.

Absalom is a famous Bible character. He rebelled against his father and paid the ultimate price for it. Yet he lives on in the pages of Scripture. Similar stories of rebellion are also told in literature, in history, and in our culture. Sometimes authors even use the name *Absalom* to symbolize a character's traits.

David, our Braveheart, has now lost three sons as a result of his personal sin. His own son rebelled against him and tried to steal his kingdom. David's life reminds us to live for the Lord and to remember that we reap what we sow.

CHAPTER 17

Returning Matters, or You Can't Go Home Again—or Can You?

"He is happiest, be he king or peasant,
who finds peace in his home."
JOHANN VON GOETHE

2 SAMUEL 19 If you have ever left your hometown and then returned to it at a later time, you have probably noticed changes. Somehow, we expect places to stay the same. But they usually don't.

In 1900 the Southern author Thomas Wolfe was born in Asheville, North Carolina. He is best known for his first novel entitled *Look Homeward, Angel.* It is a largely autobiographical novel. Apparently, Asheville was scandalized by Wolfe's book because it shed light on life in that city.

After his death in 1938, more of his work was published, including a novel his editor entitled *You Can't Go Home Again.* This novel is also largely autobiographical. According to the *Encyclopedia of Literature,* the novel presents "the story of . . . a thoughtful author in search of meaning in his personal life and in American society."[13] Americans are still searching today. For most people, this is a search for either a figurative or literal home.

Perhaps Thomas Wolfe is not the most widely read southern author in the twenty-first century. Nevertheless, many of the titles of his books have become popular phrases in our culture. This is especially true of the phrase, "you can't go home again."

David, our Braveheart, is a man after God's own heart. He is not perfect. In fact, he is experiencing the sorrowful fall-out of his own personal sin, which will plague him until his death. Second Samuel 19 narrates King David's journey after the battle with his son Absalom. Will David be able to go home again?

David returns home a changed man. He is absolutely brokenhearted. Grief and agony over his role in his son's death control him. He probably feels like a failure as a father. Absalom is dead because of his own sin. David allows his grief to rule him, and he cannot enjoy Israel's victory. Instead, he is defeated. Perhaps he is so overwhelmed with his grief, he forgets that twenty thousand of his warriors lost their lives squashing Absalom's rebellion. Grief can turn us inward, causing us to become too introspective. This is what happens to David. It is important for all of us to remember that other people have problems also.

Joab notices that the king is emotionally crushed. But Joab is not sad at all. In fact, Joab is the one who thrust the spears into Absalom's heart after David requested gentle treatment for his son. Joab is furious that his king is sulking and not congratulating the loyal troops.

Joab storms into King David's presence. Picture him with clenched jaws, grinding teeth, and eyes flashing with fire. He is not exactly diplomatic. Joab's rage erupts as he speaks to his king. Joab says, "Today you have humiliated all your men, who have just saved your life and the lives of your sons and daughters and the lives of your wives and concubines. You love those who hate you and hate those who love you. You have made it clear today that the commanders and their men mean nothing to you. I see that you would be pleased if Absalom were alive today and all of us were dead" (2 Sam. 19: 5–6).

Joab's blunt words stun David, but they are exactly the words he needs to hear. Joab helps David realize that as a king he must suck up his courage and lead his people. He needs to focus outwardly, not inwardly, because his people have problems too. The same is true for us today. If we get hung up on our own problems, we will be no use to God or anyone else. Going through hard times strengthens our faith and enables us to reach out to others who have similar problems. Joab's words work, and David turns his attention to others.

Verses 9 through 15 tell of the king's return home. People gather at Gilgal to meet their returning king. This situation presents a spiritual application for us. Our King, the Lord Jesus Christ, will also return one day. The news media report more and more events that indicate His return is near. Our redemption definitely draws near.

The people in Jerusalem ask why nobody is speaking about bringing the king back (v. 10). The same question could be asked in our culture today. Most Christians never even think about the Lord's return, but He is coming back.

There are three individuals specifically involved in David's return home. Their attitude toward David and David's attitude toward them is very telling. The way they relate to David and the way David relates to them is different. Yet their relationships foreshadow our relationship with Jesus. David's battle with Absalom has changed him. His people have changed too. Will he be able to go home again?

Shimei: Going Home to the Hateful

The first individual is Shimei. He is mentioned in verse 16, and he represents people who are hateful. Shimei has conversed with the King before. When Absalom was driving King David out of his kingdom, Shimei said some ugly words to the king. Second Samuel 16:5–8 records the incident: "As King David approached Bahurim, a man from the same clan as Saul's family came out from there. His name was Shimei son of Gera, and he cursed as he came out. He pelted David and all the king's officials with stones, though all the troops and the special guard were on David's right and left. As he cursed, Shimei said, 'Get out, get out, you man of blood, you scoundrel! The LORD has repaid you for all the blood you shed in the household of Saul, in whose place you have reigned. The LORD has handed the kingdom over to your son Absalom. You have come to ruin because you are a man of blood!'"

Shimei used hate language with his king. It probably wouldn't fly today. He basically tells David that he is old and used up. Then Shimei throws stones at his king.

Shimei represents difficult people in our lives. But David refuses to retaliate in the situation. Shimei certainly deserves it, but David controls himself. The king acts and does not react, even though it would be easier for him to react. In fact, David will not allow Shimei to be executed. The king realizes that God may be trying to speak to him through this difficult person.

But Shimei's story is not over. The scenario has changed somewhat. King David is heading home again to his throne. Absalom is out of the picture.

In 2 Samuel 19:16–18, we meet Shimei again. "Shimei son of Gera, the Benjamite from Bahurim, hurried down with the men of Judah to meet King David. With him were a thousand Benjamites, along with Ziba, the steward of Saul's household, and his fifteen sons and twenty servants. They rushed to the Jordan, where the king was. They crossed at the ford to take the king's household over and to do whatever he wished. When Shimei son of Gera crossed the Jordan, he fell prostrate before the king."

That's a change. Shimei has been converted to a new way of thinking. He says to the king, "May my lord not hold me guilty. Do not remember how your servant did wrong on the day my lord the king left Jerusalem" (v. 19). In other words, Shimei is asking for David's forgiveness. Like Shimei, some people you know may sing a different tune when Jesus returns.

Shimei says, "For I your servant know that I have sinned, but today I have come here as the first of the whole house of

Joseph to come down and meet my lord the king" (v. 20). The words Shimei utters apparently touch David's heart. Perhaps he is reminded of his own conversation with Nathan, the prophet. Remember, David said something similar to Nathan. When David confessed his sins, God forgave David. Therefore, since David was forgiven, he should forgive Shimei. Likewise, since we are forgiven, we should forgive others. David does not hold grudges. It's a human foible to hold a grudge toward another person, but the Bible says we must forgive those who mistreat us. That means living in a "no-grudge zone."

One of Joab's brothers, Abishai, says, "Shouldn't Shimei be put to death for this? He cursed the LORD's anointed?" (v. 21). He wants to kill him on the spot. Not exactly what you would call a Christian spirit.

David says, "What do you and I have in common, you sons of Zeruiah? This day you have become my adversaries! Should anyone be put to death in Israel today? Do I not know that today I am king over Israel?" (v. 22).

Then David shows mercy toward Shimei: "So the king said to Shimei, 'You shall not die.' And the king promised him on oath" (v. 23).

Matthew 6:13–15 says, "Lead us not into temptation, but deliver us from the evil one. For if you forgive men when they sin against you, your heavenly Father will also forgive you. But if you do not forgive men their sins, your Father will not forgive your sins." Forgiven people must forgive. It may take the Shimeis in life longer to learn this lesson, but they must learn it.

God also holds no grudges. When we confess our sins to Him, He fully and finally forgives our sins.

Mephibosheth: Going Home to the Faithful

The second person involved in David's return is Mephibosheth in 2 Samuel 19:24. Unlike Shimei, Mephibosheth reminds us of people who remain faithful. Remember, Mephibosheth was the lame grandson of Saul.

King David sent for him to show kindness to him. David treats him as one of his own children.

Mephibosheth's servant is named Ziba. He's an oily character. Back when King David was driven out of Jerusalem, Ziba showed his true colors. Second Samuel 16:1 says, "When David had gone a short distance beyond the summit, there was Ziba, the steward of Mephibosheth, waiting to meet him. He had a string of donkeys saddled and loaded with two hundred loaves of bread."

The king asks in verse 3, "Where is your master's grandson?" David is inquiring about Mephibosheth.

Ziba says to the king, "He is staying in Jerusalem, because he [Mephibosheth] thinks 'Today the house of Israel will give me back my grandfather's kingdom.'" Ziba is lying to David. Mephibosheth never says anything remotely like this. In effect, Ziba is slandering Mephibosheth.

Then the king says to Ziba, "All that belonged to Mephibosheth is now yours" (v. 4).

Then Ziba says, "I humbly bow. May I find favor in your eyes, my lord the king."

Ziba has staged a successful coup, he thinks. Through his lie, he believes he now possesses everything that belongs to Mephibosheth.

Later, when David returns to Jerusalem, he learns the truth about Mephibosheth. Second Samuel 19:24–27 says, "Mephibosheth, Saul's grandson, also went down to meet the king. He had not taken care of his feet or trimmed his mustache or washed his clothes from the day the king left until the day he returned safely. When he came from Jerusalem to meet the king, the king asked him, 'Why didn't you go with me, Mephibosheth?' He said, 'My lord the king, since I your servant am lame, I said, "I will have my donkey saddled and will ride on it, so I can go with the king." But Ziba my servant betrayed me. And he has slandered your servant to my lord the king.'"

The truth is that Mephibosheth could not be more loyal. But because Ziba lies about him, Mephibosheth's loyalty is questioned. In our lives today, if the devil can convince us to mess up, then he will get someone to lie about us and cause people to believe it.

God's people are often slandered. The devil doesn't like God's people. If you are living close to Jesus waiting for Him to return, be prepared. Someone may lie about you and suspect your motives.

Mephibosheth tells David that he has been slandered. "My lord the king is like an angel of God; so do whatever pleases you. All of my grandfather's descendants deserved nothing but death from my lord the king, but you gave your servant a place among those who eat at your table. So what right do I have to make any more appeals to the king?" (vv. 27–28).

"Why say more? I order you and Ziba to divide the fields" (v. 29). In other words, David is telling Mephibosheth to divide the land with Ziba.

"Mephibosheth said to the king, 'Let him take everything, now that my lord the king has arrived home safely'" (v. 30).

What does this unusual story have to do with David's homecoming? Why is it included in the Scriptures? Mephibosheth is a lame man. He cannot accomplish what other men can for the king. He couldn't march or use a sword for the king. It's as if Mephibosheth decides to be as loyal and faithful to David as he possibly can while the king is away. Mephibosheth decides to be as much like David as he possibly can. He didn't dress his feet, he didn't trim his beard, and he didn't wash his clothes from the day the king departed until the day the king returned (v. 24). Mephibosheth decides to show his support for David, no matter what. Mephibosheth would have said that indeed David can go home again because he is loyal and faithful to him.

I heard about an old lady sitting on a porch back in the Civil War days. She lived in a southern town, and the Union army was marching through one day. She held up a huge Confederate flag. One of the Union soldiers said, "Hey, lady, what do you think you can do with that Confederate flag?"

She replied, "Not much, but I want everybody to know whose side I'm on." The same is true of Mephibosheth. In effect, he holds up David's flag because he wants to support his king while he is fighting. People in that day may have wondered what was wrong with Mephibosheth. They may have asked him why he hadn't taken care of his feet or trimmed his beard or washed his clothes. It's because Mephibosheth wants to be just like David. Truthfully, there is not a whole lot we saved sinners can accomplish for Jesus because we are crippled by sin, and we fall many times. But Mephibosheth sets a good example for us because we can strive to be as much like Jesus as possible until He returns.

You may be wondering why David tells Mephibosheth that he will divide the land between Mephibosheth and Ziba. Mephibosheth says, "Let him take everything, now that my lord the king has arrived home safely" (v. 30). All Mephibosheth cares about is that his king is back safely.

The Bible teaches that there will be rewards for serving Jesus Christ. But it's not really about the rewards. The most important part is the Lord Himself. It's going to be glorious when the King comes back. The rewards will be great, but it will be greater to see the King. Mephibosheth tells David, "My lord the king is like an angel of God" (v. 27).

What an interesting character Mephibosheth is. In this final scene, he sits at the feet of his king telling him he is like an angel of God to him. Mephibosheth is the picture of praise.

Barzillai: Going Home to the Fearful

The third individual considered is Barzillai. His story begins in verse 31 of chapter 19. "Barzillai the Gileadite also came down from Rogelim to cross the Jordan with the king and to send him on his way from there." Second Samuel 17:27–29 reads, "When David came to Mahanaim, Shobi son of Nahash from Rabbah of the Ammonites, and Makir son of Ammiel from Lo Debar, and Barzillai the Gileadite from Rogelim brought bedding and bowls and articles of pottery. They also brought wheat and barley, flour and roasted grain, beans and lentils, honey and curds, sheep, and cheese from cows' milk for David and his people to eat. For they said, 'The people have become hungry and tired and thirsty in the desert.'"

Barzillai loves and is loyal to David. When others reject David or turn their backs on him in his battle with his son, Barzillai remains faithful. He brings what he has and gives it to his king. Barzillai is a generous man. Second Samuel 17: 28–29 gives the long list of items he brings to David. It is listed this way in the Bible so we can see every item Barzillai brought. The deeper meaning of the Scripture is that everything we give to Jesus is noticed and appreciated. Jesus said you can't even give a cup of cold water in the name of a prophet without the Lord knowing about it. Everything you do or have done for Jesus is seen and noticed by God.

Now David is ready to come home again. Barzillai is about eighty years of age. He is also a very wealthy man. King David remembers Barzillai's generosity upon his return to Jerusalem. Second Samuel 19:33 says, "The king said to Barzillai, 'Cross over with me and stay with me in Jerusalem.'" In other words, David is asking Barzillai to go to Jerusalem to reign with him.

Barzillai responds: "How many more years will I live, that I should go up to Jerusalem with the king? I am now eighty years old. Can I tell the difference between what is good and what is not? Can your servant taste what he eats and drinks? Can I still hear the voices of men and women singers? Why should your servant be an added burden to my lord the king? Your servant will cross over the Jordan with the king for a short distance, but why should the king reward me in this way? Let your servant return, that I may die in my own town near the tomb of my father and mother. But here is your servant Kimham. Let him cross over with my lord the king. Do for him whatever pleases you" (vv. 34–37).

David responds: "Kimham shall cross over with me, and I will do for him whatever pleases you. And anything you desire from me I will do for you" (v. 38).

"So all the people crossed the Jordan, and then the king crossed over. The king kissed Barzillai and gave him his blessing, and Barzillai returned to his home. When the king crossed over to Gilgal, Kimham crossed with him. All the troops of Judah and half the troops of Israel had taken the king over" (vv. 39–40).

So Barzillai loved David and was loyal to him in the conflict with Absalom. David asks Barzillai to go home with him. What does Barzillai do? Actually, he makes excuses. Do any of the excuses sound familiar to you? They are the same excuses people use today for not being totally sold out to Jesus. First, Barzillai says he's too old. People use this excuse quite a bit. Some say since they're retired, they can't be of much use. You're never too old to serve Jesus. You don't retire from serving Jesus.

Other people say they're too young to serve Jesus. They say they need to have a good time before it's too late. Others use the excuse of middle age. They say they're too busy with responsibilities to serve the Lord. All of this sounds like ageism to me. Any age is a good age to serve Jesus. Barzillai's excuse doesn't hold up.

Barzillai doesn't consider himself very smart either. He uses his intellect as an excuse. Yet he was smart enough to support David instead of Absalom.

Barzillai also says he cannot taste or hear as well as he could when he was younger. Yes, we change as we get older, but that's not a reason to stop serving Jesus. "Why should your servant be an added burden to my lord the king?" (v. 35). There is no way Barzillai could be a burden to David because David is already wealthy. He is the king, and has been saving millions and millions of dollars to build a temple.

Bill Gates of Microsoft is the richest man in the world. He is worth forty to fifty billion dollars. What if Bill Gates called you tomorrow and invited you to move to Seattle, Washington, to live with him? What if he offered to take care of your food, housing, clothing, and anything else you might need? You might tell him you appreciate the offer, but you couldn't handle the move because of your age or some other reason. Somehow, I doubt very many of us would turn Bill down. I guess if you have a strong aversion to a rainy climate, you might. The point is, Jesus can take care of us. He owns the cattle on a thousand hills. Philippians 4:19 says, "My God will meet all your needs according to his glorious riches in Christ Jesus."

Barzillai was loyal, but he lived in fear. He basically says he is comfortable where he is now. He doesn't want to rock his world by changing it too much. It's just as true today. Some people don't want to have their lifestyle messed up by selling out completely to Jesus. In fact, in verse 36, Barzillai says, "Your servant will cross over the Jordan with the king for a short distance."

Most Christians are in no danger of becoming fanatics. If anything, the problem is that many Christians fear that they are fanatics. Go all the way with Jesus. He went all the way for you. He didn't stop in Bethlehem or Gethsemane. He went all the way to Calvary.

Barzillai asks David if his servant Kimham can go with David to Jerusalem and receive whatever David wants to give Barzillai. David agrees and takes Kimham into Jerusalem and Palestine. Kimham is actually mentioned one other time in the Bible. Jeremiah 41:17 says, "They went on, stopping at Geruth Kimham near Bethlehem on their way to Egypt." Dr. John Phillips teaches that David gives Kimham a little piece of property in Bethlehem. Evidently, that property will become the land on which Kimham will build the inn where Jesus is born.

No matter our age, race, or gender, all of us should serve the King by living for Him until He returns. Who knows what blessing you'll get in on by doing so?

Revelation 3:11 says, "I am coming soon. Hold on to what you have, so that no one will take your crown." Don't be a Barzillai. Don't ask the Lord to give the crown to someone else. Tell Him you'll go all the way with Jesus.

Thomas Wolfe may have felt that he couldn't go home again. Maybe he thought the changes in thinking and perceptions that occur when someone leaves where they have been raised are too much to overcome if that person ever returns. King David is a changed man. His battle with his son and his son's death change him completely. But he is able to go home to Jerusalem again. And in going home, he appreciates his blessings more.

I think you can go home again. Of course, circumstances change. It may be difficult to see an auto parts store on the corner in your hometown where your best friend lived for fifteen years, but at least the corner is still there. If your heart is at home with Jesus, as David's was, you can always go home again.

CHAPTER 18

Catastrophic Matters, or The Best Years of His Life?

"Pride goes before destruction,
a haughty spirit before a fall."
PROVERBS 16:18

2 SAMUEL 24   Somehow the expectation is that once we get a little older, we won't have to deal with the same trials and temptations we overcame in youth. Unfortunately, this expectation often turns into irony.

When I was a kid, I remember a war movie entitled *The Best Years of Our Lives*. It was released in 1946 right after the end of World War II. The plot concerns "three American servicemen [who] return home . . . after the war to find their lives irrevocably changed by their military experience. . . . Together, the three must find a way to come to terms with their experiences and pick up the pieces, lest wartime turn out to be 'the best years of their lives'"[14]. These fictitious servicemen and King David, our Braveheart, have quite a bit in common.

At this point in our story, King David's life has been irrevocably changed because of his sin with Bathsheba. Even though he has come to terms with it, his sin still affects every aspect of his life.

David is aging. He is nearing the end of his life. One might say he has reached "the best years of his life." He can rest on his laurels and be proud of his many victories and accomplishments. Yet in the concluding chapters of 2 Samuel, David's life illustrates that we are never too old to succumb to temptation or to have troubles. Sometimes the problems encountered in old age are greater than the problems of youth. All that maturity and experience make life easier, right? Not exactly. The expectation is that the last years are the best years of our lives. But David's life shows us that even in the later years, it is possible to make monumental mistakes with catastrophic consequences.

In 2 Samuel 24:10, David says, "O LORD, I beg you, take away the guilt of your servant. I have done a very foolish thing." People can act foolishly at any age, including old age. Maybe you have heard the old saying, "There is no fool like an old fool."

David makes decisions at this point in his life with catastrophic results. The first component of the catastrophe includes the song of David.

The Song of David

[David] "sang to the LORD the words of this song when the LORD delivered him from the hand of all his enemies and from the hand of Saul" (Ps. 18:1). David composed almost half of the psalms in the Bible. The content of this particular psalm of thanksgiving is found twice in the Bible. First, it occurs here in the section of the Bible known as Israel's history book. Second, it is found in Psalm 18. It gives testimony to the goodness, power, and deliverance of God in David's life. The psalm also offers three main divisions.

The first division shows David as a worshiper praising the Lord. David says, "The LORD is my rock, my fortress and my deliverer; my God is my rock, in whom I take refuge. He is my shield and the horn of my salvation, my stronghold. I call to the LORD, who is worthy of praise, and I am saved from my enemies" (vv. 2–4). David creates vivid imagery of the Lord, and in the descriptions he uses personal pronouns such as *my*. That makes it very personal. Can you say the same about God?

Second, in Psalm 18:5–46, David is a warrior. In these verses, he explains how God delivered him and blessed him, in spite of all his troubles and difficulties. It portrays a life of victory. When life gets difficult, we can depend on the Lord. For example, David says, "In my distress I called to the LORD; I cried to my God for help. From his temple he heard my voice; my cry came before him, into his ears. The earth trembled and quaked, and the foundations of the mountains shook; they trembled because he was angry" (vv. 6–7).

Psalm 18:21 says, "The LORD has dealt with me according to my righteousness; according to the cleanness of my hands he has rewarded me." In other words, "God made my life complete when I placed all the pieces or compartments of it before Him. When I got my act together, He gave me a fresh start." These verses picture David as a warrior fighting the battles of life and experiencing deliverance and victory from the Lord. He tells us exactly why the Lord delivered him: "He brought me out into a spacious place; he rescued me because he delighted in me" (v. 19).

The Lord delights in you, too. You are important to Him. When you are going through life's battles and difficulties, you can always call on the name of the Lord. He will meet life's needs.

Third, the psalm presents David as a witness (vv. 47–51). Here he gives witness to his God and what God means to him and to others. "The LORD lives! Praise be to my Rock! Exalted be God my Savior!" (v. 46).

David is giving witness to the fact that God is alive. The Bible says that when Jesus Christ died on the cross and was buried, He rose from the dead three days later. God is real and personal, and David gives testimony to a real experience with God in Psalm 18.

The second component of the catastrophe includes the soldiers of David.

The Soldiers of David

In 2 Samuel 23:1–7, David's last words are chronicled: "The oracle of David son of Jesse, the oracle of the man exalted by the Most High, the man anointed by the God of Jacob, Israel's singer of songs: 'The Spirit of the LORD spoke through me; his word was on my tongue. The God of Israel spoke, the Rock of Israel said to me: When one rules over men in right-eousness, when he rules in the fear of God, he is like the light of morning at sunrise on a cloudless morning.'"

These are the last words of David (v. 1). Perhaps this verse acts as a postscript to what has just been said at the end of chapter 22. Perhaps David is referring to the words he spoke under the direct inspiration of the Holy Spirit.

David was one of the people God used to provide the Bible for us. As God's spokesman here, David may be giving us insight into how God uses human scribes. The Bible's sixty-six books share authorship between several human authors inspired by the Holy Spirit. David is one of the human authors, so this section may refer to the last words David wrote under the inspiration of the Holy Spirit. David, like Isaiah, Jeremiah, and Paul, was uniquely prepared and selected to write portions of Scripture. God raised David up for that task and anointed him to write Scripture. David is also known as the "sweet psalmist of Israel." God uses David to write songs in your Book of Psalms, which is the Hebrew hymnbook.

The Psalms touch every imaginable emotion in the human heart. There's a psalm that can apply in any situation. What David may really be saying is that God chose him specifically to write the Psalms. Second Samuel 23:2 comments on inspira-tion: "The Spirit of the LORD spoke through me; his word was on my tongue."

One example of the New Testament understanding of Scripture-writing appears in 2 Peter 1:21: "For prophecy never had its origin in the will of man, but men spoke from God as they were carried along by the Holy Spirit." Men didn't just say whatever they wanted to say or write down whatever they wanted to write. It wasn't a chance to complete creative writing exercises. The Holy Spirit inspired His human writers, and their words are the words of God.

Another example from the New Testament occurs in Acts 1:16: "Brothers, the Scripture had to be fulfilled which the Holy Spirit spoke long ago through the mouth of David concerning Judas, who served as guide for those who arrested Jesus." So the Holy Spirit did the speaking through the handwriting of David.

Second Samuel 23:8 begins by listing the names of "mighty men" who are David's soldiers. This section chronicles their exploits and their battles. One of David's men fought so long and became so weary from battle that he couldn't even take his hand off his sword. His hand just froze on his sword. Another man stood alone in a vegetable garden and fought alone for David. Another went down into a pit and fought a lion on a snowy day. When David expressed a longing for water from the well in Bethlehem from which he drank as a boy, three of his warriors risked their lives by breaking through enemy lines to bring him a drink from that well. David was so touched and moved that he poured the well water on the ground as a symbol of the blood of the warriors who risked their lives for him.

People are important to God. He never fails to notice or reward everything that is done for him. David's actions illustrate that everything these men did was noticed and "the LORD brought about a great victory." Any victory we win comes from the power of the Lord. The people listed here can challenge us today to be mighty men, women, and children for Jesus Christ.

The third component of the catastrophe involves the sin of David.

The Sin of David

David is now an old man. He is a sadder and wiser king, but he is not necessarily immune from making foolish decisions. David is a faithful man until the end, but he is also a fallible man. His situation reminds us that we never reach a plateau in life where we can lower our guard or become less vigilant. In middle age, David's overwhelming temptation was passion. In old age, it is pride.

Second Samuel 24:1 says, "Again the anger of the LORD burned against Israel, and he incited David against them, saying, 'Go and take a census of Israel and Judah.'"

First Chronicles 21:1 presents a parallel passage: "Satan rose up against Israel and incited David to take a census of Israel." Sounds like David could say, "The devil made me do it." In reality, David experiences a perplexing combination of forces many of us grapple with in life today. It's a complicated mixture of motivations. It involves David's pride, Israel's sin, Satan's temptation, God's overall sovereignty in the matter, and our human inability to see the big picture.

Life is full of unanswered questions. But nothing can happen in the entire universe that is beyond God. He can use absolutely everything for good. God is even sovereign over evil. Sometimes God allows Satan's work to accomplish His purposes. For example, Luke 22:31–32 says, "Simon, Simon, Satan has asked to sift you as wheat. But I have prayed for you, Simon, that your faith may not fail. And when you have turned back, strengthen your brothers." Somehow in God's overall providence and sovereignty, He even uses Satan to put one of God's saints in his sifter to be shaken. Life is mysterious and complicated, but knowing there is a God in heaven who is in charge of it all is a comfort. God is on His throne, and He ultimately works out His purposes and His plans.

David's sin boils down to the fact that he numbers or counts his people. In other words, David orders a census taken.

The reason why David does this is not stated. It may have been an issue of pride with David. The census he orders taken is not wrong in and of itself. But it causes David, not God, to be praised. Therefore, it is sin.

Joab appears in this chapter with some questions. Second Samuel 24:3 says, "Joab replied to the king, 'May the LORD your God multiply the troops a hundred times over, and may the eyes of my lord the king see it. But why does my lord the king want to do such a thing?'"

The gruff army commander Joab, of all people, is telling David he should let God do the counting. But David persists. He is obstinate, and he pushes the issue. Perhaps he desires to show others how powerful and important he is. Perhaps he wants to revel in the military strength he has established for Israel. It may be, however, that David is succumbing to pride, which is a typical temptation of old age. David doesn't seem content to rest on his laurels. Obviously, he has been very successful in his reign. But he seeks more praise and more glory for his accomplishments.

The administration of the census takes about ten months. Joab tries to talk David out of it, but he does not prevail. We are often as stubborn as David is here when we want our own way. "The king's word, however, overruled Joab and the army commanders; so they left the presence of the king to enroll the fighting men of Israel. After crossing the Jordan, they camped near Aroer, south of the town in the gorge, and then went through Gad and on to Jazer" (vv. 4–5).

Pride drives David to count his own people so he might garner praise and support for himself. This sin of David's is different from his sin with Bathsheba. One is passion, and one is pride.

David is approaching the end of his reign and the end of his life. He's been highly effective and successful. It seems that the closer one gets to the climax of his life's work, the more praise and adoration is needed to satisfy the hunger for acknowledgment. Whatever we may accomplish, we must always keep in mind that we are nothing without Jesus. We are absolute zero without the Lord. So it seems as if David, our *Braveheart,* temporarily becomes *Prideheart.* Just remember sin will take you further than you want to go. It will teach you more than you want to know. It will keep you longer than you want to stay. It will cost you more than you want to pay.

The consequences come, and suffering follows David's sin. The story is: "David was conscience-stricken after he had counted the fighting men, and he said to the LORD, 'I have sinned greatly in what I have done. Now, O LORD, I beg you, take away the guilt of your servant. I have done a very foolish thing'" (v. 10).

David's heart suddenly assaults him. David sought pleasure in this act. Instead, he brought himself and others much pain. David's passionate sin with Bathsheba lasted only moments. In contrast, his prideful sin endures for almost ten months. His former sin was against Bathsheba, though the nation was certainly affected, but the primary damage was done to his family. In contrast, this sin plunges the entire nation into catastrophe. David's sins represent both the sins of the flesh and the sins of the spirit. We are warned about both of these in the Bible.

God sends word to David through a prophet named Gad that he has three choices as punishment for his sin of the spirit. He can choose seven years of famine, three months of war, or three days of pestilence. David is smart enough and knows God well enough to realize he will fare better in the hands of the Lord than in the hands of people. So he throws himself on the mercy of God. "So the LORD sent a plague on Israel from that morning until the end of the time designated, and seventy thousand of the people from Dan to Beersheba died" (v. 15).

In the battle of Syracuse, over one hundred thousand Carthaginians were killed. When the atomic bombs fell on Hiroshima and Nagasaki, seventy thousand and forty thousand people, respectively, were killed. The pestilence David causes is probably the second greatest catastrophe in the history of humanity, and it is a result of pride. The sins of the spirit can do catastrophic damage.

In 2 Samuel 24:16, David has what may be the most fearful experience in his entire life. He realizes Jerusalem is on the verge of destruction because of him: "When the angel stretched out his hand to destroy Jerusalem, the LORD was grieved because of the calamity and said to the angel who was afflicting the people, 'Enough! Withdraw your hand.' The angel of the LORD was then at the threshing floor of Araunah the Jebusite."

"When David saw the angel who was striking down the people, he said to the LORD, 'I am the one who has sinned and done wrong. These are but sheep. What have they done? Let your hand fall upon me and my family'" (v. 17).

"On that day Gad went to David and said to him, 'Go up and build an altar to the LORD on the threshing floor of Araunah the Jebusite'" (v. 18).

David witnesses the possibility that the entire population of Jerusalem could be wiped out because of his sin. So David assumes the role of mediator standing between God's avenging angel and a suffering people. He goes to the threshing floor of Araunah to purchase it. He wants to have a place to build an altar. Araunah replies to David: "Why has my lord the king come to his servant?" David answers, "To buy your threshing floor, so I can build an altar to the LORD, that the plague on the people may be stopped" (v. 21).

"Araunah said to David, 'Let my lord the king take whatever pleases him and offer it up. Here are oxen for the burnt offering, and here are threshing sledges and ox yokes for the wood'" (v. 22).

Araunah is telling David he can have it all. "But the king replied to Araunah, 'No, I insist on paying you for it. I will not sacrifice to the LORD my God burnt offerings that cost me nothing.' So David bought the threshing floor and the oxen and paid fifty shekels of silver for them" (v. 24).

Faith that costs you nothing is worth nothing. Worship that costs you nothing is worth nothing. An agonizing, sacrificial, and prayerful price must be paid for faith and worship. "David built an altar to the LORD there and sacrificed burnt offerings and fellowship offerings. Then the LORD answered prayer in behalf of the land, and the plague on Israel was stopped" (v. 25).

So David does it. He stops the plague. But before the plague of sin can end, blood must be shed. David builds the altar he is told to build in verse 18 on Mount Moriah. This is the hill on which Abraham offered his son Isaac hundreds of years before. This is also the place where Solomon's temple was built. Some people believe this is the same Mount Moriah that supported the cross upon which Jesus Christ gave Himself as a sacrifice for sins.

The plague stopped because of the sacrifice. The obliteration of sin requires the shedding of blood at any time, in any place, by people of any age. Jesus shed His blood to pay the price for our sin, and the plague of sin was stopped forever.

David was supposedly enjoying "the best years of his life" when his human pride tempted him to sin. His sin of the spirit caused a catastrophe in his land. His story teaches us that age doesn't matter when it comes to sinning. His story also confirms to us that sin takes you further, keeps you longer, and costs you more than you can imagine. Let's all learn from David, our Braveheart, as we strive to live "the best years of our lives" as men and women after God's own heart.

CHAPTER 19

Final Matters,
or "You'll Be a King,
My Son"

1 KINGS 1–2

If you can keep your head when all about you
Are losing theirs and blaming it on you;
If you can trust yourself when all men doubt you,
But make allowance for their doubting too;
If you can wait and not be tired by waiting,
Or, being lied about, don't deal in lies,
Or, being hated, don't give way to hating,
And yet don't look too good, nor talk too wise;
If you can dream—and not make dreams your master;
If you can think—and not make thoughts your aim;
If you can meet with triumph and disaster
And treat those two imposters just the same;
If you can bear to hear the truth you've spoken
Twisted by knaves to make a trap for fools,
Or watch the things you gave your life to broken,
And stoop and build 'em up with wornout tools;
If you can make one heap of all your winnings
And risk it on one turn of pitch-and-toss,
And lose, and start again at your beginnings

And never breathe a word about your loss;
If you can force your heart and nerve and sinew
To serve your turn long after they are gone,
And so hold on when there is nothing in you
Except the Will which says to them: "Hold on!";
If you can talk with crowds and keep your virtue,
Or walk with kings—nor lose the common touch;
If neither foes nor loving friends can hurt you;
If all men count with you, but none too much;
If you can fill the unforgiving minute
With sixty seconds' worth of distance run—
Yours is the Earth and everything that's in it,
And—which is more—you'll be a Man my son!

You may recognize this poem. It is entitled "If," and it was written by Rudyard Kipling. He was an English novelist, short story writer, and poet who wrote the famous collection of stories entitled *The Jungle Book*.

In the poem, Kipling takes on a fatherly tone as his speaker advises a son on manhood. The title of the poem is interesting as well. *If* is one of the most inscrutable words in the English language. It is a difficult word to define. According to *Merriam Webster's Collegiate Dictionary*, it means, "in the event that" or "allowing that." It's a word that sets up a conditional statement.

Perhaps Kipling is writing what he perceives to be the established conditions for manhood. David, our Braveheart, is nearing the end of his reign at this point in our story. After intrigue and conspiracies, he is able to instruct his son Solomon on the problems and opportunities involved in becoming a king. The poem "If" may have been helpful to King David if it had been written at that time.

David, our Braveheart, is nearing death. He is old, and he is concluding his remarkable career. He began his career as a shepherd boy tending a few sheep and concluded it as the king of one of the mightiest empires in history.

David says in 1 Kings 2:2, "I am about to go the way of all the earth." David recognizes that death is an experience common to all people. He is expressing in Old Testament terms what the New Testament means when it says, "Man is destined to die once." Death is universal and inevitable.

In 1 Chronicles 29:15, David says, "We are aliens and strangers in your sight, as were all our forefathers. Our days on earth are like a shadow, without hope." David recognizes life's brevity. His metaphor compares the days of our lives to a shadow. In the New Testament, James uses another metaphor for human life. He says, "You are a mist that appears for a little while and then vanishes" (James 4:14).

Sometimes, people have trouble approaching death. In fact, many people spend much of their lives avoiding the subject of death. But death defines and completes life. A person's death makes the life that person lived a reality. Genesis 5 gives names of various people, and then it says each of these people "lived . . . and then he died." In other words, the Bible is talking about people who have lived victorious lives. We are not ready to live until we are prepared to die.

Think of Simeon in the second chapter of Luke. God reveals to Simeon that he will be able to see the Messiah, the Savior of the world. You may remember that Simeon was in the temple when Mary and Joseph entered. They had their baby, Jesus, with them. Simeon took the baby Jesus into his arms, and God revealed to him that this baby was the Messiah, the Christ. Then Simeon says some very significant words: "Lord, as you have promised, you now dismiss your servant in peace. For my eyes have seen your salvation" (vv. 29–30). Simeon's story reminds us that before we experience death, we should experience salvation.

It often seems that an impending death in a family brings out the worst in people. There is stress. There is sadness. There also may be a scrapping for the amassed wealth or power of the person who is departing. This is evident in David's final days.

The Complication of the Final Days

The final days of David were days of complication. According to 1 Kings 1:1–4, "When King David was old and well advanced in years, he could not keep warm even when they put covers over him. So his servants said to him, 'Let us look for a young virgin to attend the king and take care of him. She can lie beside him so that our lord the king may keep warm.' Then they searched throughout Israel for a beautiful girl and found Abishag, a Shunammite, and brought her to the king. The girl was very beautiful; she took care of the king and waited on him, but the king had no intimate relations with her."

David is seventy years old, and he apparently is not able to handle the full responsibilities of being king. He also has poor circulation because he is cold. He cannot get warm.

To solve the king's circulation problem, his servants devise a plan. David's servants say, "Let us look for a young virgin to attend the king and take care of him." In other words, the servants are suggesting that this young woman can take care of the king. "She can lie beside him so that our lord the king may keep warm" (v. 2). She is a beautiful young woman, and her relationship with David is not a sexual one. Her function is to serve and assist David in his last days. She is part of the solution to the problems that old age is causing the king.

Physical problems usually increase with old age. Our health deteriorates as we get older. Energy declines. Fears of unpleasant visits to the doctor increase. Grief in seeing friends lose their health and strength increases. Sorrow over the loss of loved ones who die also affects people. In T. S. Eliot's famous poem "The Love Song of J. Alfred Prufrock," his speaker shows self-consciousness regarding aging. At one point near the end of the poem, the speaker says,

I grow old . . . I grow old . . .
I shall wear the bottoms of my trousers rolled.
Shall I part my hair behind?
Do I dare to eat a peach?
Shall I wear white flannel trousers,
And walk upon the beach?

Complications come with growing older, as David finds out. Many people view dying in an impersonal way. Some of David's servants see their old king as merely a problem to be solved.

We should be grateful for everything being done today to help the elderly. The aging process actually may be a bit more tolerable now than it has been in the past. The population of this country is steadily getting older. Even the Baby Boomers are getting older. The upper edge of the Boomer generation is hitting fifty to fifty-five now. This is one reason why we are now facing problems with Social Security. It is also one reason why there is such interest and activity focusing on the issues of aging. In fact, the science of gerontology has taken on an important role in our culture today.

It's really an issue of the value of human life. In American culture today, life is cheap. The value of life is ignored and life is no longer sacred. For some people, aging is a problem to be solved. Old folks are in the way. Another area of concern is lack of sacredness and honor for human life. Life is so cheap that it's legal to kill the unborn, and it's becoming acceptable to consider ending the lives of the elderly. One state governor in the U.S. has actually proposed ending the lives of citizens once they reach a certain age. Why? Because caring for the elderly is expensive and inconvenient.

The truth is that mankind is not an accident and did not come from lower forms of life. God creates people and gives purpose to their lives. Life is sacred. The later years in people's lives should not be problematic. They should be special. There are times to focus on the future and to realize, as David did, that we are on earth only for a short time.

David confessed, "We are aliens and strangers in your sight" (1 Chron. 29:15). With age comes the stark realization that we are just pilgrims on earth. Remember the metaphors. Our lives are shadows or mists. If you are a Christian, old age brings on homesickness for heaven. The final years should be an opportunity to serve the Lord. In spite of life's complications, all of us can serve the Lord. As long as we have mind and breath, we can still serve the Lord, especially through prayer.

The Insurrection of the Final Days

David's final days are also days of insurrection. At least one person in David's household sees his impending death as an opportunity. The individual is Adonijah, one of David's son's and one of Absalom's brothers.

First Kings 1:5 tells how it happens: "Now Adonijah, whose mother was Haggith, put himself forward and said, 'I will be king.' So he got chariots and horses ready, with fifty men to run ahead of him." Adonijah sees a chance to foster an insurrection against his own father and then to become king himself. He takes advantage of his father's poor health. In reality, Adonijah knows that God's choice and King David's choice as his successor is Solomon.

Adonijah rebels against his own father and against the will of God. This carries a warning for us today. We cannot fight God and expect to win. The will of God will ultimately prevail. It cannot be blocked.

Adonijah simply takes control. His father is dying, so he takes action. David may have expected to experience peace at this time in his life. Old age is often one of the most uncomplicated times of life. Instead, his kingdom is again teetering precariously because of the actions of his son. Sounds like the whole Absalom situation is repeating itself. David will have to deal with a rebellious son for the second time.

David is partly to blame: "His father had never interfered with him by asking, 'Why do you behave as you do?' He was also very handsome and was born next after Absalom" (v. 6). This means his father never disciplined him. Perhaps Adonijah was spoiled. We might say today that David's family was "dysfunctional." As a father, he never established strong ties within his family. As a result, the family suffers turmoil until David's death. Perhaps David focused his time and energy totally on his job. He was so busy being a king that he didn't have time to be a father.

There are men in David's situation now. Perhaps a father is the head of his own company. He works hard, thinking he is serving his family by providing for them. But he may have no time to truly be a father. Situations like these cause us to examine our definition of success. Are you successful if you earn a lot of money but you blow it as a father? You and your children may disagree on the answer. Learn from King David's mistakes.

A true insurrection implies organized effort. Adonijah delivers. He simply proclaims himself as king (v. 5). He does, however, have help in his plot from various people. Verse 7 informs us about who joins his attempt at insurrection. Joab, the military commander, is one of the people. Abiathar, the priest, is another person who participates with Adonijah.

Those who chose to remain loyal to King David are listed in verse 8. The priest Zadok was one. Benaiah, the son of Jehoiada, was one. Nathan the prophet and some other people also remained faithful to their king. In fact, Nathan organizes his own plot to counter Adonijah's plan.

While Adonijah celebrates his insurrection against his father and his self-appointment as king, a plot to quell his rebellion emerges from deep within the recesses of the palace. The objective of the plan is to foil Adonijah's claim to the throne. By the way, palace intrigue is universal to all kingdoms and seats of power. Human nature causes people to grasp and to scheme for power. Fortunately for David, Nathan is savvy enough to create a plan.

Nathan meets with Bathsheba, Solomon's mother, and tells her about Adonijah's insurrection. He warns her to deal with the problem quickly. She has a vested interest in the situation because Adonijah has seemingly usurped the throne from her son Solomon. Nathan encourages Bathsheba to talk to the king to inform him about the insurrection. Nathan then plans to see the king himself to offer support for what she tells him.

Bathsheba goes in to the king (v. 15). Remember, the king is old. Abishag, the young virgin, is there attending to his needs. Picture Bathsheba in her colorful royal robes. She was probably still a strikingly beautiful woman. She enters and kneels in obeisance to the king. The king asks her, "What do you want?" She then tells him the story. She also reminds him that he has chosen her son Solomon to be his successor.

As she is talking to the king, Nathan enters. The prophet vouches for her and confirms her story. David had no clue this was happening. News of the insurrection rouses David. He realizes people in the kingdom have taken sides again. He also realizes that Joab and Abiathar are usurping him by supporting Adonijah.

The Transition of the Final Days

David's final days are days of transition because he must establish his rightful heir on his throne. First Kings 1:28 tells us that the old king is now aware of the situation. King David most likely became furious at the news about Adonijah. The situation may have caused him to think and to "dig deep" for strength and the power to solve the throne problem. You can hear echoes of David's warrior voice: "Then King David said, 'Call in Bathsheba.' So she came into the king's presence, and stood before him" (v. 28). David explains to her his plan to establish Solomon on the throne.

David says, "I will surely carry out today what I swore to you by the LORD, the God of Israel: Solomon your son shall be king after me, and he will sit on my throne in my place" (v. 30). It seems that David had not prepared for a smooth transition after his death. You might say he had not written a will. Some of us living now may think we have plenty of time to make out a will. We should not follow David's lead on this matter. It is important to take care of matters such as this so that when death comes, our families will be provided for.

David fails to make known his wishes about his successor. He has not given his people direction. He hasn't considered the transition of power. He knows Solomon will succeed him because God tells him. He just doesn't make it known in the kingdom. As a result, chaos erupts.

David calls in Zadok, Nathan, and Benaiah, some of his loyalists. He asks them to put Solomon on his mule. Now that may sound strange to you. It certainly doesn't sound like a royal action. Can you imagine Queen Elizabeth of England riding a mule? When I was a boy, I didn't have the option of Six Flags or Disney World for entertainment. Instead, I used to ride wild mules in the mule barn in my hometown. There were ropes that hung from the rafters. I would jump on those wild mules, and they would go crazy, bucking and pitching. Of course, everybody fell off, but that's where the ropes came in handy. If you found yourself about to fall, you could grab a rope to help you swing off the wild mule. Riding a mule wasn't a form of entertainment for the Israelites, but it was significant. In that culture, riding a mule symbolized peace and royalty. In contrast, riding a horse indicated war.

Jesus also rode a mule when He rode to Jerusalem to offer Himself to Jerusalem as their king. The mule signified that He came as king in peace. The Bible says the next time He comes, He will ride a white horse. This too is symbolic. He will not be returning as Savior, but as Judge to make war on Satan.

So Solomon follows David's instructions, and he rides his father's mule. He rides the mule to Gihon. Then Zadok the priest anoints Solomon with oil from the tabernacle. The people understand the meaning of these acts, and they support their new king. Suddenly, Adonijah and his camp hear the sound of a trumpet. Adonijah asked, "What's the meaning of all the noise in the city?" (v. 41). He then hears from Abiathar's son Jonathan that David has made Solomon the true king.

Solomon is now David's successor. In 1 Kings 2, David gives a charge to his son. David advises his son on spiritual and political matters. He instructs him on running a kingdom. In effect, David is telling his son Solomon that if he keeps his priorities right with God, he will be a good king. David's charge reminds me of Kipling's poem, "If." In 1 Kings 2:1–9, David tells Solomon if he chooses to follow his father's advice, "you will never fail to have a man on the throne of Israel" (v. 4).

David then calls his people together one last time. First Chronicles 28:1–2 gives an account of this meeting: "David summoned all the officials of Israel to assemble at Jerusalem: the officers over the tribes, the commanders of the divisions in the service of the king, the commanders of thousands and commanders of hundreds, and the officials in charge of all the property and livestock belonging to the king and his sons, together with the palace officials, the mighty men and all the brave warriors. King David rose to his feet and said: 'Listen to me, my brothers and my people. I had it in my heart to build a house as a place of rest for the ark of the covenant of the LORD, for the footstool of our God, and I made plans to build it.'"

The old king's words are touched with fire from heaven, and God gives him strength to address his people. God's power comes on David, and he is able to connect with his loyal subjects one more time.

David was the greatest king in the history of Israel. He started off as a shepherd boy, then God raised him up and placed him on the throne of Israel. His reign lasted forty years.

So David, a man after God's own heart, died. First Chronicles 29:28 says, "He died at a good old age, having enjoyed long life, wealth and honor. His son Solomon succeeded him as king."

There is no record of a great funeral or a magnificent eulogy from his subjects. At his death, there is still trouble within his own house. He doesn't die in peace. He dies in the midst of turmoil and difficulty. Yet he lives and dies as a man after God's own heart. In fact, it is God who writes David's eulogy. Acts 13:36 says, "For when David had served God's purpose in his own generation, he fell asleep; he was buried with his fathers and his body decayed."

God says David served his own generation by the will of God. What a magnificent statement from heaven upon the life of this man. What an opportunity for us to live so it can be said of us in death that we served our own generation by the will of God. That's a meaningful statement.

In my opinion, life's greatest tragedy is when a person lives and dies and never knows or understands the reason for his existence or the purpose of his life. The secret to the meaning of life is that we exist to serve the Lord. We are here to do the will of God and to fulfill His plan and purpose for our lives. David served his own generation by the will of God. We have the same opportunity.

In describing David's death, the Bible says he "fell asleep." That's a beautiful way to describe death. It's as if this magnificent warrior is a little baby going to sleep in his father's arms. David closes his eyes on one world, and he opens his eyes in a brighter world.

Acts 13:37 says, "But the one whom God raised from the dead did not see decay." The "one" in this verse refers to Jesus, the son of David. One of the names for our Savior is "Son of David." Death was not the final chapter for David, and it is not the final chapter for us. Because of Jesus and His death, burial, and resurrection, the desperation of death can be replaced with the anticipation of resurrection.

Rudyard Kipling's poem "If" portrays a father instructing his son on the process of becoming a man. Certainly the lessons of the poem could be applied to daughters becoming women. At the end of David's life, he is able to instruct his son Solomon how to become a king. David tells his son to "observe what the LORD your God requires: Walk in his ways, and keep his decrees and commands, his laws and requirements, as written in the Law of Moses, so that you may prosper in all you do and wherever you go" (1 Kings 2:3). In effect, David is delivering his own "If" poem to his son.

David's charge to his son and Kipling's "If" poem can be applied to our lives as well. It doesn't matter what our race or gender or earning potential. We have an opportunity to serve God and to perform His will while we are on earth *if* we accept Him and live for Him.

Notes

1. Tony Waltham, *Caves* (New York: Crown Publishers, 1974), 169.

2. Shakespeare, *Othello* 2.1.296–302.

3. *Encyclopedia of Literature*, 812.

4. Taken from www.ap.org.

5. Robert E. Norris and L. Lloyd Haring *Political Geography* (Columbus, OH: Charles . Merrill Publishing Co., 1980), 5.

6. Philip Bigler, *Washington in Focus: The Photo History of the Nation's Capital* (Arlington, VA: Vandamere Press, 1988), 13.

7. "'Amen' to a Church-free Life," *USA Today*, March 7, 2002.

8. Ibid.

9. Ibid.

10. J. D. Douglas and Merrill C. Tenney, *NIV Compact Dictionary of the Bible* (Grand Rapids: Zondervan, 1989), 227.

11. Ibid.

12. Ibid.

13. *Encyclopedia of Literature*, 1226.

14. Plot summary taken from Internet Movie Database, www.imdb.org.